Intimate
Colonialism

Writing Lives
Ethnographic Narratives

Series Editors:
Arthur P. Bochner & Carolyn Ellis
University of South Florida

Writing Lives: Ethnographic Narratives publishes narrative representations of qualitative research projects. The series editors seek manuscripts that blur the boundaries between humanities and social sciences. We encourage novel and evocative forms of expressing concrete lived experience, including autoethnographic, literary, poetic, artistic, visual, performative, critical, multi-voiced, conversational, and co-constructed representations. We are interested in ethnographic narratives that depict local stories; employ literary modes of scene setting, dialogue, character development, and unfolding action; and include the author's critical reflections on the research and writing process, such as research ethics, alternative modes of inquiry and representation, reflexivity, and evocative storytelling. Proposals and manuscripts should be directed to abochner@cas.usf.edu

Volumes in this series:

Erotic Mentoring: Women's Transformations in the University
Janice Hocker Rushing

Intimate Colonialism: Head, Heart, and Body
in West African Development Work
Laurie L. Charlés

Last Writes: A Daybook for a Dying Friend
Laurel Richardson

Intimate Colonialism

Head, Heart, and Body in
West African Development Work

Laurie L. Charlés

Routledge
Taylor & Francis Group

LONDON AND NEW YORK

First published 2007 by Left Coast Press, Inc.

Published 2016 by Routledge
2 Park Square, Milton Park, Abingdon, Oxon OX14 4RN
711 Third Avenue, New York, NY 10017, USA

Routledge is an imprint of the Taylor & Francis Group, an informa business

Library of Congress Cataloging-in-Publication Data
Charlés, Laurie L.
Intimate colonialism : head, heart, and body in West African development work / Laurie L. Charlés.
        p. cm.— (Writing lives—ethnographic narratives)
    Includes bibliographical references and index.
    ISBN 978-1-59874-104-9 (hardback : alk. paper)—ISBN 978-1-59874-105-6 (pbk. : alk. paper)
    1. Charlés, Laurie L.   2. Peace Corps (U.S.)—Togo—Biography.   3. Ethnology—Togo.   I. Title.
    DT582.82.C43C43 2007
    361.6092—dc22
    [B]
                        2007002888
07 08 09 5 4 3 2 1

Cover design by Andrew Brozyna

Excerpts of stories in Chapter 7 and 10 were published in the January/February 2005 issue of the AAMFT's *Family Therapy Magazine*. Vignettes that appear in Chapters 2, 4, 5, and 6 were published in abbreviated versions by Haworth Press, Binghamton, NY, in: Charlés, L. (2006). "Young Women Struggling for an Education: Systemic Work with a Village Community in West Africa," *Journal of Feminist Family Therapy* 18(3), 63–83. Article copies available from the the Haworth Document Delivery Service: 1-800-HAWORTH, docdelivery@haworthpress.com.

ISBN 13: 978-1-59874-105-6 paperback
ISBN 13: 978-1-59874-104-9 hardback

To My Sisters

Contents

Cast of Characters

Bernadette, a single, Togolese mother of three children; once a social worker for a Scandinavian NGO; the author's homologue (work counterpart) in the village

Marguerite Diore, 17-year-old daughter in the Diore household, where the author lives for three months during training in Kpalimé

Maxim, a Togolese Peace Corps language instructor; a charming, intelligent, mysterious man who becomes the author's close friend and, eventually, romantic partner

Nyalewossi, a tough, assertive, and charming Togolese teenager and president of the *Jeunes Filles* (young girls) group in the author's assigned village

Oded, recent romantic partner (and ongoing friend) of the author; lives in Jerusalem

Odette, a beautiful Togolese teenager who exemplifies a typical teenage African girl, who is having an affair with her schoolteacher

Patricia, sister of the author, an artist who lives in Houston

Père Antoine, a demure Togolese Catholic priest; studied five years in Rome and speaks fluent Italian; one of the author's first Togolese confidantes; eventually reported by the author to the archbishop for sexual harassment

René, a Togolese agro-economist, and married man, with whom the author has an intimate, sexual relationship

Shoshana, composite character representing three female fellow Peace Corps Volunteers (PCVs) who serve with the author—kind, impulsive, insightful confidantes and partners-in-crime

Introduction

There is one way to understand another culture. Living it. Move into it, ask to be tolerated as a guest, learn the language. At some point understanding may come. It will always be wordless. The moment you grasp what is foreign, you will lose the urge to explain it. To explain a phenomenon is to distance yourself from it.

Peter Hoeg, *Miss Smilla's Feeling for Snow*[1]

Being in a foreign country means walking a tight rope high above the ground without the net afforded a person by the country where he has his family, colleagues, and friends, and where he can easily say what he has to say in a language he has known from childhood.

Milan Kundera, *The Unbearable Lightness of Being*[2]

I sensed immediately that I was at some kind of watershed . . . you know that feeling, when you can almost see the two or several directions your life might take ahead of you, a moment when you know that the next choice you are about to make is going to be crucial and possibly final. That there is no going back and that nothing will ever be the same again.

William Boyd, *The Blue Afternoon*[3]

Prologue: June 23, 1999

Near the end of my solitary dinner of fried beef liver and fresh spinach, the phone rings. It's Cleo, my recruiter from the Peace Corps.

"I've got good news. You've finally been cleared. Your hemoglobin is now at an acceptable level and you are eligible for an assignment."

"Yea! Finally!" I yell as I jump up and down in my tiny studio apartment. I've wanted to join Peace Corps for years. Now I can stop eating these awful dinners. I've been eating liver (accompanied by lots of red wine) every Friday, in an attempt to conquer the diagnosis of anemia that prevented my Peace Corps medical clearance. I hate fried liver. When I was a child, my mother tried to feed it to us. I still remember the three of us children sitting at the dinner table in the dark, liver untouched.

"Unfortunately," Cleo continues after congratulating me, "there is nothing left for this summer in the urban youth program. But I've forwarded your name to another placement officer for a program in Africa. We received a late request for a volunteer in rural community development and girls' education. It requires a French background, which you have, and is set for a late summer/early fall departure. Are you interested?"

"Yes, absolutely," I tell Cleo. "What country is it?"

"Not sure. I just know it's in West Africa. The placement officer for that desk is Jacob Frisco. He'll fill you in on all the details. I'll ask him to call you first thing tomorrow morning."

All night I obsess about what Jacob will tell me and about my decision to join the Peace Corps. I am nearing the end of my dissertation, approaching the finish of my PhD in family therapy. At this moment, a sane person in my position is supposed to be applying for jobs in academia—not planning to live and work in the Third World for two years.

But I've waited so long to join the Peace Corps, I remind myself. Instead of joining after earning my bachelor's degree, I decided to go to graduate school and train to become a family therapist. That's the official line. The real reason I didn't follow through back then is that I was involved in a new relationship and didn't want to abandon it. Today, nearly ten years after my initial application, I am ready to put Peace Corps back on the front burner.

૧ᠥ

At the time Cleo gave me the good news about my Peace Corps medical clearance, I was thriving professionally. I had spent six years in a family therapy doctoral program, the last three working full-time on a dissertation that took me to the FBI training academy, into the "resolution through dialogue"[4] world of hostage negotiators. My dissertation was a qualitative analysis of the discourse between police hostage negotiators and a young man who had gone to his former high school to kill a teacher who flunked him. The young man shot fourteen people, including the teacher, and took more than a hundred students hostage.

As a systemic family therapist trained in linguistic and conversational styles of therapy,[5] I was awestruck by the way seven police negotiators convinced the young man, who had killed four people, to release his student hostages and surrender voluntarily. My admiration increased as I spent many hours with the hostage negotiators, conducting interviews, eating dinner in their homes, joining them at conferences, and listening to their war stories.

It was intriguing to immerse myself in another world. I had grown to appreciate the emergent aspects of the writing process, and had begun teaching qualitative research, presenting my work at several conferences. By the time I finished my PhD, my professional identity included both "ethnographic researcher" and "family therapist." I liked these new professional identities, but an important part of my personal identity remained unfulfilled.

Today, when I reflect on the strong attraction I felt to the Peace Corps, I acknowledge the need anthropologists have to understand a foreign culture, a marginalized group, an "other." However, in truth the "other" I wanted most to understand was me. I was curious about Africa, and I wanted to do something that focused on making the world a better place. But I also wanted to become more connected to the intimate parts of myself. I had spent many years cultivating my professional identity and was well on the road to polishing and refining my scholarly beliefs and values. But who was I, beyond that? What was I made of?

Since the age of 19, when I traveled for one year across the United

States, Western Europe, and Scandinavia as part of a singing group, international travel has been a powerful means of self-knowledge. In the year before I finished my PhD, I traveled alone for an extended period, visiting friends in Israel, Belgium, Switzerland, and Paris.

After earning my PhD, I wanted to do more than explore a strange new place. I wanted to live where I didn't speak the language; I wanted to work within a cultural group I knew nothing about; I wanted to challenge myself physically and mentally. I wanted to construct a new life for myself, beyond the bounds of my previous experience, outside my familiar world. What would happen to me? How would I change?

The author Paul Theroux discusses how his own "disappearance in the world" helped him develop his skills as a writer: "I was isolated and enlightened. I learned to cope, I read more, I wrote more, I had no TV, I thought in a more concentrated way. I lived in one place, and I studied patience. . . . You think of a writer as in touch and at the center of things, but I have found the opposite to be the case. . . . I found out much more about the world and myself by being unconnected. . . . It was as a solitary traveler that I began to discover who I was and what I stood for."[6]

Theroux's words portended the way I came to see my experience in the Peace Corps. Theroux wrote: "I was as full of preconceived notions as Columbus or Crusoe—you can't help it, but you can alter such thoughts. Non-travelers often warn the traveler of dangers, and the traveler dismisses such fears, but the presumption of hospitality is just as odd as the presumption of danger. You have to find out for yourself. Take the leap. Go as far as you can. Try staying out of touch. Become a stranger in a strange land. Acquire humility. Learn the language. Listen to what people are saying."[7]

I was ready to be out of touch, take a leap, and become a stranger in a strange land. Oddly enough, I sensed that only in a strange land could I become familiar with myself again—with the person, the woman, the daughter, and not just the scholar. What better way to understand who I was than to volunteer for a worthwhile project, with an organization I could be proud of, in a part of the world where the needs were great and the resources few? I was ready. I never anticipated that my background in qualitative research would be so useful to me during my Peace Corps service.

ॐ

"The country is Togo," Jacob says to me the next morning, satisfying my curiosity before I've given him much time to say anything else.

Togo? Where's that? I wonder to myself as he continues to talk.

"It's in West Africa, bordering the countries of Ghana and Benin. The job involves working with young women," Jacob states. "You'll likely deal with issues of education, life planning, health education, family planning, as well as STDs and HIV/AIDS."

That sounds interesting, I think to myself, wishing I knew more African geography.

"Peace Corps is phasing out our rural community development projects (road building, wells, that kind of thing) and basing our work more on women, as well as the education and development of communities, by focusing on the people themselves. In this project, UNICEF has partnered with the Togolese Ministry of Education, USAID, Plan Internationale, and several other Togolese and international NGOs."

Jacob's talk is fast and furious but it all sounds so inviting that I don't dare stop him, even though I don't recognize some of the acronyms he spouts off.

"The pre-service training is two-and-a-half months," Jacob adds, "and will be in French. You will learn a third, indigenous language during training."

What? An indigenous language? I barely know French. How am I supposed to learn two languages at the same time?

"You will learn the third language through French, not English. Our language trainers are host country nationals. They will train you in French using French, not English. Once your French is proficient—with the immersion it won't take long—your trainers will start teaching you the third language. The training site will be rustic, rural, and simple. All those adjectives we like to use in Peace Corps!" Jacob laughs.

I can't laugh just yet. I'm caught between Where is Togo? and How will I learn two languages at the same time?

"The program is new," Jacob explains. "You will be part of the inaugural group. You can apply your background working with at-risk youth and families, but at the village level. As this is a new program, you can expect growing pains. It will be interesting but at times frustrating. I will complete the volunteer description when I've learned more from the Peace Corps staff in Togo about the country's goals."

I am both shocked and excited to hear that this project is still in its developing stage. I like the ideas of working with young girls and of community activism, and I also like that there is no precedent. To me, that means freedom.

"Right now," Jacob continues, "all we know is that the host country wants assistance in decreasing the school dropout rate of village girls, so there will have to be community development on issues of women and girls. We don't have a name for it yet—but one idea is Girls Education and Empowerment (GEE). Hey, this is the first program of its kind in Peace Corps. Togo is the first country to have it." Jacob pauses. I hear him shuffling papers as he exclaims, "You'll be pioneers!"

I feel numb. My face is hot. I see goose bumps on my forearms. I can't believe this is happening to me. "How many volunteers will be in the program?" I ask, in a calm voice that belies my inner turbulence.

"The country has asked for twelve women to start," Jacob answers.

"How do we know if villages really want this help?" I compose myself and my academic persona kicks in. "How will the program make a difference? What do the villagers think?"

Jacob responds forthrightly, with calm, clear words I will not soon forget: "This is not a typical Peace Corps project. You'll be introducing major social change. It will take several generations of volunteers before any effects are seen."

My lingering questions, however important to me, don't really matter. I am going to accept the post, I don't need to think about it. It's as if someone has already decided my fate, and I am just following my own path. I tell Jacob I accept the placement.

"Great!" Jacob says. "Staging starts September 15. You'll have to fly to D.C. for a couple of days, then you'll travel as a staging group to Lomé. . ."

I don't hear the rest. All I hear is my inner voice admonishing me: I've got ten weeks to finish my dissertation! I've got to get an atlas and find Togo!

The Story Begins

In September 1999 I joined the Peace Corps. I went to the small country of Togo, in West Africa, to work on a girls' education project. I sold all my furniture, stored fifteen boxes of books in a friend's garage, and went in search of myself, the "other" about whom I was most curious at the time. What I found instead was a fascinating West African web of gender, cultural, and romantic complexity, heightened by the intensity of Third World conditions. In Togo, I was both witness to and participant in this complex web, and I did learn a great deal about myself and a lot about the Togolese.

In Togo, I constantly processed (in journals, essays, and letters home) my ideas, emotions, and bodily sensations as I observed and interacted with the Togolese. By focusing so intently on the discoveries of my own head, heart, and body in Togo, I was granted a window into the heads, hearts, and bodies of the young women with whom I was fortunate to work.

This book is an autoethnographic account of my trip to Togo, illustrating the experience I had there in a way that is both emotional and embodied. In my embodied presentation I heeded Paul Stoller's call for a "more full-bodied approach to textual construction" in qualitative and ethnographic research.[8]

This book takes readers inside the world I experienced in Togo. I speak as a researcher/author and also as a character in the story.[9] In Togo, I was observer and participant, scholar and woman, teacher and learner. Diverse ideas, emotions, and sensations were refracted by those multiple lenses during my work with young girls in Togo.

In Togo I practiced a recursive process to make sense of my world, and this book replicates that process, continually layering my story between self and other as I narrate.[10] This autoethnographic account ties the intimate detail, the personal story, to the larger social context in which I lived. Literary devices and inductive knowing allow me to tell a story that more truly matches the complexity of the experience. Although my identity as a social scientist shaped my decisions about how and what I wrote in this text[11] (decisions addressed in the final chapter), I have chosen to hold an interesting conversation with readers as I present the stories that drive the overall narrative.[12]

To engage readers and sustain the story's coherence, I use literary devices such as creating composite characters and collapsing certain events.[13] I use dialogue to develop characters and describe complex situations. I favor descriptions that "show rather than tell."[14] I write in the first person and in the present tense. In autoethnographic research, an authentic, first-person voice and the data generated by it are acknowledged as worthy methods of political, cultural, and social discovery.

This book is as much about myself as it is about others. I write about my feelings while living in Togo, my developing relationships with Togolese men, women, and adolescent girls, and both the incredibly joyful and the terribly unpleasant experiences I had with them all.

No doubt, this story is about a place, a people, a culture, and a country. However, it is important to remember that you will see this through my eyes, through my interactions and experiences, and through my relationships with others. What I say in this book will give you much more information about how I make sense of my world than how the Togolese make sense of theirs.[15]

ᕈᕼ

In this story I am a character in the narrative alongside everyone else. You will learn about me, about the Third World context in which I lived, and about the people who became such an integral part of my life. Through me, you will meet Bernadette, the Togolese woman who became my dear friend, my maternal and sisterly confidante, and then, understandably, my betrayer. You will meet René and Maxim, two Togolese men, one married, one single, both exquisitely handsome, with whom I had many intimate encounters, both romantic and platonic. You will meet Shoshana, a composite character who represents three women I served with in Peace Corps, all friends, partners-in-crime, and reliable confidantes.[16]

You will also learn something about the people in my life before I joined Peace Corps: my mother and sister in Texas, and Oded in Jerusalem, a man I once thought I would marry. You will also meet many young women, Togolese villagers and city dwellers, in school and out, all wise beyond their years in ways I found sometimes inspiring, other times horrifying.

To manage my reactions to these diverse relational experiences in Togo, and thus better manage their lived complexity, I documented—in letters, essays, and journal format—what I felt, observed, and thought about in Togo. I did not focus on the observations of my head, heart, and body simply to satisfy a self-indulgent urge, as critics of autoethnography sometimes suggest[17]—but instead, to make coherent sense of what I was seeing, learning, and experiencing. My focused attention on the head, heart, and body experience allowed me to reach more deeply into the world of the Togolese people to ask more informed questions about their lives.

No research endeavor is free from the indulgent impulse that drives it; nor is a researcher's indulgence necessarily a problem. Rather, what is significant is whether or not, and how, the researcher acknowledges the indulgence that drives her research impulse, method, and text production. Is she willing to be transparent about her choices? A transparent approach demands a personal, intimate relationship between the reader and the text. Social science research need neither be impersonal and distant nor written in the third person to be considered scholarly.[18] Personal experience and an intimate voice can be a powerful form of information, and be subject to critical and cultural analysis like any other data.

The unique value of autoethnography is its tacit assumption that researcher transparency is a valuable method by which to convey the management of complex social phenomena. My autoethnographic approach to life in Togo allowed me to dip into the cultural brew bubbling at its surface. It provided a lens and a method through which to examine a layer of Togolese social strata to which I could not otherwise have been privy, and it compelled me to try to live among the Togolese in ways that were socially just and accountable.

Transparency was prerequisite to my understanding of the phenomena I experienced and witnessed in Togo. I quickly learned that I would have to acknowledge, embrace, and reconfigure my own biases every day if I was to live in Togo harmoniously with myself and others. In this book, I have tried to remain true to this harmony, using the autoethnographic form as a guide toward reconstructing and telling my story. I focused on illustrating the events in this story in all their diverse complexity, much as I experienced the events moment to moment. In this account, as in the lived experience, I continually challenged myself to tie specific events to their larger cultural, social, and political contexts.

❧

I narrate this story in ways designed to invite dialogue. I share my "flaws, disappointments, and bad decisions as well as my strengths, achievements, and good judgments."[19] I do this with flourish because, like Carolyn Ellis, I believe there is great scientific value in "showing the bad as well as the good, what has been private and confidential as well as what is public and openly accessible, what makes us uncomfortable as well as what makes us comfortable."[20]

Many of these experiences have unclear resolutions, each of which can be examined from many points of view. While I address this further in the last chapter, my intention is to lay out the narrative in such a way that the reader's emotional response signals a preferred resolution more strongly than anything I say in the text. There is room for the reader to have an emotional, affecting relationship with the text.

According to Goodall, interpretivist ethnographies—those that acknowledge meaning to be socially constructed—involve writing that "rhetorically enables intimacy in the study of culture."[21] I want my reader to have as intimate an experience reading the story as I had living it. According to Goodall, an intimately written text heightens the reader's engagement. It promotes the possibility that readers will take personally what ethnographers have to say, so that our words can make a difference in their lives, and possibly in the lives of others.[22]

To make sense of my daily life in Togo, to sustain an intimate connection to what I was experiencing, I did what I was trained to do as a qualitative researcher: I took field notes, wrote process essays, and examined themes or bits of conversations that seemed to indicate a pattern not yet recognized. I even audiotaped certain phenomena: once, the sounds I heard at a funeral; another time, recordings of my friends in the village sending greetings to my family in the United States.

In the solitude of my village, I wrote profusely, out of a need to understand my experiences in relationship to the people and events that were a part of my everyday life. The isolation and bewilderment I often felt as a foreigner living in Togo, paired with the intense desire I had to understand "who I was and what I stood for,"[23] compelled me to be honest in the everyday documentation of my life while there. I have pursued the same transparency in reconstructing my story for this book.

Ironically, the issue of transparency as a research and writing method, in terms of its potential to illuminate lives on the margins, is precisely the personal issue I was to confront in my work as a Peace Corps volunteer in Togo. For the next year-and-a-half I would be consumed with methods of learning about the lives of young girls, in order to demarginalize their experiences within their communities.[24]

I had no idea that the issues I would one day face as an academic writing this book—issues to do with research transparency and social justice for people with marginalized voices—were about to become intimately familiar to me during my time in Togo, that sliver of a country I had never heard of before, which, eventually, would become a place I could not forget.

A Question of Mentalité

Maman Diore looks me right in the eye and explains, "When wives tell their polygamous husbands that they shouldn't go out with other women because they will get *le SIDA* (AIDS), the men may think that the wife is *jalouse* (jealous). It's a problem of *mentalité*," she says. "Men think only of *eux-mêmes* (themselves), not of the kids, or of *SIDA*. They do not understand and they do not want to understand. They think only of *eux-mêmes*."

Maman speaks with great determination and, at the same time, a hint of resignation. She also speaks very slowly for me. Although I now study between three and six hours of French every day, I am still a beginner in this language I've not practiced since college. I watch Maman's lips very closely to help decode her French accent as she sums up her points with a phrase I will hear over and over again during my time in Togo: *En Afrique, c'est comme ça.* That's how it is in Africa.

As a Peace Corps trainee assigned to the country of Togo, in West Africa, I am also a temporary resident of the town of Kpalimé and a guest of my host family. the Diores, where I have lived now for one month. In another two months, I will be dispatched to my village to launch a new

Peace Corps program to improve girls' education in the developing world. Togo is the first country to have the program; my training group is the first to implement it. "You'll be pioneers," my Peace Corps recruiter told me.

Maman's comments remind me how overwhelmed I am with the subject of men and women—indeed, of the complexity of all issues related to gender—in West Africa. Also overwhelming is the difficulty of grasping these issues in a language not my own. This afternoon what I find most remarkable is that I understand Maman at all—my French has not been good enough to have a real conversation with her until today. Normally, I talk to the Diore family—Maman, Papa, 11-year-old Kuku, 17-year-old Marguerite, and 20-year-old Alix—in the immature French of a child; I am forced to use sign language when I get stuck. Only Marguerite and Papa are fluent in English, however, they refuse to use it with me, so determined they are that I learn French.

In Togo, I soak up all I learn, experience, and witness, through my various identities: circumspect development worker, 30-something Latina[1] female, and ethnographic researcher. I am acutely aware (as are the fifty-three other Peace Corps trainees in my staging group) that I have recently earned a doctorate in the field of family therapy.

In this I am not the norm. Most of my fellow trainees have recent bachelor's degrees. Our first night together in Lomé, Togo's capital, I must have explained my dissertation—a discourse analysis of a hostage negotiation at a high school—nearly twenty times. Fortunately for me, of the eighteen women I see every day, three are already established professionals, with master's level graduate degrees, and are also in their mid-thirties.[2]

Today in our training class Jon, a business volunteer who has already served in Togo for a year, presents a talk on transparent accounting. He makes an interesting comment: "The French education system is one of rote learning. It is didactic. The Togolese, most recently colonized by France, maintain this system. Thus, students learn to mimic what the professor says. They do not learn how to think. It is difficult when they are put in situations where they must think. It's not done."

Considering gender roles in Togo from a different angle, Jon says the Togolese women with whom he works may intuitively know things about money, but they have not learned to put patterns together, they can't analogize. He adds, "Men don't do commerce here in Togo. Commerce is seen as women's work." Jon says if he haggles with a man, the man will say, "We're acting like a couple of women here." Not surprisingly, Togolese men don't work at the *marché*. The men you do find doing market enterprise are rarely Togolese. Thus Jon works almost exclusively with women.

After dinner one night I have a French lesson with my 11-year-old host sister, Kuku. We go over indirect and direct objects, the *passé composé*, and *le negatif*. I try to reciprocate this sweet lesson by teaching her a little English, which she, like many Togolese young people, is so eager to learn. We both laugh when I try to help her with the "th" sounds in *Anglais* (al**th**ough, **th**e, four**th**) because Kuku cannot make the sound very well; the **th** sound is foreign to her French tongue. I have the same problem with words like *reveillerai*, which Kuku tries to teach me to say correctly without much success. My mouth has difficulty with the **veill** sound in the word; my tongue has not mastered the little curl it must make to say the **veill** part of *reveillarai*. The sound does not exist in my English tongue, just as the **th** does not in Kuku's French one.

During the lesson, Kuku writes down the following sentence to help me with the conditional tense:

"If she is nice, she'll marry a rich man."

I don't realize that my surprise at the idea shows on my face until Kuku quickly adds *C'est ma professeur qui ecrire ça phrase.* My teacher wrote that phrase. Then she adds *Ce n'est pas vrai. C'est faux.* It's not true. It's false.

I nod, agreeing with her in halting French. *C'est pas une bonne phrase.* Not a good phrase.

When I am at home with the Diores, I spend most of my time with Marguerite, Kuku's 17-year-old sister. Marguerite was given primary responsibility for me by the Diore family for the three months I will stay with them. Marguerite speaks four languages (German, French, Ewé, and English) and plans to be an interpreter for the United Nations. She is assertive and has taken charge of my French lessons at home. We work every evening and weekend on my French.

One day in the *marché*, on the way home after my day of training, I run into Marguerite and see that she is upset with me. "Why didn't you come home at lunch? Will you be home by 6? After 6?"

Inwardly, I smile at her indignation but outwardly I match her seriousness. *À dix-huit heure,* I reply. At six.

J'espère, she says with exasperation. I hope so. Then she bikes away.

Shoshana, a trainee who is with me in the *marché,* comments that my host sister is feisty. I agree wholeheartedly. When I get home, I delight in trying to explain "feisty" to Marguerite; it is a perfect descriptor for her.

"Shoshana has said something about you for which I must *chercher* (look for) the translation," I report. "Feisty" is not in the dictionary, but there is something similar. I tell Marguerite she has fire (*feu*) in her. Only I mispronounce the word as "foo," not *feu.*

Marguerite frowns and says *fou* means crazy. I find "fire" in the dictionary to show Marguerite. Mollified, she says the word out loud, *feu.* Then she looks at me, exasperated again, and exclaims, "Your pronunciation!" *Feu, comme veut,* she says, correcting me again.

I can't help smiling at this, because Marguerite is being feisty again. Still, I don't give up. I try to find another, similar word to describe her and look up "attitude." I tell Marguerite she has *etat d'esprit.* Marguerite laughs, and her face relaxes. She asks, "Why did Shoshana say this about me?"

"Because of what you said to me at the *marché,*" I tell her. Marguerite laughs again, and so do I.

My nickname for Solange is *La Loi,* The Law. Solange is the supervisor of all the Peace Corps language *formateurs.* (All the language trainers are Togolese.) I love being with Solange. She has a commanding presence; she is beautiful, well-dressed, and large—just as the Togolese expect their women to be. Solange wears her size perfectly, and when she is present it is as if someone famous, someone important—someone to be reckoned with—is in the room. Thus, *La Loi.*

Solange also tries to perfect my French. She tries to teach me not to pronounce the letters at the end of every word, for instance, to say *marchande* without pronouncing the "e" at the end. "For example, it's not Solangeé," she says. We laugh together. Solange says, *J'aime la classe avec Laurie. Je ne sais pas pourquoi!* I like the class with Laurie. I don't know why. We laugh some more.

I realize that Solange has paid me a lovely compliment, both in what she says and the way she says it. Usually she is very serious and does not joke or laugh openly with volunteers. I think Solange appreciates my being near her age, in my thirties, and she likes my sense of humor. Our Togolese instructors have been asked by Peace Corps to refrain from forming personal relationships with us during training, so all of the *formateurs* remain somewhat guarded behind their big smiles and *politesse*.

I've received many compliments in the last two days, on my clothes, my colors, my legs, and my personality. An especially funny observation comes from our American Peace Corps trainer, Dani, who tells me, "You're a woman who looks as if she can handle her liquor." I love that! Cory, a business volunteer, says Larisa (one of the other 30-somethings in the group) and I are awesome because we can admit that we aren't ready to have children. I love being part of this group of women.

Fifi Rafiatu, a Togolaise *chanteuse*, is performing in Kpalimé tonight. I take Marguerite and her boyfriend Ahmet, who is 20 years old. Fifi arrives one hour late and sings one song before going back to her hotel for a break. During the interlude, a DJ plays various African dance tapes, and I dance in the back of the hall with some U.S. volunteers. A few young Togolese girls watch us timidly, but we can tell they want to dance. At Fifi's concert all the men dance, completely free and without timidity, but we avoid them and encourage the girls to join us instead. Dancing freely with them is a lovely experience. Many men try to break us up, but we don't let them into our little circle.

Maxim and Vincent, two of our *formateurs*, show up at the concert. I have developed an intense crush on Maxim, as have many of the other volunteers. While I have tried to keep my crush private, other trainees openly swoon, "Maxim! Maxim!" whenever he walks into class. Tall and lean, with a toothy smile and a charming manner, always dressed immaculately and stylishly, Maxim is popular with our all-woman training group. It has been about six weeks since we arrived in Togo. We are missing men and need someone like Maxim to fixate on.

As Fifi returns to the stadium, Maxim catches my eye and waves slightly. In a long-sleeved purple shirt, black slacks, with his shirt slightly unbuttoned, Maxim looks amazing. Just gorgeous. I had seen him earlier in the day, and told him I thought the shirt was cool.

Fifi, about to start her next set, asks four volunteer couples to join her on stage. The man in the aisle behind me, who has been yelling all night for Fifi, asks if I want to go on stage with him. "Why not?," and we start walking sideways out of our respective rows. The man stops me as I arrive in the aisle. Is it too late to go up on stage? I understand why the man halts when I hear Shoshana yell, "Maxim wants to dance with you!"

Maxim scoots out of the row and comes over to me, to me and the man, and I don't know what to do. I explain feebly to Maxim, "He wanted to come," referring to the stranger behind me. Maxim defers, stepping back. but then the other man says, "No, it's okay." I realize it's up to me to decide. I grab Maxim's forearm, and off we go!

On stage, we dance slightly behind Fifi, on stage left. Maxim is behind me, so I can't see him move. One of Fifi's staff hands me a post-card of Fifi while I dance. I hear people clap and, though all I do is shuffle back and forth, it's great fun. I'm barely aware of the people, the lights, or Fifi. I am only aware of the music. When it's over, the crowd goes wild.

Maxim whispers in my ear, excitedly, in English, "They're clapping for you." As we walk home later, he and Vincent tease me about being a good dancer. I feel very strong and beautiful and proud of myself. Ahmet and Marguerite, Shoshana, Maxim, and Vincent all compliment my dancing. Maxim takes my arm as we walk, and we hold hands briefly.

He says charming, witty things to me in French, and I actually understand his subtle, humorous nuances. His words produce the same intimate sensations I'd feel if the language were my own: I have butterflies in my stomach, goose bumps on my arms, and a smile as big as can be. I dream of Maxim this night, his hands and arms, his long, graceful fingers.

Marguerite loves to dance, dances beautifully, and can do a dance called the mapuka, which is basically a dance of butt worship. Dancers bend over and shake their butts in a way I never thought possible. It's the butt cheeks that dance! It's quite impressive, the more so when I realize that both men and women do it, and not necessarily for people of the opposite sex. Everyone worships everyone's butt. All butts are equal here!

I see the mapuka *en masse* one night at a new club in Kpalimé. Whoa! Imagine all these butts in the air, cheeks quivering, and then realize that it's completely fine for your fellow worshippers to caress your ass or snap a handkerchief at it. The butt thing is especially cool because it somehow levels the differences between women and men here. They all love butts, and they all have them, so it's quite simple. (Mapuka, my sister Marguerite tells me, originated in Cote d'Ivoire and is related to traditional African music, but here it is done with contemporary music and instruments).

After I dance one mapuka, I go to the bar to get a drink. I have trouble making my way through the crowd; all the tables are overflowing and people stand around in tightly packed clusters. As I maneuver, someone sticks his hand between my legs, in the crotch of my pants, and then quickly runs it upward, across my waist and over my breasts. The hand moves so fast that when I turn quickly I cannot discern its owner. In the sea of faces, I suspect the culprit is one of a group of older-looking Togolese men sitting at a table I just passed. When I turn around, they all have their eyes on me. I am disgusted.

Tonight is the first—but not the last—time I am groped when I dance in Africa. It quickly becomes clear that if I dance in public without a partner, especially if I am wearing pants, I am fair game. Marguerite tells me that Togolese men believe (from watching B movies) that all Western women are promiscuous. They think it is okay to touch them any way they want. (I have not seen Togolese men touch Togolese women intimately in public.)

When I dance, men have no inhibitions about touching me. Trying to keep them away tonight, I dance exclusively with Marguerite's male friends, who are very respectful. As I dance a slow dance, I notice a woman dancing closely with someone. She has been watching me all evening, and now she smiles at me. I say *Bonsoir!* to acknowledge her. She reciprocates, *Bonsoir!* Then she says, chuckling, *Vous êtes paradis.* You are paradise. I can't tell if she means it as observation, an insult, or a compliment. I just nod.

Maman tells me she has hired a girl to do my hair after church. Before we leave for Mass, the girl presents herself, and Maman instructs me to give her 5000 CFA (approximately $10 US) so she can buy two packages of what the Togolese call *mèches*, fake hair. After church, I sit on a mat under a tree for three hours while the *coiffeuse* works over me. It feels pleasant, and relaxing.

The *mèches* are long and heavy tresses. Even so, I feel a bit cooler with them hanging down my back. I don't have hair in my face. Wow! What a feeling! My hair hasn't been this long since I was a little girl. Taking my new hair for a short bike ride down the Hotel Cristal road, I hear my name. It's Shoshana, walking her bike along the shortcut to the Hard Rock Café. (We have named the *buvette*—bar—on this road the "Hard Rock Café," though no one seems to know why.) It's dusk, and the sky has bathed everything in a magical light. I feel as if anything can happen at this time of night.

Coincidentally, Shoshana also has her hair tressed. It looks lovely, but she's fretting about what she calls a "butt crack" in the front. Her *coiffeuse* parted her hair in the middle rather than the side and, because Shoshana's hair is very fine, and her skin so fair, it does indeed look like a butt crack! She hides it with a handkerchief wrapped around her head.

Eager to get the opinion of another volunteer, we walk to Larisa's house on our way home. Larisa will be the true test of the hair's success. She is our fashion aficionado; she left many Manolo Blahniks in her grandmother's attic when she came to Togo. Larisa says, very sincerely and soberly, "The crack is keeping you from enjoying the entire hair experience." Her prescription?

"My answer to any makeup question is—wear more lipstick!"

When I get home, I orchestrate an impromptu photo session with Kuku and Maman. We take photos all over the house, in various states of dress. Kuku is adorable. She is a beautiful young girl and I want her in my pictures. While Kuku and I take photos in Marguerite's room, Maman changes into more formal attire. She meets us in the living room and sits regally on the sofa, communicating without words that she is ready to be photographed. Her behavior is assertive, though in an indirect way, and I get the message.

Maman's way of communicating indirectly is in contrast to Papa, who is much more open. Maybe men are generally more open here? The other day at lunch he tells me, "Laurie, I like you! You are easy, with the food, with everything. I like you and your ways." Maman is much more reserved, speaking to me through her behavior.

After the pictures, Maman takes me with her to drop off some material at the house of her *couturier*. The Kpalimé night is very dark, so we use the oncoming motorcycle lights, a flashlight, and a few distant lightning strikes to guide us. In the dark, I pass as *une femme Africaine*. No one calls me *yovo*—the Togolese word for outsider, foreigner. This misperception is made easier because the electricity went out in Kpalimé. With my new tresses, I pass as *Africaine* tonight, and it is wonderful and liberating to blend in.

ℰ

I can't tell that it is Christmas. There have been no familiar signs. But when I get home early from language class, Marguerite is decorating for the holiday, making big snowflakes out of used school papers, and hanging them all over the house. She made balls out of colored paper and hung them from the ceiling. With leftover scraps of paper, she decorated the trees and bushes in the yard. Her decorations are lovely, creative, and simple. What a welcome contrast to Christmas in the United States!

I hear music and drumming all day long on Christmas Eve, and everyone is smiling. People greet each other in the street, *Bonne fête!* and I see the same message in chalk on the front gates in the neighborhood. All the women are getting their hair done. The Diores play religious music, both in French and Ewé. They also play African music, dance music, and Simon and Garfunkel. Papa tells me that when he was younger, back in the Sixties and way before he met Maman, he had a girlfriend who was a PCV [Peace Corps volunteer]. Before she left Togo, she gave him all her phonograph records.

On the radio, we hear about a military overthrow of the government in Côte d'Ivoire, and the news further enhances the air of festivity. The overthrown Ivoirian president is hiding out in Nigeria and the people in Abidjan are celebrating. When my Togolese friends and family hear this news, they scream with excitement. Papa Pierre tells me, "The same thing will happen here in Togo, and I will personally come to give you the news in your village when it does." When I tell Papa I am so excited for everyone, that everyone seems so very eager and ready for change, he agrees. But then he adds, with unexpected finality, "In Africa, force is the only way to change government."

For Christmas dinner, my host brother Alix (age 20) and his friend Guy (age 19), who are on holiday from their university studies in Lomé, kill a goat outside my bedroom window. I hear the goat bleat, figure out what is happening, and go outside to watch, even though I shrink from seeing it. Alix holds the goat while Guy takes a large knife and cuts its throat. Marguerite captures the blood in a pot, for some sauce, I imagine. When I see her lick the spoon I tell her, *J'ai peur.* I'm afraid. I don't know how to say "Gross!" in French.

Marguerite smiles at me as she licks, asking, "Laurie, why are you afraid?" Not knowing the answer, I go inside to take a shower and recover. I am not used to seeing my food killed. But I should be. I grew up in South Texas, and have (fairly recent) ancestors who raised and killed animals for meat, as the Diores do.

As I towel off, Alix yells at me to shut my window. They are going to burn the spot where the blood is, so the odor won't persist for days and attract animals. By the time I go outside, Alix and Guy are ready to cut off the goat's head and sear its body to remove the hair. Then they scrape the carcass and cut it up in sections, with help from Maman. When the goat is served for Christmas dinner, I do not refuse it. It is delicious!

Christmas Eve after midnight Mass, I walk with Marguerite and her friends to the dance club, Kalifornia 2000, the place where I was groped. All of the PCV trainees are now regulars at the club. We were there one night when someone threw a Molotov cocktail from the street. It hit a man on the dance floor, and he was set on fire right in front of us. We stopped dancing, but only for a second. (Why didn't we stop? I don't know.) I remember expecting an ambulance and then realizing there wouldn't be one. The man's friends tended to him, carrying him out of the club. A few minutes later Jon, a PCV, herded us out of the club. After we left, the club closed for the night.

Tonight, Christmas Eve, we dance until 4 A.M. I love dancing in Togo, no matter what. Dancing in West Africa is so stimulating, and exciting, and adventurous, and strange! In some ways it is uncomfortable and disturbing—many times men and even boys caress my butt. If I'm dancing with a man I don't know, he may startle me by running his hands over my breasts. It's hard to decide what is acceptable and what isn't. Men grab other men too, just as if they are a couple. The whole thing is sexual, and yet it's not. Dancing seems to be more about becoming rhythmic with a person, or a group—about expressing your rhythm however you want.

I dance with Marguerite's male friends, who know me. I like them. They are young, perhaps 18 to 22, but they make me feel safe. When someone is bothering me, I dance with one of Marguerite's friends.

Tonight a young man, known to Marguerite's circle of friends, takes ownership of me on the dance floor. I dance with him, while four other men dance around my butt. This is fine. But when the men touch me, my partner yells at them in Ewé and puts his hands out, as a sort of force field, to keep them away. When he wants to get a drink, he finds a friend to dance with me until he returns. My partner is an exceptional dancer with a beautiful chest. I am embarrassed to be attracted to him because he is so young! I feel as if I am back in high school, but I can't help being aroused.

Later in the evening, Marguerite pulls me aside for a chat: "Be careful, Laurie. I am worried about this young man's intentions." I don't understand.

"He only wants one thing."

This amuses me because I am twice Marguerite's age. But I can tell by her expression that she is genuinely concerned for me. Even though I want to laugh at the incongruity, I don't.

The next day, I ask Marguerite what it was that worried her.

"I became worried when you started to dance with him exclusively."

"But he didn't bother me, and in fact he saved me from other men who grabbed at me."

Marguerite just shook her head. She did not agree with me. Marguerite is Togolese; she is part of the culture. Men do not grope her while she dances. So she doesn't, or rather she *can't*, appreciate my logic.

I have a great time dancing on Christmas Eve, on any eve, always, no matter what happens. I can sit and watch the men dance and be perfectly happy. They have a way of moving like nothing I've ever seen. And the women! Togolese women must have an extra gene for dancing! They are able to move their asses without moving their hips. They can jiggle their butts at any speed, fast or slow, and when they bend over and do this, everyone goes crazy. Men can do it too, but they have a move of their own, where they gyrate their pelvis very slowly, very sexily, in a way that is out of synch with the rest of their body. It's hypnotic to watch.

The men and women dance with members of the same sex just as sexily as they do with members of the opposite sex. Men dance with their friends, as do women. They dance breast to breast, pelvis to pelvis, making intense eye contact, whether with the same or the opposite sex. Both women and men sometimes feign oral sex on the dance floor. It's fascinating.

If I saw this uninhibited behavior in the United States, I would think I was at a gay bar, or that the dancers were trying to shock or titillate those watching. I don't feel that way here. The dancing is explicit but it is not exclusively a sexual performance—and no one seems to be disturbed by it. In Africa, dancing freely is something anyone can do, and everyone does do, from women to men to children, to teenagers, to the elderly. Your explicitly sexual dance moves do not automatically imply availability, only that you are a good dancer. No one seems to expect anything from you because of the way you dance (unless you are a *yovo!*[3]). I love that.

On Christmas Eve, I watch my host brother Alix dancing near me, with girls as well Guy, his friend from school. Earlier today, I watched the two of them kill a goat. Now, they dance, pelvis to pelvis. Where else in the world would I see two young men do two such dramatic things on the same day? They are so different from the men in my country.

In our training house in Kpalimé, we've decided to post a list of the books we brought to Togo as a way to exchange reading material more easily. I crack up when Shoshana insists on adding my dissertation to the list of books, just in case anyone wants to read it. (I did bring a manuscript copy of the work with me—I won't see the bound version for two years—to remind myself that I did actually complete it.)

When Maxim sees my dissertation on the list, he comes over to talk about it. But this feels much more like flirting—we are very playful, somewhat googly-eyed (mostly me), and charming (mostly Maxim). Maxim tells me, "You are going to be rich from writing books. You are going to be famous. Like Toni Morrison. She won a Pulitzer. You will too."

"In twenty years, perhaps!"

"No. Maybe five years."

I want to tell him he has great faith in me but I don't know the word *en français*, so I ask Maxim, who is fluent in English. He says the word for faith is *foi*, and, coming out of his mouth, *foi* sounds like one of the most beautiful words I've ever heard.

"And where do you think I'll be famous? Here, in Togo? Or in the United States?"

Partout, Maxim says. Everywhere.

"You've Got Mail" signals, and about fifteen volunteers, including me, look up. We are in Pagala, an old Peace Corps training compound in the middle of Togo, because of the Y2K scare. We aren't frightened, but all the news from the States is scary as everyone wonders what the new millennium may bring. Since Peace Corps is also uncertain about what will happen, they are extra cautious, and make all the new volunteers stay in Pagala for the New Year. We spend the time watching movies and having language lessons, and will return to our respective villages—where we've been for only a week—when Peace Corps decides it's safe. We might be here for as long as ten days!

As I view the movie, I find myself longing for the following: coffee, books, New York City, Meg Ryan's clothes—and her comforter. In one scene she comes home and flops down on her bed, and I can feel the sensation in my own body. I am fulfilled just watching someone flop on a big, comfy bed!

Lunch today is a feast. I especially appreciate the food because in Pagala I seem to leave most meals hungry. I am not eating enough. Perhaps the cooks do not buy enough food? Maybe we are all eating more than we did three months ago? Because of all the physical energy we expend in Africa? It is an unfamiliar and unwelcome feeling to leave the dinner table hungry. Thankfully, today is different. We eat cabbage with goat liver, salad, fufu[4] with peanut sauce, beans, rice, bread, and wagash cheese. I finally feel full at the end of the meal.

New Year's Day, after a *sieste* of at least two hours, a group of us decide to venture into town. The cooks told us there is a drumming *fête* today. As we walk to the village, we see many people walking up and down the road, all dressed up. Children greet us properly (not a single one yells out *Yovo! Yovo!*). We get to town and hear the drumming but can't locate its origin. Following a taxi driver's directions through a neighborhood, we enter a clearing and find a swarm of people moving to the steady drum beat. They aren't really dancing, but are gyrating to the music in a circular motion.

In the circle, I see a man in a flowery print dress with a black bra strapped on the outside. Then I see two more men dressed like the first, and one of them is wearing makeup and a wig. A fourth man has a stuffed rabbit in a *pagne* on his back. The men's eyes look glazed over, as if in a trance, as they gyrate and shuffle rhythmically in time with everyone else. Finally I see the pattern: men are dressed as women, and women are dressed as men. All the adults are in drag! The men are in dresses with bras on the outside and stuffed animals in *pagnes* on their backs, while the women are wearing men's Seventies shirts and Western clothes. I plant myself at the edge of the circle to watch, and other volunteers soon join me.

Miriam, a volunteer whose mother is Senegalese, tells us the people are dressed up to disguise themselves from bad spirits and bring in good ones for *l'an 2000*, the New Year. The first thing, Miriam says, is to disguise your gender. Then you augment the disguise with fake braids, hats, and stuffed animals (representing babies) in *pagnes* on your back. Shoshana likens the scene to *carnivale* in Brazil. I agree. There is a decadent feel to it, expressing both spirituality and shock value.

I watch the women more closely, to understand why it took me longer to recognize their costumes. To look like men, some of the women have put on suits and others hold shortwave radios against their ears. (This is so clever! Many men in Togo seem to spend all day walking around with a shortwave radio held to an ear.)

The women look American. That is, they look Western—which for some reason I find disconcerting. It is not strange to see men dressed up in Western clothes; I am used to this. However, for most of the Togolese women I see each day, *pagnes* are *de rigueur*. *Pagnes* are the African village woman's uniform, worn both in and outside the home. I rarely see a Togolese woman in anything else, never Western-style pants.

I am fascinated watching the men and women shed traditional roles. Men hold hands and look sexy in imitation of women, and women wear any clothes they want and mimic men. Today's *fête* is one of the few celebrations in which we (as *yovos*) are not invited to participate. How refreshing to be excluded so forthrightly!

We leave the scene and head back to our compound, planning to stop at another *buvette* (also named Kalifornia) on the way. When we arrive, they're playing Bob Marley. We sit, drinking and watching, and soon there is mapuka music. I find myself dancing in my chair; habitually now, I jerk my ass backward, mapuka style. I think I've acquired a new reflex in my butt! Still, I don't get up right away. I try to contain myself, restrain myself. But eventually I give in to the dance.

A small boy is on the makeshift dance floor and, young as he is, he has the moves of an experienced dancer. I dance over to him. Soon, there are thirty children surrounding us, all dressed in their Sunday best for the New Year's *fête*. Shoshana joins me, and the crowd increases. The kids aren't really doing the mapuka, but a variety of gyrating and sexy moves, wildly waving their hands in the air.

The children click their forefingers and thumbs together as they dance and I think I see little castanets. But they're bottle caps! A child bites down on one bottle cap for his thumb and another for his forefinger. All of the children have these "castanets"; in unison, they sound fabulous. One little girl lends me her pair while we dance.

At first the children shyly pull away from me, but not for long. Soon they come closer, dancing like maniacs before me. They dance with the rhythms and moves of adults, yet the precociousness, vitality, and openness of children. I am exhilarated dancing with the children. If I throw my hands in the air, they mimic me. As I try vainly to mimic their moves, they do what I'm doing instead.

I dance my way to the entrance, where the air is cooler. When I start to leave the dance floor, the kids cry out in unison *Non, Non!* They think I am leaving the *buvette*. I yell *Dehors! C'est mieux dehors!* Outside, it's better outside! Once the children understand, they follow me, screaming and chanting and dancing. I feel like a sports superstar, whose fans won't let her be. Outside, the boy with whom I started dancing (age 4, I later find out!) grabs my hands and dances with me. It's just a joy.

Kids are given their freedom when they dance: they aren't doing any chores; they aren't waiting on anyone; they aren't hiding out; they aren't deferring. They are free, and it is such a contrast to what we are used to seeing them do. I love dancing here, with kids and with women, especially. Not only because they are such good dancers, uninhibited and free when they dance, but because dancing erases the roles they have inherited or been assigned, at least temporarily. The kids don't have to do chores; the women completely let go. It's great!

The Little Things That Matter

Dear Mom,

Living here in Africa makes me think about you as a little girl, living in South Texas. You know the stories you always tell about Palito Blanco? How you lived without electricity, telephones, or running water? Your stories have a whole new meaning as I settle into my new village of Kougnohou.

I'm experiencing a different version of privacy here in West Africa. I can actually wave to passersby while in my outdoor shower! The shower is about fifty feet from my front door, but away from the path to the house. It's like a short telephone booth, made out of concrete and without a roof. When I am in it, only my head is exposed. Still, when my neighbor passes by and I am in the shower, he refrains from greeting me or even looking my way. (Normally, he would go out of his way to say hello.)

In Africa I've learned to buy my toilet tissue—which I keep on my person, never knowing exactly where or when I'll need it—one roll at a time because it's so expensive and valuable. Almost every little stand on the street sells toilet tissue by the roll, but I have rarely seen it in Togolese latrines. My family in Kpalimé stacked pages of Marguerite's old schoolwork in a box by their toilet; frugally, they store lightly used paper in a second box.

Toilet tissue is expensive, and notebook paper is good for the latrine. I'm told the pit latrine can actually serve as a natural compost pile, as long as you don't put tampons and other stuff in it. I don't know if I'll be that disciplined. What the hell am I supposed to do with a used tampon?

Did you burn your trash, too? Burning trash here is a little tricky. I'm told children will reach into the fire to retrieve my trash. My family in Kpalimé went through my trash every day. I've heard little kids take tampon applicators and use them as wheels for homemade cars.

In general, disposing of things is tricky. There is no disposing here. There's a use everything—it's the ultimate recycling attitude. Even the ashes of the burned trash will go into the latrine to curb maggots.

After three months in Africa, I am constantly thinking of multiple uses for things I would normally discard. How can I use my empty tuna fish can? I need a candleholder of some kind. This leftover plastic bag, with only a bit of oil in it—what need can it serve? I am always in need of something, and in Africa I must be creative, resourceful, and quick to meet my physical needs. It's a whole new way of thinking for me.

I have had similar epiphanies about the way I use water. I never throw water away until I've used it several different ways. For instance, I use soapy water left over from washing my face or hands to wipe the floor, lantern, or propane stove. When I finally throw the water out, I'll toss it on the dirt where I dumped last night's spaghetti water, or on the spot where I spit out my toothpaste.

I don't know if I'll break down on the ground and cry (like the PCV in the book Dear Exile[1] did) when I get home and can once again use water without worrying about its eventual absence, but for now it's hard not to imagine reusing water over and over and over again. I can't believe I've written a whole letter on toilet paper, trash, and water. Suffice to say that, in Africa, it's the little things that matter. And even the little things, like bathing, using the toilet, or disposing of trash, are not done without forethought, planning, and effort.

I promise to write again soon—fewer gory details next time!

Laurie

ℰᏣ

I've been in Africa for exactly three months on the day I write this letter to my mother. Yet I feel so green when it comes to making observations about Africa. I know I've changed, I've adjusted, I am becoming *habituée* to my life in Togo. But I can't really even see or imagine what I might be like after one year, two years.

One thing that has been hard to get used to is a new conception of time. Any small errand I have can easily take over an hour to complete. This is partly because I will need to greet so many people along the way. Also, I feel the time so much because I am stared at, looked at—gawked at, really. (Today it took an hour-and-a-half to buy toilet paper, matches, and lunch.)

I am amazed at how Togolese manage time. It's not simply that no one is in a hurry. Everyone seems to be doing exactly what they are supposed to be doing—as if it's completely sensible. I am the one who can't make sense of it. I always forget how much I hate waiting and how often I must do it in Togo! I still have a First World reflex that expects things to work in Africa just as they do in the United States. Every day I relearn how Western my expectations are.

My current dilemma as a new resident of Kougnohou is how to decide when to open my front door in the morning. Although I finished my mother's letter an hour ago, I haven't opened my door yet. The open door indicates an open invitation to visitors—like a radar signal that indicates you are ready to end your privacy for the day.

Because I've chosen to live on my own, without a family and not in a compound, or *concession*, I've had to figure out things I took for granted at the Diores. I need to create a suitable place for people to visit me—and soon. Most Togolese conduct social visits outside, not inside, their homes. Most have benches or little *tabourets* (stools) outside. Also, most homes have a terrace, like the Diores' did, or a *paillote* (little grass hut without walls) in front of the house. I do not have a greeting place yet.

When people come to visit me, I must talk to them at my screen door, or admit them to my private quarters. I am not comfortable doing either. The Togolese do not permit people in their own quarters without a specific reason. You would like to have sex with a man? Show him your *boudoir*. No words need be spoken. The Togolese have a reputation for being extremely passive, but also direct! I plan to follow their example as much as possible.

ꝏ

Today Monsieur Bénoît comes to my house to talk to me about the goals of the Girls' Education and Empowerment (GEE) program. Bénoît is a social worker with Affaires Sociales (government social services) in Togo. Responsible for many villages and towns in this region, Bénoît's primary residence is in Kougnohou. He travels frequently by motorcycle, working with numerous women's *groupements*[1] in villages throughout the area. A well-built man, always immaculately dressed in Western-style *pagne* fabric shirts, Bénoît has a big, bald head that he rubs constantly when he is lost in thought, which is often. His expressive face is dominated by big black eyes and very white teeth, which appear often because Bénoît smiles all the time.

Bénoît knows the village well. He has lived here for years and is highly respected in Kougnohou. During his unexpected visit today, I take the opportunity to ask him what he thinks is the main reason girls in Kougnohou do not go to school.

"There are only 100 girls in the junior high, as opposed to 400 boys," he tells me. Such ratios are not news to me; however, I am still surprised to hear them stated so matter-of-factly. Bénoît continues, *Les filles ne frequente pas l'ecole parce que il y a la grossesse.* The girls quit school because of pregnancy.

Bénoît's observation leads me to ask him about sexual relationships between boys and girls.

"Sex is an amusement for the girls, who have sex at the boys' houses. Family planning and sex education are not as important as the need to teach *l'abstinence.*" Bénoît does not acknowledge boys' involvement in the sexual equation with girls. It's as if he absolves the boys of any responsibility—or even participation!

I am curious about Bénoît's views, even though I disagree with them, so I ask him about the problem of girls being sexually harassed (and impregnated) by their teachers. His confident response: "This is not a problem in Kougnohou."

His quick, self-assured answer makes me wonder how much Monsieur Bénoît really knows about what's happening to young girls in this village. Still, I listen respectfully to him, just as everyone else does.

Today, I have no way of knowing that Bénoît's comments represent the consensus in Togo. I will hear many similar comments—from both men and women, girls and boys, educated and uneducated, rich and poor—throughout the rest of my time in West Africa.

My first week in Kougnohou, I befriend two of the hundred girls Bénoît mentioned. The beautiful Odette is in her last year of CEG (junior high). Odette introduced herself to me my first day in Kougnohou. We sat in my kitchen as she told me about her family. Her mother has a paralyzed arm, and her father died recently; he was diabetic. Odette explains, "I am able to still attend school because my sister takes care of the household and our younger brothers and sisters. My sister makes money by selling *pâte*² at the *marché* on Fridays. Otherwise, I could not go to school."

Before she left my house that day, Odette asked to visit me in the States. She wants to go there to work with computers. When I asked in what capacity, she couldn't say. She could only repeat the phrase "work with computers." (Soon, I learn that many school kids in Kougnohou have that goal: to go to the United States and work with computers.) Odette also asked me to bring her a *cadeau*, a gift, when I go to the bank in Atakpamé next week.

I like Odette. I especially admire the initiative she takes in getting to know me. So many young girls are much too timid around me. But with Odette, I also sense a continuing expectation that I will buy her things, and this makes me feel uneasy.

The second girl I've befriended has a long Ewé name that I can't pronounce. I don't know how old she is or in what grade. She came with Bénoît my second day in Kougnohou; he introduced her as the girl who cleaned my house before I moved in. I remember feeling impressed that a teenager cleaned my entire house by herself without apparent help or complaint. I wa grateful that she did this for me, someone she didn't know.

Bénoît left the Ewé-named girl in my living room. Petite and chubby, with a huge smile and stylishly coiffed hair, the girl says her father owns a small dry goods boutique near the *petite marché*. I know this boutique; I have bought candles there. The girl admires my red toenail polish as I explain the purpose of the girls' education project. She smiles while I talk, and before she leaves makes just one request—that I come visit her in the afternoon. Her entire visit lasts fifteen minutes.

When I later go to visit my sweet teenage friend, she is not at the boutique. But I can see that all her family members—little brother, younger and older sisters, Maman—are at work, passing in and out of a door cut into the 15-foot display wall that separates boutique from family living space.

I introduce myself for a few minutes to the girl's Maman. Before I leave, Maman instructs the girl's little sister, Kafui (who Maman says attends elementary school but doesn't speak French yet), to take me where my new friend is getting her hair done. I follow Kafui, who walks swiftly down the road and through several family compounds before arriving at the base of huge tree. Under the tree, my friend sits in a chair while a *coiffeuse* works on her hair. Several teenage girls sit lined up on a bench nearby, watching the *coiffeuse* work. As I arrive, I greet everyone, *Bon soir tous le monde!* and sit with them on the bench to talk.

The second thing I say, an observation about my new friend, pops right out of my mouth before I can stop it: "Your feet are so tiny!"

The girl giggles this lovely giggle and, looking at my feet, clad in cheap flip flops, she marvels again at my red toe polish. All the girls then look down at my toes and agree, *Oui, c'est bon!*

When I leave the girls fifteen minutes later, I can't help noticing that my new friend—whose name I still can't pronounce—has distinguished herself from many others by what she hasn't said to me. She has not asked me for a thing. I like the girl.

Bernadette Dionéne is my official Togolese counterpart in the village. Recently employed as a social worker with a Swedish NGO (nongovernmental organization), which packed up and left Togo two years ago, Bernadette is now a market woman. She has a small stand on the main road near the taxi station where she sells sundries—toilet paper, individual cigarettes, small tomatoes. Bernadette is about my height, but that's where the similarity between us ends. Bernadette has arms and biceps like guns, a mischievous smile that she rarely shares, blue-black skin, big expressive eyes, and a beautiful face that can travel from animated disdain to extreme curiosity to playful teasing in a split second.

I will soon learn to love Bernadette's expressive face, which often says so much more than her words, and I will especially grow fond of her gentle way of talking. She is kind, but she is not afraid to be inquisitive and persistent, and she manages all of these with grace and poise. During the next three months, while I conduct my official Peace Corps *étude de milieu*—a study of the village I must complete before I implement any project—I will go to Bernadette's stand nearly every day. I will sit with her for hours, to chat, to learn, to familiarize myself with the town. Bernadette soon jokingly names her stand (one table, two benches, a tiny tin roof) my official *Bureau du Corps de la Paix à Kougnohou* (Peace Corps office in Kougnohou).

Bernadette has a wonderful way of making me feel good without showering me with false-sounding accolades. One day she says, "Your French is very good, Laurie, and it will just get better." I hope so.

Another day she asks, "Do women in the United States, the ones who are divorced, do they remarry?"

"Yes, of course they do," I say. "But men tend to remarry faster."

Bernadette says *Je suis divorcée*. She says she waited five years after her divorce before she married Koffi's father. Koffi is Bernadette's five-year-old son. Koffi's father works in Aného, a seaside village near Lomé, Togo's capital, a six-hour bush taxi ride from Kougnohou.

As Bernadette and I talk about the differences between women in West Africa and in the United States, I point out that I've rarely seen Togolese women in pants. Bernadette seems surprised at my comment, and I say "I've never seen you in pants!"

She tells me patiently, "Laurie. Of course I wear pants and so can you. And you can wear shorts too."

I like her enthusiasm but I doubt I can really wear shorts here. I've never seen Bernadette in pants or shorts, not even when I've been to her home. Even though I am skeptical I am glad for our conversation, because it's the first time Bernadette has volunteered personal information.

After our chat I show Bernadette some photos I keep in my purse—a colorful woven bag I bought in Kpalimé that Bernadette calls my *sac du secrets*. Bernadette comments that my mother is *tres belle* and, seeing me pictured with the Jeep Wrangler I once owned, notes that I can drive. However, she does not recognize the *Tour d'Eiffel*, or *l'Arc de Triomphe*, or the Statue of Liberty. Whoa. After this exchange, I ask each person who views my pictures if they recognize the monuments. Here I find a lack of common reference points that I assumed (perhaps we all do) are universal in the world.

❧

Père Antoine, one of two priests assigned to Kougnohou, does recognize the monuments. One day, he stops to see me at Bernadette's stand, carrying a pineapple as a gift. Although I've often seen him pass by on his motorcycle, today is the first time we have an extended chat. A young priest, Antoine makes small talk by asking about my family, my studies, and whether the people in Florida go often to Mass. In turn, he reveals that he studied five years in Italy, in Milan, and at the Vatican. He is fluent in Italian, French, Akebou, and Ewé. Curious about his readjustment to West Africa after Italy, I want to ask Père Antoine if he misses cappuccino and espresso. However, in my limited French the question comes out: "Do you like cappuccino and do you drink it here?" (How frustrating to be unable to say exactly what I want to say!)

Smaller and shorter than I am, the priest has small hands and a finely chiseled face. With his fair skin and freckles, he almost looks Italian although he is, of course, Togolese. On his huge motorcycle, he looks 20 years old, but he is 34—one year younger than I.

While Père Antoine and I talk at Bernadette's stand, I notice that everyone else who stops to chat with her avoids our eyes—mine and Antoine's—and ignores our presence. Rarely have I been so ignored in Togo, and in such a respectful way. I wonder, do the people who don't attend church feel embarrassed to be near the priest? Maybe he is the one they want to ignore (or be ignored by).[3]

I like the priest. He is intelligent, understated, and seems kind. I also like the way he watches and listens closely as we talk. He does it without making me feel as if I am someone from another planet, like many of the Togolese do. I feel normal talking to him.

Today is a major Togolese holiday and I am not sure what is going to happen except that there is a parade in town and Bénoît expects me to be there. I walk to the *carrefours*, the intersection in the middle of town, and see Bénoît, who instructs a woman to lead me to my seat. She seats me under a blue canvas tarp, which disconcertingly is emblazoned with the initials UNHCR (United Nations High Commissioner for Refugees). I sit for a minute but I'm uncomfortable. I don't want to be seen with the "authorities"; I don't want the village to associate me with them, so I walk away.

Bénoît sees me and asks, "What's the problem?"

Rien, I lie. Nothing.

I circulate, greeting young girls I've met in school, and some I don't yet know. Soon it is time for the parade and I am once more under the tent. Apparently I am one of the village "authorities" lucky to have one of the limited seats. Fine. There are lots more people now and it seems less conspicuous for me to be here.

But it is a big deal. Under the tent, there's a large picture of Togo's President Eyadema in front of the chief. The chief is all decked out in his *kenté* cloth and wears a crown of black felt with gold foil emblems. The authorities, and I, are led over to *saluer* (greet) the *sous-préfet* and the chief, and we sit again.[4] Only then does the parade begin.

The parade is hysterical and amusing and unexpectedly entertaining. I see: bush taxi chauffeurs posing on their old beat-up cars; bicyclists performing tricks; kids of all ages swishing their arms in front of the *sous-préfet*; a javelin thrower saluting the *sous-préfet* in a remarkably threatening way; a little girl who loses her flip flop but keeps right on marching; an old man who forgets he must salute and, remembering, hurriedly puts out his cigarette; and young CEG girls with whom I fall in love.

The man next to me (a teacher) says, as the girls pass, *Les maitresses de la future*. The teachers of the future. I beam with pride. The parade continues with: thirteen boys watching from atop a tree; Bénoît's great laugh when the chief dances; a Rastafarian soccer team player; girls *en sport*; Kabyé dancers holding tree branches and kicking up dirt as they dance; and, finally, the police, all decked out.

The spectacle of the parade is a huge success in the village, because, I now see, the Togolese are hams! Yet they take themselves very seriously even when hamming it up. They give one hundred percent to the effort. They are also a well-behaved and orderly audience—no protests, no antagonism, no upset. This, despite its being crowded and hot. Not to mention that 13 Janvier is a political holiday.[5] In the States such an event elicits a protest of some kind. Today I see no sign of dissent.

Bernadette invites me for lunch after the parade. I can come only if I watch her prepare the sauce for the *rix* (rice). Of course, I agree, and I spend an hour-and-a-half, maybe two, at Bernadette's sitting outdoors watching her cook on her mud stove. She puts oil and fresh tomato sauce in a pot with chicken parts (including feet, which I have never eaten) and a *pâte* of some sort. It's peanuts—*écrasé*, ground up. This takes thirty minutes and she gently ensures that I watch her. Bernadette's *leçon* makes me want to cook here like the Togolese do. Outside.

Bernadette tells me "Your skin is the color of river water!" and I laugh. We eat a delicious lunch, and we even share a beer. Yum. It is a true fête day, and so nice to eat with Bernadette and her family. I feel so comfortable here.

Later Bernadette pulls out tons of family photos to show me. Many are of Yawi, her 9-year-old. In the pictures, the family members rarely smile. Bernadette looks very beautiful in all of them.

Bernadette walks me partway home and, as we leave her *cloture*, I explain why I did not want to sit with the *sous-préfet* at the *fête*. She says, "The *fonctionnaires* (authorities) sit there. And you are a *fonctionnaire*."

Everyone seems to know this but me.

Bernadette tells me there will be a soccer game this afternoon, to mark the fête. After my *sieste* I arrive late, accompanied by a CEG girl, Marie-Claire. Again I am given a seat on a bench near the *sous-préfet*. More than an hour later I realize that everyone but the people on this bench are standing to watch the three-hour game.

I love being at the soccer game. Seeing *le sport* makes me want to run and play and shout out loud. How demure I've become in Togo! I can no longer easily imagine doing any of those things. I am focused on blending in, not standing out. I feel sad thinking how I've changed. Am I just *bien integré*? After all, this is how so many women behave in Kougnohou. I don't know how to evaluate my observation, but it doesn't feel good.

The gender gap really strikes me when there's a break in the game.

The boys and men are everywhere, but where are the girls? I find them in the crowd. They watch the game, passively. It's the girls who bring the water, serving the men, the dignitaries, and me. I sigh heavily. Leaving the game, I suggest to the *sous-préfet*, who I met formally on my first day in Kougnohou, "We need a girls' soccer team in Kougnohou!" He doesn't respond, other than to shake my hand and smile.

Undeterred, on the way home, I tell my CEG friend the same thing. "We'll do it!" she says.

I am lost in thought as we walk, reflecting on what I saw and how I felt at the soccer game. But Marie-Claire bursts with questions for me: When will you start working? What will you do? When can we start?

The questions shake me out of myself. I tell Marie-Claire, "I am still doing a study of the village, and am still not sure what my project will be. However, my goal is to improve girls' attendance at school. Right now I am very curious about how pregnancy prevents girls from reaching their full potential."

Marie-Claire gets very passionate when she hears me talk about pregnancy. "*La grossesse! La grossesse!* This is a serious problem here in Kougnohou!" she exclaims.

Marie-Claire's fervor has the effect of making me more curious about what she thinks. She is so believable. Then Marie-Claire surprises me: *Avec vous, ce sera mieux.* With you here, things will improve.

I feel a sharp pang of guilt. Although I've taken an oath to serve as a Peace Corps volunteer for two years, in my heart I have many doubts about the task with which I've been charged. Eradicating the problems that lead to the marginalization of girls in education is an overwhelming mission. What can I really do about it? Will forming a girls' club, as Peace Corps recommends, really help? What about the problem of *mentalité*? Besides, I am just one person, an outsider. I will leave Togo after two years; I don't know what decisions Peace Corps will make for this village once I am gone, nor do I have control over it. I feel so helpless, already, and I am only at the beginning of my *étude de milieu*. I have not even begun my project.

Yet, when Marie-Claire looks at me with such hope in her eyes, something shifts. I felt the same thing earlier today when I visited the *lycée* (high school) and met the thirteen girls who attend there—13 girls alongside 212 boys. I can almost count the high school girls on both hands! When I saw this statistic come alive in such a graphic way something woke up inside me. Seeing these eager faces, I can feel myself falling in love with the potential here.

I look back at Marie-Claire and say *Avec vous aussi.* With you too.

Bernadette has hired a woman for me. Her name is Honorine, and I am to pay her $10 US a month (Bernadette negotiated the fee) and for that she will do my laundry (by hand of course), and bring me drinking water (from the pump in town) and bathing water (from the *marigot*, the river).

Before I came to Africa, and even when I first arrived in Togo, I was disturbed to hear about volunteers who don't do their own laundry or get their own water. But the truth is that it is so much easier to have someone Togolese help with these difficult chores. (I had to wash my own clothes, all of them, by hand in a *cuvette*, a small basin, in Kpalimé. I learned to wear my clothes many times over before I washed them.) I don't mind it so much now.

I am still uncomfortable about the way Honorine defers to me. For instance, I have noticed that she eats the food I leave behind. When I returned from my shower yesterday, I found Honorine eating my leftovers with her daughter.

Honorine walks with a quick, determined stride, which she often punctuates with a harsh look or curt comment. One night, she took me to the Mobil gas station (which sells only lamp oil) to show me how to buy petrol for my lantern. About ten or twelve people were waiting in line for the same reason. The petrol has to be pumped by hand, and it takes time. After just a few minutes, however, Honorine pushed her way to the front of the line. She managed to get the petrol even though it wasn't our turn. She's tough, like all the other women. But she is also deferential to men, and deferential to me, as if I am a man too.

Tonight I talk some more with Honorine. She is thin and wiry, and her bright, animated face is full of wrinkles. Imagine my surprise when I learn that Honorine is close to my age, in her mid-thirties. However, she tells me, "I don't know the exact year or day I was born. *En Afrique, c'est comme ça.*"

❧

I love *marché* day. If I get tired at the *marché*, I can go home and have a nap and when I return I can eat whatever I want—kind of like the food court at the mall. Today I eat fufu with beef, I see the Fan man (who sells Fan ice cream), the rice woman, and buy bread and tomatoes and batteries and a mat and serving dishes and a *pagne* to wear to the shower and one to have made into a dress.

I make myself at home at Bernadette's stand, sharing a beer with her at lunchtime. We drink it in sips between her sales. I joke with Bernadette and a male friend of hers from church; he tells me I am *bien grosse* (fat)—bigger than the last time he saw me. He thinks it is good I am fat, so when I go home people will think well of Africans. We have a good laugh at that one; I tell him, joking of course, that I must stop eating. He tells me, joking back, that my mother won't recognize me when I go home. I say I'm fat because of Bernadette's food. He agrees the food is good in Togo. I say it's the fufu that's making me *bien grosse*, and he jokes back, "No, it's the *pâte!*"

Every market day, I walk to see the Muslim merchant at the end of the *marché*. He sells the dead *yovo*[6] clothes—the attire North Americans and Europeans give away, which often ends up on sale in African village markets. I am fascinated by the donated clothes, particularly the t-shirts, which look quite amusing on Togolese citizens who don't know what slogan they are proclaiming. They assert:

Johnny's Mom

Cheerleaders Have PMA: Positive Mental Attitude!

HORNY
(This last with a crude drawing of a little devil face)

The village seems to triple in size on market day. As I walk the marché, I am mesmerized by the crowd—the *tatouage*, the *pagnes*, the eyes of the children. I see tiny children caring for even tinier children. I smell coffee, but never find it (nor fresh bread—am I fantasizing?). I see the grace of the women, no slouches, naturally posture-perfect. I hear girls I don't yet know, but who already know me, yell out, "Mademoiselle Laurie! *Bonsoir!*"

How I love the energy of *marché* day! It is here I first start to see court-ing rituals. I see adolescent boys turn their heads when a girl in a short skirt (in Togo, knee-length) walks by. How comforting it is to see their universally recognizable reaction.

I go back to Bernadette's stand well-rested and full. I love days like this. They are full of nothing and everything at the same time. As the afternoon starts to wane, I run into Honorine and her kids. I tell her, "I cooked some extra rice last night. Will you come by and take some?" Honorine thanks me over and over. "*Grand merci! Grand merci*, Mademoi-selle Laurie!" It feels good to give.

Bernadette told me it's a custom to walk your guests at least part way home, but at dusk she leaves her young daughter to dismantle the stand and walks me all the way. As night falls, the village takes on an air of mystery, much more subtle and more beautiful than I see during the day. The skies, trees, stars, and even the cook fires are beautiful. The encroach-ing darkness is also scary as hell, because I cannot see anything familiar; without the moon and Bernadette's flashlight, I would be walking in pitch blackness. The dark night—the *nuit noire*, as Bernadette calls it—seems more natural than the daytime and also deeply rich with life. I can't see it, but I can smell it. I can hear it.

When I take my outdoor shower, I gaze at the stars; they feel like a reward from the heavens. Tonight is clear and I can see many constella-tions that I do not recognize. The stars are diamonds sprinkled over deep blue velvet.

Early morning in Kougnohou is magical in its own way. In the early mist I hear foreign tongues: French, Akebou, and Ewé. Uniformed chil-dren march to school, market women prepare to sell soap and *bouilli* (breakfast porridge) by the roadside, women carry water jugs on their heads as they pass my window.

The peace I feel as I greet each day is routine in Kougnohou. It's the first time in my life that I can truly appreciate dawn, dusk, constellations, the phases of the moon, the fragrance of the air at different times of day. That I can watch the sky for rain, for dust, for clarity. That I can smell earth, trees, and cold. That I can distinguish people's footsteps. That I can be wide awake every day at 6 and be happy for it. Here in Kougnohou, I can finally be with nature. I can feel, see, and appreciate nature.

As I get ready for sleep, Honorine comes to my front door to tell me the rice I gave her wasn't well cooked. She says I don't know how to cook it and that's why I'm always sick. Tomorrow she's going to show me how to do it right! A man who accompanies Honorine steps out of eyesight, behind her, and laughs in the background.

༉

Tonight I am compelled to write down the bits of conversation I hear nearly every day in Kougnohou: Hey, *Yovo*. Got a *cadeau*? Book for me to read? Address? Give me that watch, backpack, purse. I'll take your clothes, CD player, tape recorder. Can I have some money? Twenty-five francs? A ticket to the United States?

Can you get me a visa? A bank account? Mail this for me. Give me a copy of the photos you take. Tell your mother to send me something. Will you take me with you to the United States?

Will you sleep with me? Marry me? Buy me a beer? Show me all your belongings?

Did you buy that here? Can I have your sunglasses? Love those sunglasses. Love those shoes. Love that running bra. Your bike is nice. Can I touch it? Ride it? Wash it?

What's that? Wine? I'll take some. *Il faut me donner*. It is necessary to give it to me. What's that? Lipstick? *Donnez-moi*.

I like your hat. You'll give it to me when you go. Where's the bread you brought me from your trip? Bring me something nice from Lomé. Kpalimé. Atakpamé.

Can you introduce me to a sports team? A woman I can marry? Someone I can correspond with?

Do you have any work for me? A magazine I can read? A book? I'll be here tomorrow. I'll come Saturday. Will you be here?

Can I know your house? Can I visit you? Can I come to you? Here are some things I've never heard, or heard only once or twice, which make me take a step back: I have a gift for you. Can I take you to dinner? When you return home, I will send this to you. I want to give you something. Please, allow me to pay for that—you paid last time. In Africa, we have so much to give. We are smart, we know what we're doing. History is on our side. We can teach you. We can help you. We have a richness about our world that you don't have. You are lacking. You Americans need our help. Why is money so important to you? You don't need money to live a good life. To laugh. You don't need money to be happy. Money is the root of all evil.

You could learn something from us. From Africa.

Yet nearly every day, and often several times a day, I hear words, from strangers, friends, acquaintances, that I rarely (if ever) heard in the United States, and certainly not with the regularity that I hear them in Togo: Come to my house. I'll make fufu—I know how much you love it! Watch me cook, then, we'll eat. *Viens. Mange.* Let me help you with that. Let me carry that. Can I go get you bread? Wine? Candles? My daughter will take dinner to you. Are you hungry? I've cooked food, come have some. Do you like beans and rice? Monsieur Bénoît made some for you. What beer will you have? What do you take to drink? *C'est pas grave*—it's not serious, don't worry.

I'm very content you came to visit me. I am happy you are here with me. I've missed you. You are welcome here. Welcome. We'll take breakfast together. I'll buy the bread, you can buy the *pâte*.

I will write you when you leave.

My other very big excitement today was my BM after lunch. Finally, solid! I am so happy! It's just as psychiatrist Erickson[7] rhapsodized: a "rectum can really be pleased by having a good bowel movement." Exactly! I came out of the latrine smiling—I loved watching myself shit. As I was watching the two BM's go I felt I'd earned some sort of medal. An accomplishment. Very exciting.

How true it is that what you eliminate is a barometer of your health; it can be vital information about the state of your body. In a country where health is so closely (and clearly) tied to your water source, your food preparation, your own cleanliness, well, it's an accomplishment to be healthy, to have a solid BM. It means I'm in good shape.

One of the Crowd

Bernadette is part of a small commotion on the side of the road. As I walk closer, I recognize the crowd from the funeral that I passed earlier. Before I can reach Bernadette, a man in the crowd—someone I've met at the Kougnohou *dispensaire*, the health clinic—calls out my name. He seems to recognize the confusion on my face as he approaches.

"I am Jerome," he says. He grabs my hand and doesn't let go. Jerome seems a little too friendly. Has he been drinking? Suddenly he seems less appealing. When I first met Jerome, I imagined him as a potential lover. Now he is just another of the men I try to avoid.

Bernadette walks over, and together we stand at the roadside watching the activity at the home of the deceased man. The well-dressed, animated crowd looks more like a party than a funeral. A circle of people look downward. Some women wail, others sob, and the coffin rises as if by magic. One woman lays a purple-and-white striped *pagne* over the coffin.

"Laurie, the mourners are about to form a procession to the cemetery," Bernadette tells me. I notice that all of the other women stand alone as they cry—some loudly, others softly. No one consoles them, yet there is a feeling of shared sadness, of caring, of community. I am the only one who seems to find it strange that all the criers walk alone.

I think of the funerals I've been to at home. My grandmother, from whom my Charlés surname originates, is the most recent. She died after a long illness that included Parkinson's, heart disease, and diabetes. A very gentle, kind, and humorous woman, she died in a hospital, not at home as she had wished. This polarized my mother's brothers and sisters and my mother refused to go to the wake or the funeral. She did not want to deal with family conflicts arising from her mother's death.

I did attend both the wake and funeral. I remember seeing my aunts take turns consoling each other. One would cry, and another would arrive within seconds, cooing those terribly trite, insincere words: "She's in a better place now," "You have to be strong," "Think of the others." I saw unwelcome hugs, and the memory stings.

Here in Africa, the grief over death, the sentiment, is implicit. You can be alone *and* together in your grief. No one tries to tell you your experience. They just let you be. Watching this play out at the man's funeral, it seems to me that we in the States have an awful way of shutting down this experience, and we end up cheapening it. In death, there are no words to say to a family who has lost a father, brother, or husband. In Africa, people seem to know that.

After I witness many more funerals and *veilles* (wakes) in Togo, I begin to wonder: Is grieving a luxury of the developed world? People grieve here in Togo, but it is intense and brief and then it is over until the next death. Back home we say that death is a part of life; here, people don't say it, they live it. There's no haggling with funeral people. Grieving is quick, intense, and clean. I have great respect for this way of grieving. Still, I hope that no one I know here dies.

As the procession departs, Bernadette and I start to walk away from the dead man's house.

"He died yesterday, after a long illness," Bernadette tells me. "Laurie, I have been up all night." That's when I realize Bernadette's eyes are red—and everyone here has the same red eyes. Oh! Jerome needs sleep—he hasn't been drinking! He is slightly delirious from lack of sleep.

I see the crowd move collectively in a sort of jog, chanting as they follow the coffin, a huge procession of jogging, chanting, red-eyed Africans. Death is a two-fisted affair in Africa. It's as if the grieving is turned on full force, all at once, to the point of complete and absolute exhaustion. It seems that everything exists in extremes in Africa—even grief.

To bid me goodbye, Jerome takes my hand again and says, with a drunken look I now understand, "Now I am leaving to go to sleep, like the dead man."

He smiles as he says it. But maybe that's the point. Grieve yourself to exhaustion. Then sleep the sleep of the dead. Maybe that's what it takes to grieve well. That's what death—and life—deserves. To give hard and fully, to exhaust yourself in one fell swoop.

ॐ

At 7 o'clock one evening, I am writing in my journal when I hear Honorine on the path to my house. To my surprise, she chastises me for not stopping by her house after my walk. She has made fufu she says, because of me: *À cause de toi.* Honorine makes a big show of her upset, Togolese style. To appease her, I give her some cabbage I cooked today. She sees the box of Sangria on my kitchen table and says, "I'll take some of that too!"

Honorine's house is just across the road and up the hill from mine. She has put the fufu on a *tabouret*, a tiny bench. Although it's completely dark, we seat ourselves outside on *tabourets*. Honorine serves the sauce for our fufu while she tends the fire with one hand, a lantern in the other.

Honorine and I share one bowl of fufu and one bowl of sauce with chicken and peppers in it. Two of the boys who live in Honorine's concession pound the fufu for the children, who in Togo eat after the adults. Honorine and I eat and chat about the weather and the African *nuit noire*. Then Honorine pulls what I think is a chunk of chicken from the sauce. Only the chunk she pulls out has the head of a small rodent! I can see sharp teeth and even make out small ears. Honorine takes a big bite out of the back of the head and I must look shocked, because Honorine and all the kids start laughing at me.

"You eat the head?" I gasp.

Oui! Honorine answers back.

Everybody laughs as my eyes grow bigger.

When I munch on chicken pieces and toss the bones on the ground, Honorine tells me, "I would normally eat that and so would my kids."

I suddenly feel ashamed for tossing a chicken bone, something I never twice about. Thereafter, I give the bones to Honorine instead of tossing them. She eats them like corn chips.

I love eating outdoors, and I have a wonderful evening at Honorine's. Normally, I do not like my routine to get interrupted. After five months in West Africa I have developed an orderly existence. My body has become accustomed to having what it wants when it wants it. Sleep, a warm bath, and preparation for a night's rest are important to me. No doubt, living in Africa has made me much more conscious of my needs and much more direct about getting them met.

When Honorine invites me to dinner, I cannot say no. I don't really want to. That's why I'm here, isn't it? So I leave my letters, my reading, my quiet time before sleep. I leave my bucket of bath water outside. When I return later, the water is still slightly warm. Rather than walk the fifty feet to my shower, I bathe outside my front door, in absolute blackness (*nuit noire*).

In hindsight, I am grateful to Honorine for her invitation. I loved the banter with her, her kids' laughter, our strange relationship, the rodent episode—the whole enchilada. It makes me feel happy and loved and appreciated and part of something. Even though I'm still new and strange, I'm becoming part of the woodwork. It feels so normal, and it feels so good to feel normal! It's just like home. Only now I get to see beautiful stars, shower outside, and fend off disease. Mmmm, I'm happy.

Oh I almost forgot! Earlier tonight I learned that Nyalewossi—my CEG friend whose family owns the boutique—is in *4ème* (ninth grade), and that she is 17 years old. Her name is pronounced without really saying the 'n' or the 'w': Ya-Lossi.

At her house tonight, I met Nyalewossi's father for the first time. An *ecole primaire* (elementary school) teacher in a nearby village, I am surprised to learn Nyalewossi's Maman is his first wife. He has two others in nearby villages. Although I am disconcerted by the polygamous revelation, I like Nyalewossi's father immediately. He has a ready smile, a chatty demeanor, and is youthful. He walked me home because I forgot my flashlight, and we had a very nice chat. I'm so glad I stopped at both Nyalewossi's and Honorine's tonight. That's how things happen here. You have to stop.

ᕫᛠ

Susan Blake, who wrote *Letters from Togo*, insisted travel in Togo was easy.[1] I'm not sure she ever rode in a bush taxi. On today's trip we stop so many times. Near Atakpamé we drop people off 50 feet from each other: Stop, go, Stop, go, Stop, go.

A baby throws up in the car, we stop. The chauffeur sees a friend in the road, we stop. We stop to fix a loose wire on the frame, to add bags of charcoal waiting on the side of the road, to drop off passengers and pick up new ones. We stop to bribe police, and to buy baobab juice, roasted corn, bits of wagash cheese, or bread. It doesn't seem to occur to anyone that it is a waste of time and energy to stop so often, yet that is so clear to my Western efficiency-driven mind.

How can I begin to describe the bush taxi experience? Imagine all the problems you've ever had with cars happening simultaneously, but somehow your car still runs, barely. Imagine the body of your car held together with wire, boards, plastic wrap, and nails. Imagine having a contest to see how many people could fit inside. Remember there is no such thing as a seatbelt or a gauge for mileage, gas, or oil. Only the radio works. No rearview mirrors. No mufflers. Add a few chickens and a goat to the top of the van, throw in four to ten huge bags of charcoal, flour, and millet, and there you have it.

Now to the trip itself. Be prepared to climb over people, have them climb over you, feel their legs and ribs, smell their armpits, watch them pick their noses, have them sleep on your shoulder. (I've been doing this myself lately!) In the bush taxi, I have been so smushed between other bodies that I have felt my pelvic area fall asleep. Miraculously, you can entrance yourself in the midst of such discomfort. In Africa, there is no such thing as just getting there.

At the Atakpamé station, I am told that the taxi to Kougnohou is full and there is no place for me. I pay anyway, still hoping to get a place, while the taxi takes off to get gas. While I wait two handsome, albeit obnoxious, Togolese chauffeurs hit on me. They bat their eyes, they tell me *Je t'aime! Je t'adore!* They motion for me to sit next to them and, when I don't, they follow me around. At one point they both make eyes at me from opposite ends of the station, not realizing that while they can't see each other I can see both of them. Laughing, I tell them, and they say I must choose between them.

The chauffeurs' playful flirtation becomes the source of an unpleasant scene when the taxi returns. I can see that there is absolutely no place for me to sit. One of the flirting chauffeurs starts to argue with the passengers. The language switches from French to Ewé. I suspect the chauffeurs are asking people in front to move to the back of the van or get out so I can have the front seat next to the driver. Four people are already seated in the front seat, including the driver.

One man carrying a large display board with watches for sale storms out of the van and walks away. Then another does the same. One of the chauffeurs, now in the driver's seat, motions for me to come on board. He dusts the place next to him with a jacket. I am still outside, standing next to an older man who had been in the front seat before the commotion. I ask him what is happening.

C'est à cause de toi. It is because of you.

"I told them I could wait for the next vehicle, but the chauffeur told me I should take this one." I sound very unconvincing, even to me.

As the old man and I climb into the front seat, I see that the chauffeur means for me to sit on top of the gearshift. I have seen men sit in this place, with the gears between their legs; however, I can't do this because I am wearing a skirt, so I stay to the right of the shift. This means I am taking up the space of two people.

"Is this happening because I am a foreigner?" I ask the old man.

"It is because you are a woman." He is polite.

The people in the van are angry about the commotion I have caused. I want to be different; I want to take the high road. Part of me wants to give up and wait for the next taxi. But I don't because, more than anything else, I want to get home.

I knew that, when it came down to it, I was going to take advantage of my outsider status, my gender, my foreignness, my skin color. And I do.

At the first checkpoint we pick up an elderly woman with a small child. She will ride in the space over the gearshift, only there is no place for the little boy. He stands at my feet, scrunched between the dashboard and my knees. I pretend to be in a New York City subway, not noticing what is right in front of me. I try to think nothing as I feel the Ewé woman's concern about holding on to the child while she sits on the gearshift. I am torn between my desire to hold on to, and let go of, my foreign values.

When I allow myself to wonder—What would my grandmother do? What would a Togolese do?—and come up with the same answer, I am annoyed at myself. I pull the child onto my lap. The woman offers to take my large water bottle so I can have more room, but I decline. Holding on to both the bottle and the child, my position is awkward and uncomfortable, but I don't care.

As we ride like this, I am appalled and amused at the chauffeur's persistence in flirting with me. He shifts gears over the lap of the elderly woman while asking: "Do you have a boyfriend?" "Can I come to your house to visit you?" "When can I come to see you?" "When will you come back to Atakpamé?"

An hour passes with the child sleeping on my lap, before I finally, completely, let go. Without words, I hand the old woman my water bottle. Now I can hug the child to me so he can sleep more comfortably. He sleeps through it all.

At one stop, a passenger from the backseat sees that I am holding the child and smiles approvingly. I keep thinking how weirdly things turn out. At the end of the ride, I give the child a candy and he opens it very slowly, as if the candy is going to eat him and not the other way around. The old woman thanks me in local language, *Akpelo!* as she steps out of the van.

At times like this, I see how easily two years can pass. When I let go of everything but the moment—talking to Père Antoine about cappuccino, watching children at the *marché*, flirting with sexy Togolese chauffeurs— how far away my old life is! I don't feel sad, I don't feel upset, I don't feel unfortunate in any way. I feel this is how it is. This is my life now.

Nyalewossi and I snack on koliko—a favorite fried yam snack served with pimente sauce—and make plans to eat dinner at her house the next day. Kafui, the younger sister, runs around as if she is looking for something.

"Kafui is looking for the chicken we bought today," Nyalewossi explains.

We follow Kafui until she finally catches up to the chicken. Nyalewossi's 10-year-old brother Yawi and his schoolmate Atsu also watched Kafui chase the chicken from the commissariat across the road. The boys dash over to help, but the chicken hides in the bushes. Kafui can't see him there, and she looks lost. She is so expressive! So is Atsu. He rubs his head just like Monsieur Bénoît and wears a very serious face, but his quick laugh comes out of nowhere.

All of sudden, I see the chicken's head inside the commissariat.

Nyalewossi, her Maman, and I yell, "He's in the commissariat!"

I think this chicken will provide the sauce for our fufu dinner tomorrow. In fact, Nyalewossi and the others make me promise to return for the ceremony of strangling of the chicken, which the boys will do tomorrow. "You must bring your camera to commemorate the event."

The chicken-chasing episode is an opportunity to ask Nyalewossi a question my mother asked me in a letter: "With all the chickens running around Kougnohou, how do people know whose chicken is whose?"

Nyalewossi's face becomes studious. "If you buy a chicken, keep it at your house overnight, and wrap it in a *pagne* or tie it to a chair, it will always remember where you live. Then, if it goes out during the day, it will always get home again."

This is not the first time I've heard this explanation.

According to Nyalewossi, today's chicken, being freshly bought, did not have an opportunity to know its house.

Near 5 o'clock the following day, I walk over to Nyalewossi's again. I almost choose not to go because it is already late and I don't have my flashlight for the long walk home in the dark. I also feel a cold coming on. But, I go.

Nyalewossi has a big pot of sauce on her mud stove, which sits on top of a large brick. She sits on a *tabouret* while she cooks, and her little sister Kafui pulls one up for me so I can watch the action closely.

Nyalewossi adds oil, tomatoes, onions, and then the cubes of the beef she's already cooked. After the mixture has simmered a few minutes, I watch while Nyalewossi adds a huge portion of cooked white rice. The entire process takes two hours to complete, but Nyalewossi and I visit so easily it feels more like ten minutes.

During the visit, a number of everyday things happen in the family's concession. The fire dies a little and Nyalewossi has to add more charcoal to keep it going; a neighbor from the nearby concession walks over to get some of Nyalewossi's coals for her own family's fire; night falls and Kafui lights the gas candle; Nyalewossi's Papa arrives home from work, stops to say hello, and serves me a shot of sodabi (the local liquor); Kafui brings my bike in from the storefront, around back to the family's living space; I fan the fire too strongly and oil spills out of the pot.

When the meal is cooked and we are ready to eat, Kafui places me at a small table with Nyalewossi's father and his colleague. Nyalewossi's mother sits at the fire, and Nyalewossi and her siblings sit together in a corner. I don't even get to eat with Nyalewossi? That's not why I came.

When I ask Papa where Nyalewossi will sit, as she has cooked the meal, he laughs, "With her comrades, of course!"

"But I'm her comrade," I protest.

He just laughs. Nyalewossi stays where she is, smiling. I am the only one a little indignant.

Nyalewossi's father, his colleague, and I have another shot of sodabi before we eat out of one large dish, using spoons. (Typically we would use our hands to eat. You can form a little ball with the rice and it's easy to eat, except when really hot. However, we are still strangers, thus the spoons.)

Big sister Didi minds the store with Nyalewossi's help while her brothers eat together, and Maman eats with her hands, alone by the fire. It was Maman who sat at the fire immediately after the food was cooked, she who served up the bowls of food. It seemed to be her role to do this, a coveted one I believe.

The men and I talk amicably while we eat, but I am extremely aware that I just became one of the men. I became a male, a dignitary, some-one whose presence was too important to waste on an adolescent or a Togolese female. Although I enjoy eating with Nyalewossi's father and

his friend—they ask me about Texas, what food I eat there, what *viande*—
I miss eating with Nyalewossi and her brother.

When I've had enough of the fine meal Nyalewossi cooked, I shake
hands with Maman and the men, thanking them, and Nyalewossi and
her brother walk me home. When we arrive, I invite them in my kitchen
to show them my new *garde-manger*, the stand-alone kitchen cabinet the
menuisier has made for me. We compare in French and English the words
of the vegetables—*chou* for cabbage, and how *gingembre* and *l'oignon* are
so similar in French and English. They look at my tuna and spices. The
brother tells me, "If you eat the ginger with sugar it will cure your *rhume*,
the cold you're catching." Before they leave, I begin to heat my bath water,
and they *ooh* and *ah* at my propane stove.

Later, I am brushing my teeth when I taste something unpleasant. I
look down and see that some of the Klin soap, the African laundry soap
sold in tiny powder packets, accidentally got on my toothbrush. Hmmmm.
Not awful. Here I am, washing my mouth out with soap! Amazing, how
you can actually tolerate something you had thought absolutely awful.

❦

Today I have been invited to the *dispensaire* by Jerome, the sleepy man I
saw at the funeral. On Wednesday mornings the staff holds an open clinic
for pregnant women and young children; they give vaccinations and lectures. I arrive by 8 but the women do not start arriving until 10 or so, and
they make quite an entrance. The woman are all dressed beautifully, in
rich-patterned fabrics, long skirts, big blouses, a head wrap, and a baby
wrapped on their back with a third *pagne*.

I discover today why Togolese women wear such loose blouses: to let
their breasts out so they can breastfeed! I did not think I would get used
to seeing breasts all the time, but I have. Most of the women are breastfeeding, and at first I am shocked to see how no one takes any pains either to hide or to notice. Several breastfeed during the lecture, one as she
holds her child to get his vaccination, another as she is being chastised
by a staff member.

In Kpalimé, I had a dress made by Maman's *couturier*. It was halter
dress, a bit sexy, cut out of a silky, flower-covered fabric I'd found at the

marché. I gave the *couturier* a picture from a magazine as the model for the dress. However, when she was done, the dress was not sexy at all; actually, it came out a bit matronly. There was no place for cleavage, which defeats the whole purpose of a halter dress. I am not sure the Togolese conceptualize cleavage the way I do. Maybe next time I'll tell the tailor I need room to breastfeed!

It's not just at breastfeeding when breasts are out. Around the house, cooking, pounding fufu, women just wear the *pagnes* as a skirt and leave their breasts out. The breasts are like a tool here, like an arm or a leg. At the *dispensaire*, I watch the men closely; to them, it's as if the women are just using bottles, not breasts, to feed the children.

In Togo, women hide their legs and butt. To show your legs is very *risqué*. You don't see women in shorts here, or short skirts. In Lomé, you sometimes see women wearing miniskirts; many of these women are commercial sex workers. Young girls sometimes wear running shorts or skirts that go to their knee. Here, legs are like breasts —very sexy!

I learn this lesson the hard way one morning, as I walk to town in my favorite khaki skirt, which has a slit up the middle front. The skirt goes past my knees but the slit goes to my mid-thigh; it is unnoticeable, except when I walk. When I walk, the skirt swishes back and forth and my thighs are clearly visible.

As I walk to town one day, I am aware that my thighs are showing but I pretend to myself that it is not a big deal, even though people stare. No one stares at my breasts, as I expect; they stare and gape at my legs, which I don't expect. Each time I have worn this skirt, I have had trouble. One night, a stranger yelled out, *Est-ce que je peux coucher avec vous? C'est possible?* "Can I sleep with you?"

On the way to town, I stop at the *menuisier* (carpenter) to borrow a hammer. I carry it in my hand, swinging it back and forth, as I proceed to Bernadette's stand. A man walking through town rudely yells at me to stop.

He calls me *yovo* and says he wants to tell me something.

"I'm here, what do you want to say? I can hear you." I keep walking as I talk to the man in French. The man keeps my pace but stays about twenty feet behind me.

"Do you speak English?"

When I don't answer, he begins to yell in pidgin English. I repeat in English what I've already said in French. I'm carrying my hammer; he has his *coupe-coupe*, a machete farmers use. We each have props for what feels like a cultural performance of belonging and identity.

I tell him in French, in a very Togolese way, "You must not be from here because the people in Kougnohou are nice and you are not nice." I can't imagine saying this in similar circumstances in my country but in French-speaking Togo it's the perfect thing to say.

When we arrive at the town's main intersection, the market women walk out to get a better view of us. Everyone knows me; this man is the outsider, not me. But he hasn't guessed that yet—he just sees a white woman with skin the color of river water whose legs are showing.

Bernadette meets me in the road. She doesn't smile at me but our eyes connect and we both know what will happen next. I turn around, and Bernadette and I wait for the man, still thirty feet away.

"I am here, what do you want to say?" I speak in French.

Before the man can respond, Bernadette intervenes. She scolds the man in Akebou, the local language. She demands, with plenty of chutz-pah, that he explain himself. She insists he apologize to me. She berates him for his behavior. The man seems to get smaller and smaller as Ber-nadette speaks.

When Bernadette takes a breath, I repeat to the man: "I am here. What do you want to say to me?" I feel strong and confident, but I am borrowing all of it from Bernadette.

Not expecting to be accosted by two women, the man finally says, meekly, "Oh, you don't want to play."

Je ne suis pas un enfant. I am not a child.

The man doesn't bother responding to me or to Bernadette, he just walks away. Bernadette walks back to her stand, and everything returns to normal. But not for me.

The performance was more difficult for me than I let on. I was very much aware that I was being bothered by a stranger in what I now see as my village, and this was not acceptable to me. I was surprised by my upset. I was also pleasantly surprised to discover that the episode—espe-cially the reactions of others who witnessed it—made me feel so much more a part of the village.

ᲓᲮᲝ

My routine in Togo is now established and comfortable, and for the most part I am happy. Although I find many things difficult, I am surprised to discover they are not what I expected. To some degree, the things I find difficult also happen to be issues for the Togolese people. However, the issues are compounded for me, because I am a citizen of another continent, an outsider from the United States.

I'm having a lot of difficulty appreciating the country's political, economic, and cultural milieu. I hate that the schools are only open three months a year, because the teachers are always on strike, because they don't get paid, because the government says they don't have money, while the president of Togo travels all over this continent and Europe and still manages to pay the police force.

Like the Togolese people, I find myself very upset at the government, but I am also upset at the Togolese people for not getting angry enough to change things. (This is very much the luxury of an outsider's perspective, *non*? I won't have to fight the war that the Togolese fear if they have an uprising, will I? I won't risk losing family members—they will.)

I hate that, as a Peace Corps volunteer, I can never speak critically about the Togolese government in public. The president of Togo, with only a sixth-grade education, has remained in power thirty plus years, by force. He pays police and soldiers, while hospital workers and teachers go unpaid for five or six months at a time. (As frustrated as I am about this, I am a citizen of the U.S., not Togo. Eventually, I will leave Togo and her problems behind me.)

I hate the inequities between men and women here. I hate that I have to wear pants and long skirts so my legs don't show because I'll lose credibility if people see too much of my skin. I hate that I can't drink a beer by myself at our corner café, because I will be harassed by men who want to "marry" me. I hate that my skin color (brown to me, but white to everyone else) seems to be an invitation for people to ask me for money, gifts, or trips to the United States, all before they introduce themselves.

I hate that the poverty in Togo is incredible, pervasive, and persistent. I hate that it is safer for the Togolese to approach me for assistance than it is for them to question their government or demand economic justice. I hate that they are much more accustomed to pursuing foreigners for help than challenging their own government. (Togolese do ask other Togolese for money and favors, particularly people who are perceived as well off, like nuns or priests. In a way, a sense of colonialism pervades the culture, and it is not directed solely at people who are strangers here.)

I hate that Peace Corps is asking us to create girls' clubs here, when I know in my heart it's going to take more than that to improve girls' lives. I think that the economy must be improved and, for that to happen, I believe the government must change. Still, I think cultural nuances, gender expectations, and historical traditions stand in the way. The predictable direction of my thoughts reminds me that I have a Western view of the situation in Togo. The people here may see problems, but their way of life is their way of life.

I could not see or understand these things before living here. The suffering and the problems I've experienced these past few months are not at all what I'd anticipated. I thought it would be sickness, or living conditions, or heat, or insects that would challenge me. Certainly, the sun is fierce and the insects are huge. But what unexpectedly troubles me is gender oppression and cultural differences, political injustice, and human rights concerns. These are the elements that underline my most challenging moments in Togo.

Life is hard everywhere. But in Africa, life is hard in a way that is difficult for those of us from the developed world to understand and appreciate. Despite the incredible sunsets, the shining stars, the lush forests, the lively people, the fierce music, the faces of children, despite the acceptance I feel in my community, I can't *not* see the things I see now.

I can no longer romanticize Africa.

Back in the World of Ideas

Okay, it's official. I am living a Third World life. Most of my daily tasks are intended to sustain myself, and there is nothing to show for them except that I exist. As much as I love reveling in ideas, I can't do it whenever I want to. It takes so much time just to get through the day in a way that maintains my health and well-being. I need a timeout. It's full-fledged now: *Je suis un peu Africaine.*

However, there is a certain sweetness to my deprivation. I love antici-pating the taste and smell of cheddar cheese. Of milk. Of ice cream. It's not the deprivation that is sweet; rather, it's the deprivation that creates the sweetness.

Last night I dreamed I was in line at Whataburger, that wonderful Texas-based hamburger chain where we went so often when I was a child. I didn't dream the burger, mind you. I never even saw the burger in my dream. Rather, I dreamed the anticipation of it as I stood in line.

Ɋⅉ

Today I sweat so much in the bush taxi from Atakpamé, it's unbelievable. I glow, I stink, I am burning with heat. I put my ubiquitous bandana on my forehead for the first time, tying it back behind my head, just like everyone here. Just like my mother used to do when I was a little girl.

In my mind I take some imaginary photos for Mom. I imagine myself in the floppy pink hat she and I bought at Wal-Mart, along with a *pagne* and flip flops. Oh, and African beaded bracelets—I'm collecting quite a few. I have a tan, and I'm thin; I'm smiling. I'm outside, eating at someone's hut, or in my yard. I feel integrated. Suddenly, the khakis and Gap shirt I wear nearly every day feel strange. I have envisioned myself dressed differently—not Western, more African.

My presence is so routine now in the Kougnohou bush taxi that I can read undisturbed. I can make small talk of my own volition. I can relax into the head-nodding sleep that comes with not caring how you look. I feel the same lethargy as I do when flying. Only I'm in a West African bush taxi that is twenty years old, held together with wires, with seats mended by hand, and chickens to the front.

⚭

In the middle of *étude de milieu*, I decide to undertake a study of the Kougnohou *dispensaire*, which is the largest clinic in the Akebou region. The staff of five *assistants d'hygiène* and two midwives maintain a small lab, a place to dress wounds, some overnight beds, a birthing room, and a large terrace that serves as a waiting area. I observe a young girl vomiting blood and am told she has malaria with seizures (*neuro-paludisme*).

The *dispensaire* staff members keep routine office hours, hide a cash box in a small desk dwarfed by a huge accounting book, use a small (dorm-size) refrigerator for medications, and display huge piles of cotton balls—not new cotton balls, but used cotton. Posters about *santé* decorate the walls. One says, *Contre le SIDA nous avons choisi la fidélité* (To avoid AIDS, we have chosen fidelity). The poster shows a young couple with kids, listening to a radio while gazing at their wedding picture. Another is about breastfeeding, "A gesture of love and good for health"; a third tells about preventing misery by planning your family. The latter depicts a worn couple surrounded by eight kids.

After giving her a vaccination, an *assistant d'hygiène* tells a mother, *Donne-moi cent francs.* Give me a hundred francs. The woman pays immediately.

Today I quiz everyone who works here about the situation of girls in this country: why girls don't go to school, why they get pregnant, why they refuse to use birth control. Many things aren't clear to me, and I just heard something I want to write down. An *accoucheuse*, a midwife, told me, "The parents don't support the kids well."

"What do you mean? Are the parents too busy?"

"Parents here have too many kids, 11 or 12. Not like *chez toi* or in Europe. It's hard for parents to meet the needs of the kids. The girls get their needs met elsewhere. With boys."

(Where do the boys get their needs met, I wonder? Oh! I just had an *Aha!* The boys have school, extracurricular activities, and sports for fun. The girls don't have these outlets.)

"Planning *familiale* began about twenty years ago, in Lomé, but not until later in this region of the country," the midwife explains to me. "The *dispensaires* see a lot of girls who have tried to get abortions. They do this in secret and end up causing more harm than good. So they come here."

"Why don't they practice birth control?"

"They are embarrassed. They are afraid of their parents. Also, school isn't regular, and it's easier to quit."

"This is where the *sensibilisation* (consciousness-raising) comes in," the *infirmiere* pipes up. "We are only here until noon. We don't have the capability to go to the kids' homes at night, or to visit the parents. That's where you can help."

I still don't clearly understand why the girls fail to use birth control. Where exactly does the gap exist? Do they not know how to use it? Not care? Not want to? Do they want children? Do they have bad information? What do boys think? Do they carry condoms? I have so many questions.

"I will send girls to you, the ones who've had children, so you can ask these questions, " The midwife tells me. She goes on to say there are many more villages close by, and I must visit them. She says I will also find smaller *dispensaires* throughout the Akebou bush.

Later, on my routine stroll before dusk, I run into one of my neighbors, a feisty old man who walks with a cane. He and his companions chat me up about why I am in Togo, and why girls' education—as opposed to education in general—is my project.

I've devised a few stock phrases that succinctly describe my work in Togo. Resorting to them, I say, *Il faut augmenter le nombre de jeunes filles qui fréquentent l'école. Les jeunes filles ne terminent pas leurs études.* (It's necessary to increase the girls' attendance in school; Girls do not finish school.)

The men nod in agreement.

"Why don't you raise money at the church? You are Catholic, aren't you?"

Yes, I am. But I don't answer the question because I am taken aback by the immediate acceptance of my project; I am so accustomed to defending it. Instead, I tell the men about my idea to form a soccer team for girls. They like the idea of a girls' sports team, and one old man suggests a theater group.

"How about a girls' center, for *formations*, studying, and sports?"

Quelle bonne idée! I tell the men. I did not expect the older men to understand what I am trying to do in Togo. When they do, I feel a part of the community.

Before I go home, I stop at Nyalewossi's boutique to buy candles and batteries, plus a box of old Spanish wine. Nyalewossi sneaks up behind me and covers my eyes with her hands. She laughs, "Next time I go to Atakpamé to buy inventory, I will buy more Sangria for you." I am grateful because that old wine has become one of my most appreciated luxuries in Togo. For the first time in Africa, I don't feel self-conscious buying alcohol by myself. Togolese women don't do that.

☙

While I am at the boutique, a gendarme asks whether I can find him a pen pal in the United States—preferably a young girl, about fifteen? He asks me this in all seriousness. The Togolese regard all government officials with mistrust and the Kougnohou gendarmes also have a reputation for laziness. This particular gendarme had seemed to be less wily than the others; however, his question sets off fireworks in me.

"Did you know that such a relationship can get you arrested *chez moi?*"

"No, I didn't know," he says, seemingly surprised. A moment later, the gendarme is watching Nyalewossi coo over a baby.

"And when will you have a baby?" he asks her in a sleazy, seductive way, as if he wants to father the baby.

"I am going to wait until I am 40 years old before I have kids," Nyalewossi says confidently, without any help from me. She never ceases to impress me with her assertiveness, her absolute faith in herself at age 17. I look at Nyalewossi and smile. She doesn't look my way, as if I am not there. But I am so glad I am.

"Too bad," the man says.

Nyalewossi doesn't miss a beat. "Oh? For you? *Chez toi?*"

I love Nyalewossi!

Last Sunday, I saw Nyalewossi's *etat d'esprit* again. After church we sit outside together eating beans for breakfast. The older, married brother of Imma, another student I've met, strides past very determinedly. All of a sudden, Nyalewossi jumps to her feet and runs after him. The man approaches a woman, his wife, pulling at her shirt and hitting her face. Without a second's hesitation, Nyalewossi gets right in his face and yells at him. She speaks in Ewé, but whatever she says makes him stop.

Nyalewossi stayed the course. She did not flinch for a second. At home in the States, bystanders don't want to get involved in other families' domestic disputes. Here, even for an adolescent girl, it's an obligation.

Dear Patricia,

Hey chica! Comment ça va? I hope you are OK. I am doing well. Very well, actually! I've finally figured out what project to do with my village. I am going to teach a 14-week course (kind of like a women's studies course) for the girls in Kougnohou. I plan to utilize all the training I received in Kpalimé (on the educational system, gender role issues, historical and current trends for women) and what I've learned in the last two months while soaking up life in Kougnohou. Human sexuality issues will loom large, as well as reproduction, love and marriage, courting, AIDS, and STDs.

I will have to handpick girls for the course because the village is too big to work with all of them at once. There are 14,000 people in Kougnohou, and only 160 girls are in secondary school. The ratio of boys to girls is preposterous, I know, but even so, 160 girls is a lot of girls to teach! I will train one group of girls first, then use them to help me train other girls—as well as everyone else in the village.

So far the villagers have responded well to my idea, although at first the men and boys seemed hesitant. Usually they ask right away why I'm just here for the girls, not the boys. It's a valid question. But it is easily explained once I start giving statistics. The men will have to support what I propose if the program is to work here. They have to back me up, or the project will fail.

I already have a tentative syllabus, constructed with the input of several key community figures, the village clinic staff, and the school directors. This Wednesday I plan to meet with all 160 middle school girls (plus the 13 high school girls), to get their names, ages, and other basic info. I may assign a short task. I want to give girls in the large group a chance to shine early—there are so many I don't know. I'll start there. Class begins in March.

I've got to run for now. Write soon!

Love,
Laurie

At Bernadette's I talk a long while about my project. She listens carefully and seems to understand what I want to do. As usual, Bernadette's questions stimulate more ideas: How will you work with the men? How will you work with the girls? Will you divide them into groups?

"I'll come with you when you present the ideas to the CEG director." Bernadette realizes I am talking about instituting an American style of teaching. She knows the class will be different than those the girls are used to—it is meant to be a place where they can participate openly and freely in their learning.

Brainstorming my ideas with Bernadette, I get so excited it makes me tired and hungry. Sweetly, Bernadette offers some beans she'd cooked earlier. While I eat my beans, Dopé, one of the high school girls, stops by for a visit. Dopé tells me school adjourned early because the teachers are not getting paid. As a compromise with the village, the teachers make their own hours; each *lycée* teacher has agreed to teach two classes every morning.

"These teachers are lazy," Bernadette comments derisively. "The CEG teachers have the same problem, but they keep going to work."

"If Bonnekinder, the NGO you worked for, had stopped your salary would you have continued to work?" I ask her curiously.

"The salary was guaranteed," Bernadette replies.

"But what if it wasn't?"

"Yes," Bernadette says quietly but firmly. Then she adds, "There is no money to pay the teachers because other countries have pulled out of Togo. They have stopped giving aid to Togo."

"But my family in Kpalimé says there is no money to pay teachers because the president of Togo uses the money to travel in France."

"That's not it," Bernadette says.

Bernadette and I may not share the same views about Togo politics. Bernadette is mad at the teachers, not at the president who won't pay them. If she continues to think teachers are the cause of the problem, how can the government be reformed?

Is it really that people are lazy? If the teachers just stop teaching, what happens then? Shouldn't someone address this situation directly? If teachers teach just a little, what good is that?

Although the situation still bugs me, for the first time it doesn't frustrate me. My goals aren't hopelessly unreachable. Instead, I think, "That's free time for the girls to do the assignments I give them!"

The next day Bénoît takes me on his moto to the *lycée* so I can talk to the girls about my *Études des Jeunes Filles* class. The director walks me to each class himself, introducing me each time by saying, "I have a special message to the *filles*: Madame is here, she wishes you to come to the CEG at 3 next Wednesday afternoon." We go from class to class and, each time, students stand at attention when we enter the room.

Twice, however, after the director announces me, boys ask, "What about the boys? Is it only for girls?"

I address these comments immediately: "First, the girls. After, everyone."

One boy asks for my name and I say it. The director snaps back.

"Why do you need her name?" The boys laugh loudly.

The director is commanding and very handsome. After the greetings we chat in his office. He tells me he is from Togoville, having only been in Kougnohou for two years.

"I am a stranger here," he says. Oh. I can relate to that. How odd it feels to hear a Togolese person say it. Kougnohou is much more transient than I expected. It's not a village at all, but a town, and full of strangers.

"Why does school end at 10 each morning?" I ask the director about Dopé's comment from several days before.

"The teachers are on strike. They have only agreed to teach a little bit each day."

When I tell him about the topics I am thinking about for the girls' class, he says, "That is exactly what the girls are already preparing for, so it's good."

On the walk home, I run into Dopé and two of her friends, Judith and Anne-Philippe, leaving *lycée* at 10 A.M. Dopé says, very charmingly, *C'est midi . . . à lycée Kougnohou!*" (Generally school stops at *midi*, noon, in Togo; it's too hot for anyone to work when the sun is high.) It's awful to see school stop so early; the kids are so smart and eager to learn.

The next morning, eager to get to work, I rise at 5:30, make coffee, and wash my face. It is still dark outside my bedroom window, the full moon evident. At the window, I see the shapes of women, flashlights in hands and buckets on heads, walking to the river to get water. In the moonlit darkness, this is exceptionally exotic and graceful. It is a vivid reminder of where I am. Not in Kansas, Dorothy!

At Bernadette's stand later today, I am deep in reflection and full of new questions: What sicknesses are most problematic in Kougnohou? Specifically, what sicknesses keep people from working, studying, or even living in Kougnohou? What illnesses contribute to girls' absence from school? When I ask Bernadette, she suggests I visit the clinic again. Saying I'll be back for lunch, I get on my bike and arrive in the middle of the Wednesday *formation*. I sit down next to one of the *assistants d'hygiene*, and whisper to him, "I have some questions."

Before I realize what I've done, the assistant has interrupted the *formation* to tell his colleague who is giving the talk that I have questions for the women. Wait! My questions are for the staff, not the women. But it's too late. Sixty eyeballs turn to look at me as my request is translated into Ewé. I quickly explain the misunderstanding in French. The speaker recovers easily and continues his talk to the women.

Wait! Of course I should be asking the women my questions! This time, I interrupt the speaker myself—*Un instant, s'il vous plait!*—and jog over to where he stands. Speaking in French, I ask the women what they think are the biggest health problems in Akebou. The speaker translates to Ewé, and the women respond like gangbusters.

La grossesse! in French.

Le palu! also in French.

"Girls are not serious about school! They like boys too much!" (laughter)

"But many girls are smart! They need our help!"

When the women have finished, I say, "Thank you, that is very helpful to my work. Thank you."

The women applaud. All I did was ask questions. I keep forgetting how important it is to ask questions.

I love the experience at the hospital. Researching, talking, reflecting, and planning puts me back in the world of ideas and I feel so productive. Perhaps this is why I'm so tired lately—too much thinking. Three nights in a row I have not slept. When I tell Bernadette, she says, "It's the same with me—too much thinking!" A man, who is sitting at Bernadette's stand killing time, joins in our reflections. He tells us he is not well either because of too much thinking.

"Five months, no salary. Too much thinking," the man nods sagely.

That puts it in perspective, doesn't it?

Early one Monday morning, near the end of my *étude de milieu*, I walk over to Bernadette's to pick up a taxi. It's early, Bernadette's stand isn't set up yet, but Bernadette comes out to meet me and surveys my attire. When I see her face, I assume she doesn't approve of my black t-shirt and khaki pants. But no. She only wants to warn me, with a big smile: "There's a lot of dirt where you're going!"

Standing next to Bernadette is Père Antoine, who has hired the 7 A.M.

taxi. He says I should wear the black sweater I have tied around my waist: "It will protect you from the dust." I notice Antoine wears a jacket, as do the others in the taxi. In fact, I can see the driver wearing a sweatshirt with a hood on it; he has covered his whole head to protect himself from the dust.

I bid goodbye to Bernadette and get in the backseat of the taxi next to Antoine. He has planned for us to visit market day in a small village twelve kilometers up the mountain, deeper in the Akebou bush. I am excited and curious, because I've never traveled in this direction before. Usually I head the other way, to the city of Atakpamé.

With only four people in the taxi, I can move around in my seat as much as I want. We are traveling through a cloud of dust that I can't really see unless I look at the trees, bushes, and palms; their leaves are orange, not green, covered with a layer of dust. This is all because of the *harmattan* wind, which comes in from the Sahel for several months during the year. The *harmattan* wind parches our throats, dusts our belongings, and dries out our skin.

In thirty minutes, we arrive at a small village. The taxi negotiates its way onto a path that seems more appropriate for feet or bikes, not cars. Slowly, we turn into a small *concession* (compound) and stop in front of a house that seems faintly European. Its stone is in stark contrast to the adjacent mud huts.

When we get out of the car, Père Antoine goes inside the house and retrieves a towel for me to wipe my face. He beats his sweater in the open air, and I do the same. Then we sit on a bench to drink water and recover from the dusty journey. Looking around, I see the village of Djon perched at the crest of the mountain with vistas below. Sniffing, I sense a difference in the air. It is crisp, fresh.

Antoine and I walk through the courtyard and up three steps into a large, open foyer. He tells me to sit on a sofa while he opens a locked door.

"Is this your house?" I ask Antoine, needing to orient myself to my new surroundings.

"No; it's a room I have," he says. "I live here when I'm not in Kougnohou."

I stay in the small foyer while Antoine busies himself in his room.

I can hear him opening windows and unlocking another door. "Please enter now," Antoine calls out. I walk into what looks like a life-size doll house. There is an area to receive people, a dining area, and a bedroom. Is this the house where Antoine's family lives?

"My family lives in the *concession* next door," Antoine continues, as if reading my thoughts. "This room used to belong to another priest, who has since moved to a larger house. It is mine now. Just mine."

As Antoine moves around the room, tidying, I see his ordination photo on the wall and walk over to get a closer look. The picture next to it makes me catch my breath. Most Togolese people have calendars on their walls, rarely a picture, unless it is the standard propaganda picture of President Eyadema. But Antoine has none of this. On his wall, next to the ordination photo, is a picture of a small group of priests standing next to the Pope. Antoine has been photographed with Pope John Paul II.

I sit down, impressed, and drink more water.

A woman comes into the miniature house to greet Antoine. She says hello to me in both French (*Bonjour*) and Akebou (*Ouru clackaleur*).

"This is my sister, Marie-Therese," says Antoine. As soon as she leaves, another woman arrives. This woman is much older, and very slight in build. Antoine tells me, "This is my mother." She smiles at me and speaks in Akebou to Antoine. I can't make out anything but the word fufu, and my ears perk up immediately. Fufu has become one of my favorite foods.

"When do you need to be back in Kougnohou?" Antoine asks me.

"I have a French lesson at 3."

Antoine and his mother continue in Akebou and, after she leaves, as he goes on arranging his things, I have two epiphanies at once. First, Antoine is a quiet person, not a big talker. Although he invited me here and is turning out to be very generous, I will have to initiate the conversation. Second, Djon is the village where Antoine was born. Antoine has brought me to his private residence, in his family's village.

When Antoine first invited me on this trip, I had assumed it was so I could see market day at a small village in the bush. I had no idea we were coming to his native village. A wave of gratitude washes over me for the intimate gesture Antoine has made, and I thank him. My words seem very small compared to my feelings.

Antoine stops what he is doing, looks at me very seriously, and says,

"You are a stranger, from another country. If people do not receive you, you will be alone. And that is not good."

Silently, I agree.

"I studied for five years in Rome. I was very happy there. But I was also lonely. I know what it is like to be alone in a foreign country. I want you to feel welcome and at home here. That is why I brought you here today."

I am touched by Antoine's words. I did not suspect him of such thoughts; suddenly, I am much more curious about him. When did you last live in Djon? How many brothers and sisters do you have? He has one sister, whom I met, and a brother in Lomé, who is an attorney. Antoine has been a priest for three years.

After this brief interaction, I feel an intimate connection to him, perhaps because he's traveled, is educated, and seems aware of all of the cultural complexities involved in transcontinental migration. His Catholic priesthood reminds me of a dear friend back home, Jimmy, with whom I went to high school. Once a San Antonio cop, Jimmy is now a beloved priest in my home city.

The newfound and unexpected intimacy I feel with Antoine results in my telling him all about my plans for the *Etudes des Jeunes Filles* course. No doubt I overwhelm him with talk about my project. I am so grateful to be able to talk to a thoughtful person like Antoine. Unconsciously, I attribute many qualities to Antoine as a result of his kindness to me. Antoine interrupts my soliloquy by bringing out a bag of Italian bonbons.

"Would you like one of these? My friends in Italy sent them last Noël."

I take one, then another, and another. Filled with creamy nougat and almonds, the bonbons are delicious.

Abruptly ending my long-winded speech, Antoine says, "We can talk while we walk to the CEG. I will introduce you to the director and if you want, perhaps you can speak for a few moments to the girls?" What a great idea.

Antoine and I spend the morning at the CEG with another priest who teaches there. Hugues, from Ghana, is dressed in a long white cassock. He greets me in the Ghanaian way. Although he speaks English, the way he puts his words together sounds foreign to me.

"How are you, Hugues?"

"You are welcome!" he responds enthusiastically.

Hugues tells me he has just taught a religion class. "The girls are so quiet in Togo, so deferential. The boys speak up, but the girls aren't used to it. This is not a good thing." His words thrill me; my heart starts pumping and I want to sit and talk, talk, talk with this priest.

Antoine seems very comfortable in this setting. Everyone seems to know and greet him. He brings the school director to meet me, and the director offers me an opportunity to speak briefly to the girls. (How lucky that I am comfortable in these sorts of impromptu situations; it's not hard for me to make something meaningful out of these stolen moments.)

The director and I step inside a classroom, and the noise of fifty chairs scraping the cement floor is followed by entire class rising to say, *Bonjour, Monsieur Directeur!* The director returns the greeting, introduces me, and the teenagers sit down.

"My name is Laurie Charles and I am from the United States." Silence. "I am in Togo as a Peace Corps Volunteer—*Corps de la Paix*." I hear oohs of recognition—they all seem to be familiar with Peace Corps.

"I am in Togo to promote girls' education." Quickly I add, "No one has forgotten the boys, or men, or parents, or teachers. However, it is the girls I will work with first."

The class—mostly the females—smiles at me. I ask if they have questions, but in my excited state of mind, don't wait very long to hear them. It's one thing to respond to complex questions in your own language, but in a language that is not yours? That you've barely just learned? Not yet confident in my ability to have a conversation in French, I take my leave with the director.

Nevertheless, I feel as if I am floating. How wonderful to see the girls' eager faces, to see both boys and girls nod when I talk about improving girls' education, to have the experience of being understood in French— even if only a little bit. I knew I was giving a small performance, and I felt strong and powerful, as if the whole world was encouraging me in that moment. I could feel the girls' pride and surprise upon hearing the reason I am in Togo.

At *midi*, Hugues takes us home in his car. I had not noticed the little car under the big, shady tree of the school courtyard. Seated in the front seat, I come face to face with a bumper sticker on the dashboard: "I'm proud to be Catholic. Are you?" and smile broadly. I've never thought of my religious beliefs in that way, but I think it's great that Hugues does.

Antoine and Hugues want me to see the village, so we take a short tour. First, we drive past the Catholic church, which is big, with beautiful stained glass windows and a bell tower. It looks exactly like San Fernando Cathedral back in San Antonio, which for some reason I find very disconcerting. Inside the church I am further disoriented. The church has actual pews, not hard benches like the church in Kougnohou, or even the Kpalimé Cathédrale I visited several times with the Diores.

Hugues wants to take me to a center "where nuns offer assistance to girls who want to learn to sew, cook, or make clothes." A hundred feet down the road from the church, Hugues maneuvers his tiny car behind the small village *dispensaire* to the nun's "center," a *paillote* with two sewing machines under it. Hugues tells me, "The nuns work primarily at the health clinic."

A young girl at one of the sewing machines sees us and runs inside a two-story concrete building adjacent to the *paillote*.

"That is where the nuns stay," Hugues tells me.

Our arrival causes a nun frenzy. Two nuns, dressed for business, hurriedly come out of the building with surprised smiles on their faces.

"We are here just to say hello," Hugues says.

"Don't do anything complicated," Antoine adds.

But this advice is wasted in Togo. Visitors—even neighbors you see every day—require attention and respect. To show respect, you participate in formal greetings and the sharing of snacks or drinks.

I sense a rash of behind-the-scenes activity as we three are taken into a living area. We sit on wooden frame couches softened with colorful square-foot pads of *mousse* (foam). A young girl brings a bottle of honey and a plate of cookies. The two nuns have disappeared temporarily, but they return in minutes with a third nun. All three smooth down their robes and adjust their coifs as they sit down. Immediately they rise again to shake our hands and greet us, a bit more formally this time.

"*Bonjour, Ma Soeur. Bonjour!* How are you? How is your health? How is your work? *Merci Dieu.*" Everyone repeats the greetings, re-ordering the questions slightly to personalize the process.

Antoine introduces me and my work, and before I know it I have launched into a discussion for which I am not quite ready. I am so excited to see these educated women that I hint at their coming to talk to my Kougnohou class before I make a formal invitation. I forgot it's not possible to propose things halfway to the Togolese.

The moment the words leave my mouth, the nuns want to know: What are we supposed to do? What will we discuss?

My open-ended musings confuse them. All my ideas for the class are still forming in my head. The circular style of conversation I am used to clashes with their more-linear approach to life and ideas.

Things are complicated further when Père Hugues tries to translate for me. Being unfamiliar with me and my project, he translates inaccurately. I can tell this, but my French is not good enough for me to refute the misunderstandings that are flowering like weeds. I think the confusion is not a language barrier, but a cultural one. I am grateful when the conversation winds down; we are just here to greet the nuns, after all. The time for this discussion will come. I am learning to be more patient in Africa. Silently, I vow to visit these nuns again, but next time without a translator.

Our next stop turns out to be the home of the Djon priests. At this house, which has a large porch and a yard with numerous trees, I meet yet another priest, Didier. We walk into the living room as Didier, who wears a huge smile, washes his hands at the far end of the room. "I'll be just a minute," he tells us as we seat ourselves.

A woman sits on the sofa, and another woman is close by. I don't know who these women are—they are not in nun's habits—but they are beautiful. One of them leaves and returns moments later with an *apéritif*—*crème de menthe*. I had this drink once at the house of the *sous-préfet* in Kougnohou, on the day I formally introduced myself and my project. The syrupy taste and green color did not agree with me.

This time, I don't drink, nor do I refuse to drink. Instead, I pretend to drink. I am definitely learning how to socialize in a Togolese way! Antoine tells me quietly, "Didier also studied in Italy, before me, and speaks fluent Italian. He has been a priest for ten years."

When Didier sits down with us, all three priests chat with great animation in exquisite French. I am captivated by Didier, who is expressive and unrestrained. I lose track of the priests' conversation as I notice details of the house that did not register earlier: videos near a television set; a small, plumbed sink in the corner of the room.

"You have electricity! And running water!" My unrestrained shout interrupts the priests.

"The house has generators and batteries. We have a large pump at the top of the house that provides water," Didier explains to me, smiling. Now Hugues officially introduces me to Didier as a *Corps de la Paix* volunteer.

"The reason she is here is to work with the *jeunes filles*, to promote their attendance at school."

Didier looks directly in my eyes. Almost in a whisper, he says, "I have had a dream of this! A dream that so far I've only said to one person. It is a dream for the *jeunes filles*."

Père Didier has worked on this for years. He considers girls' education, particularly in Akebou, necessary for the development of his country. However, he has done this work unbeknownst to many of his colleagues. Didier seems both amazed and genuinely appreciative that my entire charge is to work with young girls.

"When a young girl sees you, she will know you are here for the *jeune filles*. You are not here to build water pumps, you are not here to teach English. You are here just for the *jeune filles*."

Didier is the first man I meet in Togo who talks about girls' education with passion, and vision. For nearly an hour, we engage in clear, provocative, and ripe conversation. It is the kind of talk where you feel the seed of an idea is planted, where something is set in motion. This is the sort of experience I took for granted back home, as a doctoral student. Now I am crossing cultural borders and still, unbelievably, smack in the middle of a community of ideas that I find relevant and familiar and intoxicating.

"I am on sabbatical this year, and I plan to travel as well as to work on several projects for the *jeunes filles*. I am so glad you are here in Akebou with us!"

A young man arrives at the priest's house to say our meal is ready. We walk across the road into a maze of family compounds positioned creatively around dusty red stones and petrified wood boulders. I have to watch or I will trip over all these natural obstacles. Now I see we have arrived at Père Antoine's house, this time from a different direction.

Our meal is long and leisurely, and, although he didn't cook, Antoine is in charge of the hospitality. It is the first time I have shared a meal with men only. There is no Togolese female in sight, neither to serve or clear. I actually serve myself, just as I would back home. The food is abundant and delicious. Fufu with chicken, and then rice with another meat sauce, and beer, and a bottle of wine. (Not a box of wine, but a bottle!)

"This is Akebou. There are many ideas here. Akebou is full of them," Antoine tells me proudly. Antoine has been very quiet all morning, but his intuitive comment makes me feel as if he has been inside my head. At lunch, I finally acknowledge openly what I am sure Antoine has known: I will not be home in time for my French lesson.

C'est pas grave, Antoine tells me. It's not a serious problem.

"It's Togo," I say, *"c'est pas grave toujours."* Nothing is ever a serious problem. We all laugh as I, the outsider at the table, say something a Togolese would say.

The meal ends as it began, with grace, and an Italian candy. As I savor the moment, I think to myself, I am back home. I am back in the world of ideas. I didn't realize how much I have missed it. (Sometimes, as now, I let myself think, this is all taking place in another language! A language that is not my mother tongue! And I let myself be impressed.)

At Antoine's today, I realize how much I have missed being looked after. I have missed the pleasure of someone's attentiveness. That realization comes after lunch, during the *sieste*, when Antoine arranges his bed for me. I will nap in his room; he will take the sofa in the living room. His bedroom is sparse, except for a large bookcase, messily loaded with books—many in Italian. Oh, I've missed this.

Afterward, I find Antoine outside, reading a book in the afternoon quiet. He shows me photos of his ordination and his training in Milan, and we talk about how travel changes you. Antoine has a quiet charm, and he is matter-of-fact and brief in his statements. He tells me his first impressions of the world once he stepped out of Togo, "I couldn't believe all the things I saw." He also talks openly to me about his views of the situation in his country. He says, wisely and quietly, "The mentality of the people in Togo has to change before the country can change."

More than 150 girls come to my first meeting in Kougnohou. They continue to arrive for an hour, and they spill out into the courtyard. I take a picture of them at the end but, because there are so many girls, I have to divide them and take two photos.

My French is passable but I am nervous, and there are so many girls! They laugh at my mistakes in grammar, as adolescents laugh, and I am so very aware of their eyes on me. I tell them I am putting together the program for a girls' class. I tell them what I have learned so far in their village.

As I talk, I force myself to walk down the rows and rows of girls, just so they can see me. It is important that they see me up close. I want to establish an atmosphere of informality and approachability. I do not want them to be afraid of me. I talk as I walk, with passion and enthusiasm, which is easy to conjure among the lively girls.

As I walk, I look at the young women. I am mesmerized by their faces—eager, open, and inviting. I tell them, "I want to know your interests. I want to know your ideas as young girls in Togo. Also, I need more information from you in order to organize my project. I want to know what you think."

I put five questions on the board and ask them to write answers:

1. What are the reasons that girls quit school?

2. In your opinion, what are the causes of this problem?

3. If you could say something to all the young girls in Togo, what would you say?

4. If you could create a girls' club in Kougnohou, what activities would you want?

5. What do you want to be when you grow up? What is your plan for your future?

As the girls write seriously in their notebooks, I tell them to bring their responses to my house the next day after *sieste*.

I'll never forget the moment Bernadette said to me, *Tu va reussir, Laurie.* You are going to succeed. Bernadette was referring to my project, but the timing of her comment is especially significant to me. It comes right when I need it. For months, I have been preoccupied with terminating my Peace Corps assignment early and leaving Togo. My difficulties in adjusting to the country have given me ample reason to think I should have stayed home. Many times, I have wondered if it was a mistake to come to Africa instead of pursuing a job in academia. In hindsight, I see I have fought any sense of settling down in Africa.

But today, something changes. Bernadette's words make me visualize something I've never been able to picture before: A future, with Togo—not Peace Corps, but Togo, and Kougnohou. When Bernadette tells me, "Laurie, you will succeed," I realize, vividly, that I've committed myself to Togo. I am no longer on the fence. I'm engaged, I'm here—and I'm not going anywhere. I've had so many rich moments in my life lately, I can't keep up with them.

The next day after *sieste*, girls visit me one by one to return their homework—the papers on which they have answered my five questions. They ask: Will you correct it? Will you correspond with us? Can we come visit you? My answers: No. No. Yes.

All afternoon, I stand outside greeting the girls. The salutation is what's important here in Togo, don't forget. You must participate in it. No matter what you say, or how long you stay, but that you take the time to do it.

Colette Eweli, 5ème

1. Girls quit school for the following reasons: *They lack support for their studies; family problems; they are too lazy about school work.*

2. The causes of these problems are: *Girls become orphaned by losing a mother or father; girls are in a poor family; their families have had divorce between mother and father; or, she has a mean mother.*

3. The thing I wish for the girls of Togo is: *To tell them to do their work with courage, to not chase boys, and to have faith in their studies.*

4. If I could create a girls' club I would want: To help girls with their studies and create diverse ways to help them achieve success in their studies.

5. When I grow up, I want: To be a sage-femme and open a clinic to help people with their health problems. My plan for my future is: To succeed in creation of a health agency that provides free health care to the poor.

Sandrine Agbero, 3ème

1. Girls quit school for the following reasons: Young girls quit school because they do not have much success in their studies and they become discouraged.

2. The causes of these problems are: Young girls don't learn enough because when they fail or don't do well, then they become embarrassed to continue. Boredom also sets in and eventually they stop going to school.

3. The thing I wish for the girls of Togo is: I hope to tell all the young girls of Togo to face their embarrassment in their own heads and continue to study hard. This is the best way to approach one's difficulties.

4. If I could create a girls' club I would want: I can propose a girls' club that does theatre activities specific to young girls' needs, and also dancing and performing groups could go a long way toward those who need help to forget their embarrassment.

5. When I grow up, I want: I hope to become a journalist. My plan for my future is: To finish my studies quickly and then to reach for my own voice.

❧

A few days after the meeting, Shoshana, my fellow GEE volunteer who was posted in the north of Togo, arrives for a brief visit. We cook spaghetti mixed with tuna, and I tell her how my hair caught fire eleven days ago.

I was writing a letter at my desk one night, with a candle close by. All of a sudden I smell this putrid smell, and I see little balls of black thread fall on the desk. It was my hair! My hair caught fire! I slapped at my forehead to put out a fire I could not see, only smell. I wasn't even scared! Rather, I was cracking up. I couldn't believe my hair was already burning a bit before I realized what was happening!

Still laughing about this episode after dinner, Shana and I decide we want a cold beer, so we walk over to a *buvette* near the *marché*. Excited about my project, I give Shana more details about the course I plan to teach. I will conduct most of the classes myself, but will ask volunteers from other Peace Corps programs to visit Kougnohou as guest speakers. I will ask a health volunteer (Geeta) to speak about AIDS, two business volunteers (Jon and Kate) to speak about feasibility studies and the role of women in the economy, and an environmental protection volunteer (Monica) to discuss gardening and soil conservation. I will also use community resources, such as the *sage-femme* to discuss birth control and family planning. "It's all coming together!" I tell Shana, unable to contain my excitement.

I've forgotten that it's market day. We search for cold beer, but we won't find it because market day means that cold beer runs out by noon. So, we go to Nyalewossi's house. They don't have a refrigerator, but they do have beer. We wanted to visit Nyalewossi anyway. We'll drink beer at her place. It doesn't matter if it's cold or not.

I can see Nyalewossi's shape in the moonlit road as we approach the boutique. When we are close enough, but before she squeals a greeting, I whisper, "Nyalewossi! We want to drink a beer. We've already bought our koliko. Can we drink here at your house?"

I am surreptitious because I know if Shoshana and I drink in a *buvette*, or even in the front of Nyalewossi's boutique, we risk being accosted by strange men. Nyalewossi understands this by now, and she knows exactly what to do.

Wordlessly and quickly, Nyalewossi takes my hand and Shoshana and I follow her inside the family boutique. We march straight through the store, back to the family kitchen. With silent authority, Nyalewossi seats us on a bench and drags over a small table. She arranges it so we are hidden from view, in a corner and yet able to see out through the cracks in the *clôture* fence, which protects the family's privacy.

We are extremely grateful for Nyalewossi's intuitive care of us. While Shoshana has probably grown accustomed to the virile reactions she gets in Togo, I am not. With her Nordic looks—porcelain skin, deep blue eyes, pale corn-silk hair—and healthy breast size, Shoshana really stands out in West Africa. She is a man magnet.

Shoshana and I rest silently, enjoying the life we see around us—the *video de Kougnohou,* as Nyalewossi calls it.

"This is great," Shoshana says out of the blue. She sits back and sighs, then adds, "You've done well here."

I like the way Shoshana and I can talk to each other. Earlier today, she told me I come across as very confident, but that I had made her feel comfortable even though she is ten years younger. She is completely without pretense, and is respectful and thoughtful about Togo in the way I try to be—with a stance of curiosity, rather than the boredom or derision of some volunteers.

Shoshana is different in other ways, too. Many of the volunteers in our training group jockeyed for position the first night we arrived in Lomé: Who knew the most about Africa? Who had already studied in Africa? Who'd just earned a degree at Harvard? Who has the PhD?

Shoshana was not like other volunteers in our training stage. Shoshana has studied in Tanzania, and knows much more about the continent than I do, but she doesn't advertise it. And she is neither overly impressed by nor put off by my doctorate.[1] Shoshana reminds me of friends back in Texas, though she is completely unique. She is in her early twenties, fresh out of college, with limited sexual experience. Her parents have been married more than thirty years.

I agree with her assessment of our relationship. Shoshana apparently does not think it significant that I am ten years older. I respect her opinion, her observations, and her choices. I value what she thinks about how I am doing in my village.

"They love you here. Already," she says.

Nyalewossi returns with two warm beers. We call her younger sister to the kitchen to take a picture of the three of us. Nyalewossi blushes with excitement; she giggles and hides her face with her hands. Shoshana and I find this so adorable that we giggle too.

Formation of a Committee for the Education and Promotion of the Young Girls of Akebou

Syllabus

Laurie L. Charlés
Peace Corps Volunteer
Girls' Education and Empowerment Project
Akebou, Togo

14-Week Course Themes

Week	Date	Theme
1	30 October	Introduction
2	6 November	History of the Education of Young Girls in Togo
3	13 November	The Rights of Young Girls in Togo
4	20 November	The Role of Women in Togo
5	27 November	Women and Marriage
6	4 December	Sexual Education for Young Girls
7	11 December	Sexually Transmitted Diseases
8	17 December	AIDS
9	24 December	no class
10	1 January	no class
11	8 January	The Role of Women in the Togolese Economy
12	15 January	Feasibility Studies
13	22 January	The Role of Women in the Protection of the Environment
14	29 January	Round Table Discussion on the Future of the Young Girls of Akebou

Course Objectives

- Raise awareness about the lives, rights, and future of young women in Togo
- Train students to raise the community's awareness about the well-being of young women and girls, and thus, of all the people of the country
- Create a place where young girls can discuss their ideas, develop confidence in themselves, demonstrate their aptitudes, develop their capacities for reflection
- Inspire and educate youth about the value of girls' education to the country

Students will also be able to:
- Give brief presentations on girls' education issues and train others to do the same
- Obtain important experience in working in groups and learning to work as a team
- Discuss, reflect, and better understand the potential of young girls and women of Togo
- Develop the capacity to give and receive counsel and encouragement
- Share their experience in the class with the Akebou community

Lust, Passion, and Tactical Adoration

As Odette and I stroll to 7 A.M. Sunday Mass, she tells me that her boyfriend came back to Kougnohou last night. Odette told me about her *petite-amie* when I first met her; however, she has not mentioned him since.

Near the end of the Mass, Odette whispers to me, "My boyfriend is here, I'll show him to you." I wonder why she whispers.

When the Mass ends, Odette and I walk outside. In the crowd I see Bernadette and a few of the *dispensaire* staff. I also see a tall man whose face I recognize but whose name I cannot remember. Odette grabs me and whispers loudly, *C'est lui!*

The tall man walks by, holding the hand of a small boy. His eyes flash from me to Odette and back to me. Odette does not greet the man, nor does she introduce us. Despite his apparent indifference, the man's eyes tell me he knows Odette has told me about him. The brief exchange goes by in slow motion.

The moment breaks, and Odette and I start to walk home. She tells me, in a normal voice, "He is a teacher at the *lycée*."

Now I realize that I met the man when I visited the *lycée* shortly after arriving in Kougnohou. Oh, my God! Odette's boyfriend is a teacher at the high school. Odette is in *4ème*, her third year of secondary school in Togo. Secondary school in Togo, like the French system, is four years long; *4ème* is the equivalent of eighth grade in the United States.

"Is he really your boyfriend?"

Oui.

I am stunned, I don't know what to say. In a few minutes, the teacher catches up to us. Although he is inches away from Odette and me, she still does not introduce us. Nothing is said aloud until Odette, again in a whisper, explains, "It is his son."

I remember when I first met the teacher. I had visited his classroom to talk to the young women. He was wearing a white lab coat. He wasn't especially welcoming and seemed uninterested in my project. Today on the road he poses all sorts of questions about my work. He may actually be interested in my project, but after what I've learned he sounds completely disingenuous. I feel sick in my stomach.

Here I am, walking with a *jeune fille* for whom I am supposed to be an advocate and a man who is taking advantage of her—contributing to the problem I was sent here to ameliorate. Yet we are walking together, business as usual.

Even worse is the way Odette morphs before my eyes. Odette, always talkative with me, sometimes even pushy, transforms into a quiet, deferential creature. She fades into the background, but the teacher doesn't seem to notice. He peppers me with words as Odette fades away. He is so engrossed in his own talk that he remains oblivious when I turn away from him to greet another student on the road—and even hold a brief conversation with her. He simply continues to talk at me, business as usual.

"I would like to come see you and talk more about your work," the teacher concludes as we stand in front of my house.

I want to laugh when I hear this. No, I want to cry. Really, I want to scream. Instead, I say nothing. I am complicit.

At home, as I ponder the episode, I feel many different things. I do not like that I am judging Odette. I am the one who had asked, Do you have a boyfriend? Is he *beau*? How old is he? Odette told me he was a teacher, and that he was in Lomé. I had assumed he lived and worked in Lomé. It didn't bother me then that Odette's lover was a teacher, although I did note the ten-year age difference. I remember asking if Odette's parents knew about him.

Still, something about this is wrong. Marguerite's parents would never allow her to have a teacher as a boyfriend! But Odette? Her parents aren't available; her father is dead, her mother sick. One of the women at the *dispensaire* told me that girls here search for boys because they don't get their emotional needs met at home.

I am less upset, but still preoccupied with this news when I go *chez* Bernadette for lunch. It is soothing to watch Bernadette prepare the food and eat together. But I am anxious. I want to ask Bernadette what she thinks about Odette. Unfortunately, there is a visitor from church, and I cannot speak about Odette. As I prepare to leave, I tell Bernadette that I have something on my mind I want to discuss later. But she sees the worry in my face, and decides she will listen now.

"Laurie, just a minute. Wait for me." Bernadette walks down the path with me.

"Do you know Odette well?" I bring it up slowly.

"Yes."

"Do you know that she has a boyfriend?"

"Yes, it started last year. She gives in to the urges."

"This is against all the things I teach in the program! What can he do for her!"

Bernadette says she will talk to Odette.

"No," I respond with alarm. "I want to talk to her."

There are questions I want to ask Odette: Is it a sexual relationship? Are you monogamous? Do you use birth control? Long hours later I realize these questions are intrusive and none of my business. Worse, I really don't want to know the answers. By the end of the day, Odette and her teacher cease to be one of the statistics in my notes. They become a couple, entitled to their privacy.

I remember reading somewhere about a doctor who joined the staff of an institution rife with problems. His first day, he had a person shadow him with these directions: "Write down all I say. Only today, with fresh eyes, can I see the problems. After today, I will not see them so clearly. So write it down for me."

This morning, I was outraged. Now, I am resigned.

Is this what I was afraid of in the beginning? The time when I will no longer be able to see the compromises I make in Togo, slowly, surely, one by one fading from memory. Perhaps so.

I saw my position clearly when I realized, with horror, that Bernadette knew of Odette's relationship. Of course she was not outraged. How do you sustain outrage at something you see every day? That many people are keen to accept? That makes perfect sense in its own context?

Isn't it easier to resign yourself? To accept what you cannot change? Of course it is. None of what I witnessed today is new to Bernadette. It's only new to me.

To her credit, Bernadette appreciated my outrage, and she saw the contradiction I had spelled out. She seemed to understand my dilemma. She even acknowledged it: "You have spoken well, Laurie, you are right."

But Bernadette's eyes are old. All the eyes here are old. Now, after six months in Africa, mine are old too. I wish Shoshana or Grant had come to visit me this weekend. I need to talk to someone about this. But who? An American? A woman? I don't know—just someone. Someone with new eyes.

The rituals of the early evening have a calming effect on me. I heat my bath water and sit on my front stoop to watch the colors in the sky. The atmosphere at this time of day never fails to humble me. The sky is the color of dusk. It's late, close to 6, yet there is still a faint glow in the sky, right above my house. It's a pink cloud. It's actually pink! My bath water boils over, bringing me back to the present. The world is heaven right now. I can't do anything but sit in awe.

Taking my bucket of water outside to the shower, I catch sight of a small neighbor boy. If I peer at him through a crack in the fence, I can just barely make him out as he walks down the path to my house. He can't be more than two or three, but he looks like a tiny adult, dressed in a *pagne* suit shirt and matching pants, with a pensive expression on his face, his eyes focused on the ground ahead of him.

Usually I am the one being peered at. Now it's my turn, and I can't help staring at this adorable young boy. I grin, just as they do to me, because it's such a joyous sight. It's even more precious because it's private, a moment with myself.

Before he is completely out of sight, the boy looks up, catches me staring at him through the fence, and stops. The spell is broken. What will he do? He simply looks at me, lifts his right hand, and makes a small wave. I wave back. Then he continues on his way. I want to cry at his small, meaningful gesture. I feel the emotion of being taken for normal. Is there such a thing? Whatever it is, I felt normal in that moment.

෫෯

I arrive late to Nyalewossi's house one afternoon, but it doesn't matter because she is not ready. I wait for her on a bench in front of the boutique. The man we are going to visit, Nyalewossi's uncle René Kuma-Dunyo, stops by unexpectedly. He too is running late. His right hand is chalky white.

"I am teaching," he explains abruptly. Then, *Tu prends quoi?*

Vin, s'il vous plait.

René buys a box of wine and leaves quickly. He seems unremarkable to me, but Nyalewossi is acting strange. She changes clothes several times and glances repeatedly in the mirror before we finally leave. Nyalewossi's uncle has moved here from Lomé; his employer relocated him to work with the coffee and cocoa *groupements* in Akebou. Nyalewossi is clearly nervous about the visit to her uncle. She peppers me with questions as we walk to his house: What are you going to ask my uncle? Ask this! Ask this too!

René's house is at the end of an old road that used to be the main route out of Kougnohou. The house is large, with a back terrace that faces the river. Beyond René's house, there is nothing but trees and brush and it looks very forbidding. A young girl sits on the terrace, working on her lessons.

Uncle René turns out to be charming and conversation is easy. He laughs quickly at my jokes, and is intelligent and observant. When I ask him to contribute to the tape recording I am making to introduce my mother to the village, René grabs the recorder and announces in loud and dramatic French, "Laurie is doing very, very well here! She is doing so well here, so very well! In fact, she is doing better than she ever did in the United States!" His comment makes me burst out laughing; he doesn't know me but he sounds completely convincing.

During the visit, René shows photos of his many female (always European) friends, which I can't help contrasting with the photos of his wife,

95

who, he tells me, "travels a lot." The photos of his female friends—young, white, laughing, sexy—are vastly different from those of his wife, who in her pictures looks mature, stately, and serious. René doesn't seem to fit both pictures; he is having much more fun with the friends.

A woman in a swimsuit poses seductively, her hair wet. René says she is French. As I look at the picture, René touches my face, almost caresses it. I jerk away, surprised. He smiles slightly, asking if I am upset.

Is he reading my mind? It seems he knows these women intimately and, as I looked at the pictures, I had been putting myself in their shoes. For an instant I think maybe he has seen through me. Then I realize he is asking if I am upset that he touched me. Laughing, I tell him he is like the children who are always touching my skin. But his caress felt lovely.

My earlier sexual liaisons began with a moment like this, by a touch that was intimate and unexpected. I don't mind that René has apparently known so many women, that he has a wife and children. In fact, I like that he is so open with me.

We drink too much. We laugh too much. Our visit lasts more than two hours, not the expected twenty minutes. If things were different, no doubt we would sleep together. But Nyalewossi is here, a colleague of René's has arrived, and we are in a small village in rural Togo. My comings and goings are newsworthy events in the village—my visit to a man's home particularly so, even given Nyalewossi's presence.

Later that night, I dream of René's body, of being with a man. Not just any man—but one who is intelligent, sexy, observant, and funny. A man who is fearless about showing emotions and sensuality. René is the first Togolese man I have met who fills the bill. Yet I know the fire was fueled by cheap wine, a full moon, and lovely Orion in the sky.

Six months after my arrival in Togo, the day after I meet René, I am primed to start my project. I make a brief trip to Lomé to type my syllabus on the computer in the Peace Corps bureau, and make a hundred copies for distribution.

In Lomé, on a whim, I call Maxim, who I have not seen since the end of training three months ago. He gave me his cell number before we parted, but I haven't had the nerve to call him until now. Maxim agrees to meet me later at an Internet café, Cybercité, and we reacquaint ourselves while we surf the Net together, check email, and look at photos sent by my Uncle Mike in Santa Fe.

Finally, at Cybercité, I am able to see Maxim up close. In fact, he is so close that I can smell him, and I touch his big bald head when he bumps it on the computer cubicle. Later, we hold hands—something Togolese friends do in public—for wonderful minutes as we cross the street to find a place for dinner. I can feel his slim fingers between mine, as long as pencils.

"We must hurry or the taxis of Lomé will run over us," Maxim smiles, only slightly in jest.

"With your long legs, it's easy for you to cross quickly!" I tell Maxim he will have to pick me up if I am to walk as fast as he does.

"I am too big, you are not strong enough!" I challenge him further. Maxim scoops me up in his arms. I can feel his hands on my back and my butt, and his arm at the side of my breast.

We dine at Big Mak, Maxim's favorite hamburger bar, until midnight. We talk about both mundane and serious things, and I learn some personal things about him.

"My father died this past Christmas. We buried him before the New Year. He was very sick the entire time we were doing your training in Kpalimé. That is why you rarely saw me outside of class. I came home to Lomé to see him as often as I could."

I can't believe Maxim's father died in the midst of our Peace Corps training, and that no one knew about it.

C'est la vie. That's how life is. Maxim responds simply. We are silent for a bit before he shares another intimate piece of information.

"My father raised me and my brother and sister. My mother left us when I was 11 years old. She did not want to be in a family so she left us. She was gone for 14 years." Silence.

"She is back now, but it is not the same," he adds.

As Maxim talks about his mother, his face changes and his voice gets hard. Is Maxim afraid of women? Does he find all women untrustworthy? I feel sad and I am surprised by my feelings.

Quel dommage. That is too bad, I tell him.

"I was very close to my father," Maxim continues. "He made everyone happy. I want to be just like him." Maxim's face lights up, only to darken again when he adds, "However, I think my experience with my mother has made me careful with women. I have dated many women, too many. I used to be very bad about this!"

Maxim laughs at himself, a great big smile on his face. "But I'm different now, I've changed."

I tell Maxim there seems to be a part of him that does not want to be cynical about women, and Maxim nods in agreement. He denies that his unfortunate views of women are *terminale*, permanent.

"I will not be forever defined by my mother's departure."

"You are young, you can change."

"No, I am old. I feel very old." He smiles wistfully.

Tonight, Maxim seems very young to me.

At Bernadette's the morning after my trip, we catch up with each other and I talk about my preparations for the girls' class. We chat, we joke, we playfully tease each other, but something is different. Bernadette laughs less than usual, and she places the items roughly on her stand. When I ask her if something is wrong, Bernadette tells me she has to go to the *sous-préfet* office. She thrusts a piece of paper in my face.

Although by now I can easily translate the French, my understanding of the document is still limited because I am not Togolese. I can't appreciate how serious the paper is. So, I ask Bernadette to tell me what happened while I was in Lomé.

"Oh, Laurie! Did you see the military officer who was leaving on his motorcycle just as you arrived?" I did recognize the man. I met him in a village I visited once with Monsieur Bénoît.

"The officer has been relocated to Kougnohou. He has begun to build a house directly behind my stand."

I look behind Bernadette's stand and see piles of mud bricks not four feet away.

"His house will put me out of business," Bernadette continues. "Although this man is a stranger here, he did not ask permission to build his house here. He did not get the chief's permission as he is supposed to." Bernadette breathes in deeply before continuing.

"Laurie, you know the chief. You know I am related to the chief, that we share the same family name. This man does not know. He has lied when he said he got the chief's permission. He has chosen this spot, he does not mind lying, and he does not care that he will displace me."

This man does not know of my relationship with Bernadette. When he moved to Kougnohou, he came by to see me, acting as if we were already great friends. I now realize that when he did, he had already begun plans to displace Bernadette. Now I am upset too.

I have never seen Bernadette so angry! Bernadette is many things—strong-willed, straight spoken, assertive. I have never seen her distraught.

"I wanted to hit this man when he handed me the notice to go to the *sous-préfet* office," she fumes. I have never heard Bernadette say a harsh word about anyone.

"I told him, 'I am not from the bush. I am not some village woman you can control.' He thinks I will not go to the *sous-préfet*. He thinks I will not answer his challenge to have the land. He thinks I will be afraid. He is wrong!"

I realize in this moment that I would do anything for Bernadette. I don't know if I *can* do anything. As if reading my mind, Bernadette asks me if I will accompany her to the *sous-préfet*. It is the only favor she will ask of me the entire time I live in Togo.

I say yes without any compunction, with none of the hesitancy I so often feel before making any social/behavioral decision in Togo.

Bernadette and I march together all the way across the town of Kougnohou. We march as if we are soldiers going to war. Bernadette's righteous indignation and the regal way she bears it makes me so proud to be with her. She is a pistol! When we arrive, I realize I am in no way disturbed that I have come here on business not my own. By my presence I am aligning myself with Bernadette, not the police officer. However, because I am the village foreigner, my alignment with Bernadette confuses the authorities. The chief of police greets me, but he does not smile as he usually does. The *sous-préfet* also greets me, but without enthusiasm. The authorities assume that, as a guest in their village, I will automatically defer to them; they do not expect me to side with a market woman.

The social dynamics of the visit interest me. I have to be polite to the people in charge, even though I don't like them (I have to be Togolese). If I were at home in the United States, I might ask the *sous-préfet* directly about this problem. Here in Togo it is better for me to keep each culture clear and separate. I'll be nice (save face for him) in public. I cannot speak openly to him about Bernadette's issue. In private, I can speak. Each interaction will be respected and taken seriously.

❧

Nyalewossi finds me later in the day.

"I came to your house with my uncle three times this weekend while you were in Lomé. Saturday night we looked for you. Then Sunday at noon. Then Sunday at 3." I am surprised and happy to hear this.

"René was mad that you weren't there, and sad. We must go to his house tonight."

"No, I am too busy. I have to see the director about my class." Nyalewossi agrees that the visit can wait until tomorrow.

When I finally get home, I run into Honorine, who chats for a while at my front door. We hear a motorcycle. I think it might be the *assistant d'hygiene*, coming to check on my progress with the class schedule, but it is René. Honorine leaves quickly.

Getting off his motorcycle, René tells me, "I have come to invite you to my house for dinner."

René has caught me at a very bad time. I am consumed with my plans for the class, which starts tomorrow. Tied up all morning with Bernadette, I've had no time to prepare.

"I cannot tonight. I am not finished with my work."

René says he is afraid I won't come because I am worried about what people might say. I haven't thought of that yet. I haven't thought of René at all, actually.

"No, I am not afraid. Only tired and busy. I will come, but tomorrow is better."

"I left you a note, did you get it?"

I now see the note, wedged in the frame of my window. It is written on a tiny piece of paper, in lovely cursive French: "Please come to my house. We must eat together. I am so sorry I was not here to invite you sooner. I was busy today in another village and did not get home early." René writes as if he's been courting me, the way he addresses me and the way he apologizes profusely. It feels strange.

René insists we have dinner tonight. Because I am too tired to argue and I have nothing to cook for dinner, I give in, and René smiles triumphantly.

"I will come to get you at 7 o'clock." That leaves me just over an hour to bathe and meet with the CEG director about my class.

I tell René, "8 o'clock is better." It's a date. When René says goodbye, we hold hands for what seems like a long time.

I sit outside my house, waiting on the steps, enjoying the cool air. I carry only my flashlight and keys. Should I bring a condom?[1] That feels a little slutty, but also powerful and smart. I think, if I don't take a condom, that's a reason to avoid having sex. I know I won't have sex without a condom, so I just won't take one. (It seems like stupid reasoning in hindsight.) I decide I will put the condom in my little coin purse. No one has to know but me. Unless we use it, of course, and then it won't matter. I'll look smart and strong, because I am! The condom will confirm this.

René is here right at 8 and tells me I look pretty. I get on the moto and we're off. We take a little spin around town, and villagers I do not recognize watch us as we pass. I've rarely been out so late. Without the harsh African sunlight, the village looks completely different to me.

I'm a bit nervous at dinner because I don't know what René intends. Once the meal is served, René dismisses his daughter and the young *domestique*. The girls giggle, avoiding our eyes as they scoot away. And what did they prepare for us? *Lievre!* Rabbit. Couscous. Rice. Peas with sauce. Water and wine.

Again there is a moment when I sense René and I will be lovers. Our eyes meet, we touch. I am aware of conversation, but I am not paying attention. René makes a couple of trips to my side of the table. He finds opportunities to touch my neck, and I know what is coming.

His lips are on my neck, and they feel lovely. If I turn my head, I will be kissing him. I turn my head. His mouth is hungry as it devours my lips. I can feel his teeth and it's as if he wants to eat my throat. I'm still sitting at the table, but I don't want to kiss timidly. I want to stand and feel the full force of his kiss. And return it. I raise myself and I am bigger than he is. His hands find my bra and unhook it. Soon he has lifted off my sweater and bra.

ↄ⅊

Dear Oded,

Are you ready? I have a lover, a married man. He is 36, with two children, and he is a Togolese businessman with the coffee and cocoa organizations in my village. When I first met him, I wasn't sure I liked him. But I do. He is very different from me, but also similar in a lot of ways. He is confident, self-assured, and romantic. I would like him in or out of Togo.

But it's the married part that is so interesting. His wife lives in another country, so we are deceitful mostly with the community. I told you what it is like here; people watch everything I do. So he comes to me very late, in the dark, on his motorcycle. We are polite in public. In private, in bed, I am very comfortable with him. It's very good between us in bed.

Kissing him is when I notice something missing. I don't feel I can give myself to him completely in a kiss but I'm surprised to find it doesn't bother me greatly. (Nor that he's married.) I am not worried about my reputation in town, but I should be. I may regret what I am doing.

There's so much I want to tell you. I hope you are well, my dear. I think of you often, and promise to keep you posted on my love life. You please do the same.

Yours,
Laurie

I was thinking this morning how *habituée* I've become. It's strange, but I am starting to like the smell of my own armpits. They are clean but they still smell because I don't use deodorant anymore since I don't have any. Everybody smells to some degree, everybody sweats; you can't help it, so it doesn't matter. I realized how strange this new appreciation is when I pictured myself telling Jani, who will meet me when I vacation in France two weeks from now. I see her wrinkling her nose and saying "Gross!"

ↄ⅊

I feel such incredible momentum. In four days I will be on a plane to Paris! I want to be on a plane, to change countries, to see new sights, to live a different life for ten days. Nothing can bother me, I am so strong and confident.

Or so I think. I sit with Nyalewossi and Bernadette when the *moulin*, the man who runs the flour mill, walks past. The *moulin* has been hitting on me lately. This time, he asks about my friend Grant. Grant is a fellow PCV with whom I have grown very close; he is a male Shoshana, a triathlete, an intelligent, articulate, and adventurous person. Grant is a health volunteer in the same region of Togo as I am. But he lives in a dry, desolate village on the opposite side of the country, a few kilometers from Benin. Grant's work focuses on HIV/AIDS training and, especially, guinea worm eradication.

Grant visited me recently in Kougnohou to do a health session for my class. He helped me manage unwanted suitors by pretending to be my boyfriend. We held hands and acted like lovers while we sat at Bernadette's stand, so the *moulin* would stop bothering me. (It apparently works only when Grant is here.) I am annoyed by the familiarity with which the *moulin* teases me, and his questions feel accusatory.

Why are you going to Paris? Why do you travel so much? What is there for you in Atakpamé? Why don't you bring anything when you travel? Why can't you tell me when you are leaving? Because the questions presume some sort of familiarity, I get angry and snap at him.

"Laurie, *c'est pas gentille*," Bernadette chastises me gently. The ill feeling left by the exchange with the *moulin* leads me to snap at her.

"I am ready to leave on vacation. I have been six months in Togo and it is time for a break."

"Oh," they say, in that passive Togolese style. Immediately, I realize my offense and try to explain it away.

"It is necessary to understand. I am bothered by people asking questions, every day there are people who grab, touch, and stare at me."

Their faces show interest and concern. The more I try to explain myself, the worse I do.

"I want to be in a place with a lot of *blanches*. Then I won't be bothered." I don't realize how racist my comment is until I have said it out loud. Again, I try to backpedal.

"I am always a stranger here, I'm always noticed. In Paris, I will just be like everyone else." I feel a little better, saying this, but not much. Nyale-wossi and Bernadette remain silent.

This is such a strange feeling. I have made one of those dumb racial *gaffes* that politicians sometimes make and trying to correct it sounds even more stupid and racist.

The truth is, what I said *was* racist. Yet I was being honest. I do want to go where I don't stand out, where I am not bothered, where I can be unremarkable. I do long for a place with more white people, but not solely *les blanches*. I want to be in a place that has diversity so I can blend in. I want to be somewhere I am not ostracized because of the color of my skin.

I am still not sure they understand.

I spend the night before my trip to Paris as a spectator at René's church. René is the leader of the chorale, and tonight he's invited me to come and watch the group practice. I can see that René loves music as I watch his complete involvement with the group. Later he told me had written the song they were singing and showed me the music.
Watching René makes me wonder what kind of teacher I am. With the CEG girls I have had several moments when I felt completely at ease, when I was centered in myself, even in West Africa, even in French.

A big kerosene lamp lights the inside of René's church. Someone sets it on the floor near the chorale. Now, I can see on the wall the shadow of the choir members with René above, directing. He looks like a big shadow god, a big singing deity. At the end of the practice, René insists I introduce myself and the work I am doing in Kougnohou. I do, but halt-ingly. As I walk back to my bench, the small audience claps, and a young man grabs my hand and kisses it when I pass him.

Because it is dark, René manages to sneak me on the moto without our being noticed. When we arrive at my house, René says he hasn't eaten and seems concerned this could be "a problem." I make him laugh by insisting on feeding him tuna and mayonnaise.

"You become very nice when you want something." Now it's my turn to laugh.

After he eats, I tell him *Viens*. Come.

We lie on my bed with our clothes on, kissing and caressing. I shut the window so my neighbors won't hear us. This time, we feel more familiar. And so the sex is also better, more personal. I enjoy myself. René laughs when I pull the condom from my medical kit.

"Normally, it's I who keeps that," René observes, smiling. His forthrightness and intuitiveness surprise and delight me.

We have the kind of sex in which you ignore the bed's disarray and the clothes strewn all over the floor. We turn every which way. It is completely dark and we rely on our bodies and hands.

I can kiss him now. Easily. Openly. I feel enough . . . what? Love? Affection? Enough of something so that I can kiss his face and eyes and hold his hands during sex and after. I like him more.

"You have a need of me, and I have a need of you. We are both alone here in Kougnohou." René tells me that his wife works in Europe. It is clear that he is proud of her, and also that he misses her. "She has been gone a long time."

For the first time I see how much René loves his wife. But he is lonesome for company, for intimate conversation as well as sex. As I am.

René tells me he feels trapped. It is a lot of responsibility to be married, with a family, a job. There are a million things he may never be able to do because of choices he's already made. He tells me marriage is a burden for men in Africa. The sadness in his voice when he says this makes me believe him without question.

René tells me he wants to share my bed and laughter and conversation. I love his openness about this. I feel the same way.

"When you start to love, you know already you are going to suffer." René tells me it is always a risk when you start to like someone. Ah, he is wise too. He knows himself.

"I am a stranger in town, just like you," he continues.

"I don't want to be a stranger."

"Whether you want it or not, you are."

Can I handle this kind of honesty? I change the subject to ask René what he wants for himself.

"To be free."

Even in the dark I can see his face become pained and ugly. My heart jumps. I want to hold him, to touch him, to ease his pain. René is essentially a stranger, so it feels false when I reach out to him. He sees this. When I caress his cheek, René turns his head. Leaving, he is very abrupt.

"Time! *l'Heure!* He slaps my ass goodbye.

Alone in bed, I replay René leading his chorale. I see his smile. I see his *pagne* shirt, his leather slippers, his *boubou*. I see myself comforting him. I see his receding hairline. I laugh when I remember his calling condoms *chapeaux*. Mostly I see him at the choir lesson. I see him excited, doing something he loves. And I love him in that moment.

I have many such moments in my life now. Moments of peace that come from seeing people do what they love, in the center of their universe. Maybe it's a sign I am in the same place? Am I at my center now? Is that the source of the peace? All of this feels wonderful and strange and new. My heart was closed before. I had so little love in my life. Now, it seems as if I have too much.

જી

Sophie finds me in Lomé at the Peace Corps bureau one day after my vacation to France. "Laurie," she asks, "can you stay in Lomé until tomorrow to participate in a women's conference before you return to your village? Other volunteers are here for it." The conference is sponsored by WILDAF, Women in Law and Development in Africa. The theme of the meeting is sexual harassment and young girls. Of course, I say yes.

"What are the reasons for sexual harassment of girls?" our moderator asks. The group of attendees, which includes teachers, lawyers, and other professionals, both women and men, have ready answers: Men have no conscience. Men consider girls and women to be property. Parents do not talk enough with young girls about sexuality.

The moderator, a woman, tells us that 38 percent of girls in Togo will experience sexual harassment at least once in their lives. Typically, that harassment will occur *au niveau du scolaire.* It will occur in school.

It is difficult for me to follow the rapid academic French used in the conference, but I manage. One comment by a female participant catches my attention.

"We often talk with young girls about this issue, and they also talk among themselves. It is necessary to add teachers to the discussion."

A man speaks up. "It is a problem for teachers. If a young girl sees you with another female student, she gets jealous and there will be tension."

This comment surprises me. Why does he address ways that girls' behavior affect the teachers? Isn't the teacher responsible for his behavior with the girls, and not the other way around?

The moderator points out that *harcèlement sexuelle* is a systemic problem in Togo.

"We treat women as objects. We are not shocked by this behavior. We have even begun to consider it normal. This shows how deeply inferior women are perceived in our society."

The moderator and most of the participants don't want to discuss specific examples. Rather, they focus on how institutional beliefs promote the behavior. The moderator continues.

"Subordination is always a story of inequality. So, specifics are not important. We must discuss the system that produces these consequences. The phenomenon has to do with the stature of women in Africa. This makes it about the stature of men in Africa as well."

While I agree with these comments, the discussion has me evaluating my own experience in Togo, and the women and girls I've met here. Just off the top of my head, I think of two examples of this phenomenon: Nyalewossi with the gendarme who said he wanted to father her baby, and Odette with her teacher/boyfriend.

Nyalewossi set her boundaries with the gendarme clearly and without incident. However, Odette is another story. Odette reminds me of women back home who strategize clearly and comprehensively to achieve their goals in life. In my own world, that meant planning what university to attend, what classes to take, what to major in, and whether graduate school is necessary.

For Togolese girls like Odette, higher education is not an option. So, how does such a girl plan for the future? She thinks strategically about money. One path is to develop an intimate relationship with a man who will give her money. She looks carefully for just the right man. The effort is as clearly strategized as any American woman planning to attend college. Odette's future is more likely to be assured through an intimate relationship with an educated, affluent Togolese (or better yet, European) man.[2] My new theoretical epiphany is like a block of cement in my gut.

"It is a system that allows this. It is a problem of *mentalité*," our moderator says. Sophie, who is also a participant at the conference, agrees. Her legal background makes her a formidable and skilled speaker.

"There is the law, of course. There are documents that say this sort of behavior is illegal in Togo. However, if people do not know the law, if people do not respect the law, if people do not think it is a serious offense, it is as if there is no law."

"Yes," the moderator reiterates. "it is a question of *mentalité*. We must change our ideas before this behavior will change in our society."

The next morning I visit Cybermonde 2000, the Internet café Maxim has opened for business. He is not there when I arrive, but his office manager tells me he will be soon. In the meantime, I check my email. The office manager, unbeknownst to me, calls Maxim on his cell phone to tell him I am here. I am very happy to see him when he arrives about a half-hour later.

We spend several lovely hours together at Cybermonde. I tell Maxim about my trip to Paris and my recent discovery of Aného, a seaside village in Togo. Maxim surprises me by telling me that his family is from Aného, once Togo's capital city. We begin talking about his family name, da Silva. Maxim gives me a brief history of his family.

"They were Portuguese traders of the Guin coastal tribe. They were Spanish-speaking, but also German-speaking, and they had some English too. They were business-oriented, involved in trade in several West African countries. Their names are all Spanish-sounding. They were very intelligent, very festive people. The sole purpose of family *fêtes* was to remind you not to get involved in politics. It's family tradition to avoid politics."

I am spellbound. Maxim manages to be matter-of-fact, confident, and humble all at the same time.

"My Portuguese name is Manoel; my father's name was Africo, and my grandfather's was Candido. Candido's family were slave owners, and very wealthy."

As Maxim finishes his story, a young, gorgeous man strides into the café; he heads right over to us. Our eyes lock as if we know each other, however I've never seen the man before. He is Maxim's 21-year-old brother Luc. Luc speaks superb English, just like Maxim, and after we are introduced he insists to me, "You must let me know when you are returning to Lomé. I would like to invite you to our house."

I look at Maxim; he has never extended an invitation like this. He blurts out "Okay!" with surprise. Maxim has already promised me a trip to Aného. I will not forget that. But Maxim has never asked me to his home. Maxim asks me, somewhat sheepishly, "When will you be back in Lomé?"

When we kiss goodbye, we kiss international style, three times on the cheek, right-left-right, just as we did when we kissed hello. Except that, I swear I'm not imagining it, Maxim, on the third kiss, makes sure less cheek and more lip is involved.

Before I leave Lomé, I stop by the medical unit in Lomé to stock up on tampons and baby powder before I head back into the bush. Beatrice, the extremely professional Ghanaian nurse, gives me a quick once over. Upon seeing sores on my feet from the new sandals I bought in Paris, Beatrice admonishes me to take better care of them. She reminds me of the risk of infection here—how a small sore can turn into a full-blown seeping injury.

"Don't forget, my dear, you're in Black Africa now!"

On my way upcountry, I make another stop—this time in Kpalimé. I have not seen the Diore family since Christmas. Papa is the only one at home when I arrive in the middle of day, and we have a very adult chat together while waiting for the rest of the family to come home for lunch. Having just been back in the developed world, I tell Papa how hard it is to return to West Africa and see so many needs unmet.

"Oh, Togo, Togo, Togo. It is because of our government that we have these problems. The president is giving my pension to Sierra Leone."

"Why? Where do you think the money's going?" I know Papa used to be a teacher, and that he is retired, but he has never talked to me about problems with his pension.

"The money goes to Sierra Leone, to pay for the diamonds, of course." Papa adds sadly, "I haven't received my pension in six months."

I can't believe I actually know where the path ends, and still we can't do anything about the corruption. Papa sums up simply.

"The only way things change in Africa is with civil war."

Later, after lunch and *sieste*, I take 18-year-old Marguerite with me to a *buvette* for a *sucrerie*, a Coke. Marguerite seems to have something on her mind; she is unusually quiet. I sense that she wants to tell me something. Finally, she speaks.

"Maman doesn't want to know I am serious with Ahmet." She adds, *"en Afrique*, people do not like to hear the truth."

Our ensuing discussion about sexual mechanics, safe sex, and romance is surprisingly rational and clear. I don't tell Marguerite about my affair with René, but I do tell her about Oded, who is in Israel, and how I hope one day we will be together. After hearing me out, Marguerite asks me questions that force me to be honest with her.

"Can you really wait three more years to have children?"

No one has asked me that question before. Most of my girlfriends back home want to know the same thing but are too polite to ask.

"Well, I have just earned my PhD. Now I've got to look for a job. You don't know how long job searches take in academia. . ."

Marguerite sees right through my explanations, and her assessment is stark and wise beyond her years.

"You Americans, you have your families, but you work too much, you study too much, you don't have time for life."

Back home in Koughnou, my first class post vacation will focus on the difference between sex roles and gender roles. The girls arrive for class all dressed up, and we talk for about an hour-and-a-half. I show the girls slides of my sister Patricia's abstract paintings of young women. I use a map of the world to talk about how, across the globe, women do many different things and also many similar things.

Some of the girls look at my sister's paintings and say they are *Très jolis!* When I tell them some art critics found the paintings scary or ugly,[3] the girls say *C'est pas vilain!* After a few minutes a couple of the students agree, "Only boys think that, and are afraid."

I describe my sister's professional and educational experience as an artist to the girls: "She went to school a long time and did not have money when she was a student. Eventually, she earned two baccalaureate degrees, one in art and another in art history. Now she is working on a master's degree, also in art history."

The girls' faces show disbelief. There is only one university in the entire country of Togo; it is hard to enter and is often shut down due to teachers' strikes. Compared to the opportunities in Togo, the fact that my sister can earn three degrees in one city, in a space of a few years, seems unbelievable. I see that now.

"Do you see this painting?" I pass around a slide of a painting that represents an adolescent girl sitting in a pink landscape that is interrupted by pastel drips of blue, gray, and yellow. "My sister told me that she sold a painting just like this one for $3000. It is the most money she has ever made from one painting."

Kuh! Kuh! The girls say, shocked at my revelation.

The girls have a difficult time believing anyone can make a living this way.[4] I realize how unusual it might sound to the girls to hear that my sister's sole means of financial support is through creating art.

It doesn't occur to me until I get another letter from my sister after telling her about the class discussion, that I'm not sure if the girls had trouble believing Patricia can live as an artist because she is a woman, or that they can't imagine that anyone, male or female, can make so much money for creating what looks like a colorfully messy drawing.

The priest I met in Djon, Père Didier, has invited me to attend a *Jubilée de la Jeune Fille*. Held in the small village of Seregbené, deep in the Akebou bush, the event is in concert with the Catholic Church Year 2000 Jubilee. The Jubilee will be held in Seregbené because it is the largest of the tiny villages, and has a grand church that will serve as our meeting place.

The late afternoon drive to Seregbené is beautiful. About twenty girls ride in the back of Didier's truck, while seven of us are up front. Père Didier talks nonstop while he drives about plans for the next day. We arrive in Seregbené very late. Although it's pitch dark and impossible to see anything, I remark that Seregbené is smaller and more isolated than any village I have yet seen in Togo.

"There are many small villages in the vicinity of Seregbené, much smaller than this one!" Didier chuckles.

We walk to the Catholic compound and Didier introduces me to several nuns from the monastery in Danyi, a small town near Kpalimé. I will stay with the nuns in a dorm, complete with running water, electricity, sheets, towels, and blankets. When I see this oasis of city life in the middle of the African bush, I can't help but marvel: "If all Togo was like this!" This atmosphere is conducive to critical thinking; it is easier to luxuriate in ideas when you have amenities at your disposal.[5]

The next morning after breakfast we walk to the church for the meeting. To my astonishment, I learn that nearly 800 girls await us inside the church. Girls and their families have come from Seregbené and the many smaller villages surrounding it. Even though many of the girls have traveled for hours to get here, even though we are late and they are cramped into too few benches, sweating and uncomfortable, they sit patiently and quietly. Sitting on stage left as I wait for my turn to speak, my eyes lock on the face of one little girl crammed at the end of a pew not far from the stage. The little girl won't stop staring at me. She is probably no more than five years old; her small head is cocked to one side as she regards me, smiling ever so slightly.

Looking around, I see many of the girls' eyes on me, despite the procession of priests and nuns speaking at the microphone. For once, the constant collective staring I experience in West Africa doesn't bother me. I'm not annoyed, I don't want to hide from these stares. I do not experience these stares as scorn or ridicule. Rather, these stares feel like innocent, simple curiosity. You wouldn't think there's a difference, but there is.

When it is my turn I speak in French, and someone translates what I say into Akebou. I tell all 800 girls my reasons for working in Togo, and the goals of the project I am doing in the Akebou region. I speak no more than ten minutes, and I receive thunderous applause not once, but twice! First, when I say I have earned my PhD, and am a *docteur de lettres*. Second, when I say "You too can become anything you want to be!"

The young girls' applause overwhelms me, and I am high for the rest of the day. Not until later will I reflect more critically on the words I chose to speak. Once the high wears off, I feel ashamed of telling the girls they can become anything they want. Why did I say that? Do I think it's true?

After the Jubilée, Antoine departs for a sojourn in Italy. When he returns a month later, I smile uncontrollably because he is so chubby. This happens to nearly everyone who goes abroad from Togo. They all gain weight! Antoine is still very slight, but his face is fuller, and his cheeks look different. I agree to have lunch with him at the priest house in Kougnohou.

We didn't have much time to chat in Seregbené, and there's a lot to catch up on.

Antoine then tells me exciting news. Some of his friends in Italy have bought him a truck, which will be delivered to Lomé next week. I congratulate him, but my attempt to be cheerful does not last long.

"You are not in good humor," Antoine observes frankly. "What is wrong?"

Antoine is right, and my mood will only worsen throughout the afternoon and evening. I am full of disquiet. I don't feel like talking to anyone, not even my friend Antoine.

Dopé is dead. Beautiful Dopé with the big smile, the tall posture, the huge eyes, the intelligent face. Dopé, who sold rice at the *marché*, lived near me, went to *lycée* every day, and often stopped by to say hello when I first got here. Monsieur Bénoît stopped by very early this morning to tell me. His eyes were red and puffy, and he openly cried as he gave me the news.

"She died in Ghana, where she'd gone for treatment of an illness. I don't know what the illness was, and her family doesn't know either. They took her to Ghana because it is closer than Lomé. She died there unexpectedly, and her family had to bury her there. They arrived back in Kougnohou last night."

Dopé's house is not far from mine, and all night long I had heard singing at the *veillée*. I even recognized René's choir. But I did not know it was Dopé who died.

After Antoine leaves, I visit Dopé's sister, who is in my girls' class. All day I walk the village, talking with every student I see about Dopé's death. One of the few young women in high school (one of thirteen girls in a village of 14,000 people), Dopé also worked at the *marché* to help support her family. She was well known by everyone. Dopé was tall and graceful, with a direct gaze and a kind face. I cannot believe she is dead, and neither can anyone else. The whole village is sighing.

Nyalewossi tells me everybody who attended church last night cried throughout the service.

"The parishioners put Dopé's dress on display. They hung it at the front of the church to signify her absence." The image of Dopé's dress hanging alone, silent, in the same church where René's choir practices, takes my breath away.

Nyalewossi and I both sniffle. She adds, "It was very, very, very sad."

We had planned to go out for dinner tonight, walk to the *marché* and eat *pâte* with peanut sauce. It starts to rain, and I think it might be better to just go home. I want to go to bed and hide from everything. But Nyalewossi doesn't want me to leave.

"It won't really rain, it will stop." There is her usual assertiveness, and I hear a bit of playful mischief in her voice as well.

"Oh, how do you know this? Are you God?" I respond accordingly.

"Yes!" she says, without hesitation. "I am the second in command. I watch over the earth and the sky."

"Really?" I make a quizzical face, pretending to be impressed.

"*Oui!* God takes care of the dead and I, the living."

"Then we'll have a new life," I say.

"Yes," she says with assurance. "A boy."

Sometimes I just adore Nyalewossi.

A few weeks after Dopé's death, Antoine invites me to lunch again, this time at his house in Djon. He wants to meet members of the Djon Village Development Committee (CVD). The CVD would like to arrange for me to accompany Père Didier on trips to smaller villages in the Akebou coffee and cocao farms, to discuss my project. The Djon priests regularly travel to the numerous tiny villages in Akebou to celebrate Catholic Masses there.

I've already traveled with Antoine—on the back of his motorcycle—to villages west of Kougnohou, where he performs Masses on alternate Sundays. It's pleasant to assist him with the rituals of the Mass, usually in someone's private home. However, Didier's work will take me in a northern direction, higher up the mountain, deeper into the Akebou bush.

Antoine and I arrive in Djon at lunchtime, and after some fufu and discussion, it is time for *sieste*. Antoine opens the wooden shutters of the bedroom windows as I stare at his overflowing bookcase. I will take *sieste*, as I usually do, in Antoine's bedroom; Antoine will take the sofa in the living room. Once the shutters are open, Antoine takes a seat on the bed next to me. When I turn to face him, he surprises me by planting a big kiss on my cheek. The kiss is definitely unexpected, but Antoine has a tendency to be sentimental, so I think nothing of it.

Antoine leaves the room, and I go to sleep, *sans problèmes*. When I wake up two hours later, Antoine is already preparing to leave for the CVD meeting. Still groggy, I sit down on the living room sofa, and Antoine sits next to me. Before I realize what is about to happen, Antoine leans over to kiss me—this time, on the lips.

Antoine's mouth feels like a little minnow attacking my face. Then he puts his hand inside my shirt, inside my bra, and his rough fingers caress my left nipple. Although I feel slightly repulsed, I try not to show it.

I do not want to hurt Antoine with my impulse to recoil. I don't want to risk damaging our friendship (at least no more than he is by kissing me!). I do enjoy the sensation of a hand, any hand, on my breast. How strange it is to feel repulsion and enjoyment at the same time.

When Antoine tries to push me down on the sofa, as if to lie on top of me, I stand up. Enough. Antoine stands up too, very quickly, and immediately moves to the opposite side of the room, looking nervous.

"Does it bother you?"

"Yes." When he remains silent, I add, "Antoine, you are a priest."

"Yes. You are right." Antoine says he will never do it again. Then he goes back to preparing his things for the meeting. Wait a minute. What just happened here?

"I don't understand why you kissed me."

"I've been thinking about kissing you for the past two months."

The desire on his face saddens me. Antoine tells me, very matter-of-factly, that he's broken his vows once already.

"I've made love before. I do not regret it." He says it as if he were just another man—a mature one, even, in the matters of love. *Je suis seul.* I am alone.

"You need someone." This I understand, too well in fact.

"Yes," he says, a forlorn look on his face.

After the meeting, Antoine takes me home to Kougnohou on his motorcycle. I want to believe things will not change between us. I don't want to ignore what happened, but I think we can get past it, because Antoine and I have always been able to talk to each other. We have had a wonderful friendship and I don't want it to go away. On the way to Kougnohou,

Antoine repeats that he doesn't regret his sexual liaison because he was in love with the woman.

I don't know what to make of Antoine's confession, nor of his behavior toward me. Frankly, I never thought of Antoine as a sexual being. Part of that is because he's a priest and, I've naïvely assumed, celibate. I've always seen Antoine as a platonic friend, asexual. I feel confused when I learn he sees himself differently. I don't know why I think this is so strange. Why does it challenge me to imagine a priest who is sexually active? (Now, who is the immature one?)

"I have learned something from kissing you." We are still on the motorcycle.

"Already?" I say, disbelieving. I am so disoriented and so engrossed in my own thoughts that I don't bother to listen to what Antoine learned.

At the end of this day, one thing is clear about Antoine's kissing me. I felt desire. Not sexual desire, mind you. Rather, I felt a desire to meet Antoine's need for companionship, for attention, and for love. I felt compassion for him. I understood his longing for intimacy with another person. Antoine needs what all of us need. In that way, he is no different from anyone else; he is no different from me.

Except for the vows.

Antoine's kiss raised many questions for me. Would this have happened if we were in the States? Why, or why not?

What if René wasn't meeting my sexual needs? Would I have responded to Antoine?

What if I really was attracted to Antoine, not just as a friend but as a man? What if I did see him as a sexual being? Would I have allowed him to continue to touch me? What if I'd been more turned on by his hand on my breast? What if I had no scruples?

I feel incredibly naïve. I completely misjudged Antoine. I never saw this coming.

A Change of Future

Dear Mom,

A strange thing happened to me the other day at the post office in Atakpamé. A smiling woman about my age comes up to me and says "You are beautiful!" She asks where I come from. When I say Texas, she gets misty-eyed.

"I want to marry a white man." She speaks with such longing that I jokingly say, "I have two brothers!"

"I must have your address in Togo so I can send my photo to send your brothers."

"One is spoken for," I say, still joking. I give the woman my address. In Africa, my address is the simplest it has ever been in my life:

Laurie Charles
Akebou CEG

I give my address to anyone who asks. In Akebou where I live is public knowledge. Everyone in the village knows how to find me.

Several weeks pass, and I forget all about the incident. Monday, however, the woman arrives at my house with a friend in tow, who "also wants a white *man for a husband." Odette spotted the women asking about me at the Kougno-hou taxi station and accompanied them to my house.*

I must have looked profoundly shocked when I saw the women because, although they had brought baggage with them, they were flustered and said they could not stay.

I felt slightly put upon, and very confused. But I liked the women, and it was not hard to be kind. The four of us talked for about an hour in my kitchen. To ease conversation, I showed them my photo album. I didn't think David (the "available" brother) was in any of the pictures, but he was.

"That's my brother."

"My husband, my husband!" The friendly woman gets very excited. Then there was a picture of you. "My mother in law!"

We all laughed at their excitement, but I am certain we were laughing for very different reasons!

Despite the cultural mess I had made, it was fun visiting with the two women. The pictures brought up all kinds of comments on men, women, same-sex relationships, and cleanliness (the women commented that I look so clean and well-coiffed in the photos). They loved the swearing-in picture of me in a Togolese dress—called me une femme Africaine. *When they saw Maxim, they said he was beau. Then the friendly woman adds, "It is terrible that African men need more than one wife. It is terrible that they think they must always have filles."*

"Africans treat Europeans and American women differently," Odette's eyes had flashed at the woman's comment. She looked ready to kill. Then, a bit sadly, "Laurie does not want an African man."

I was not serious about helping these women, but they actually believe I will find them husbands. I feel too ashamed to tell them that it was a joke to me. They left me with addresses and pictures, and we parted as friends.

All week I have consulted my Togolese friends for advice about the situation. Most of them, especially Bernadette, were appalled at the women's behavior. Some thought it made perfect sense for the women to do what they did, because "Togolese men aren't faithful." Another woman said, "She is right, you are beautiful, why wouldn't she want to join the family?"

But the best advice came from Nyalewossi: I should explain to the women it was just a joke. Sounds simple, right? I'm not so sure. I may just tell them David got married! The women would understand that better. What is a joke at home is not a joke here. All the rules are different. I keep learning that.

More later,
Laurie

༄

In April, my eighth month in Togo, Peace Corps celebrates "Take our Daughters to Work Day" (TODTWD) for the second time in the country, and it is a rousing success.[1] Through an essay contest each volunteer in the Plateaux region has chosen three girls to meet for one week in Atakpamé, the regional capital. Following the essay contest among the girls in my class, I chose Imma, Beatrice, and Akossiwa. Beatrice's mother has died recently; she lives with her father, who was impressed with the idea of TODTWD and, after a lengthy talk, gave me permission to take his daughter. Akossiwa lives in a small *concession* with her mother and sister; I don't know anything about her father. Her mother was extremely appreciative of the TODTWD invitation, and gave permission immediately.

Imma lives with her parents and siblings in a *concession* near Nyalewossi's boutique. When I visited to ask her parents' permission, I saw firsthand the way so many people with disabilities move around in Africa—by dragging themselves on the ground.

Imma had polio as a child, and although she pedals a heavy, three-wheeled bike with her arms, she cannot use her bike in the *concession* because the ground is covered with medium to large petrified rocks. After he gives permission, Imma's father asks if I can get her a new bike. At 14, she has never left the village. To take the girls to Atakpamé, I rent a 12-person van and pay the chauffeur extra money to put her cumbersome bike on the roof.

For three days, the Plateau region's TODTWD girls, nearly twenty of them, stay in dorm rooms at Affaires Sociales headquarters. The volunteers stay at the volunteer *maison*, and elect two PCVs each night to chaperone the girls in the dorm.

Throughout the first and second day, the girls are extremely quiet, timid, and deferential. By the last day, we can't believe how animated they have become. They are full of questions for the working women they visit, and full of attitude about the answers they get. For instance, instead of listening passively, as they have done for two days, on the third day, one of the girls asks how the manager of an Internet café got her job: "Did you apply? Did you know the owner?"

The manager is a young, attractive woman. Although we've included her on our TODTWD speaker list, we volunteers stopped frequenting her Internet café months ago. The system at this café is always down; the manager, although she certainly looks the part with her professional clothes and well-coiffed hair, doesn't know how to type or use a computer.

The young woman tells the girls she got the job because she knew the owner, an older man who is a friend of her father's. Oh. The inference that the woman likely has an intimate relationship with her boss is not lost on the girls, and they seem fed up.

"Is that the only way a woman can get a job in Togo?" Imma blurts. "Why do we need a man to give us something we can earn on our own?"

The speaker dodges the question, responding limply, "Just don't pay attention to boys."

On the last night, we have a *soirée* at a fancy hotel with many local dignitaries as guests. In a celebration, we let the girls drink beer and soda, even though some of the dignitaries, overweight and bored-looking *fonctionnaires*, eyeball us with disdain. Traditional dancers entertain before dinner, and some of the girls give short speeches. The girls' speeches are sweet, funny, and full of hope. One girl, Beatrice, says, "We must stay away from boys because boys are always lying." Another girl says, "We can be proud because we can do anything boys can do." Some of the men in the audience laugh.

"That is why I said what I did in Seregbené!" Saying out loud that girls can do whatever they want to do defies the hearers' disbelief. It shines a much-needed light on beliefs about gender and other issues in the girls' lives.

The girls are quiet after the *soirée*, as we walk to the main road to get taxis. Before we can hail taxis for the fifteen of us it starts to rain and we all get soaked. Shoshana, who is visiting our region to help out (her region's TODTWD took place last week), takes most of the girls in one car when it arrives, but Grant and I have to wait for another taxi to accommodate Imma and her polio bike.

The bike, as long as a small car, is too large for the taxis that do appear. Finally we agree that I will take Imma in a taxi without her bike, and Grant will jog Imma's bike back to the dorm room in the pouring rain.

When I arrive at Affaires Sociales with Imma, Shoshana helps me transport her to the dorms. The rest of the girls are dancing the mapuka in their underwear to songs they sing and chant. They are waiting for a volunteer to bring our house stereo and some recorded music. They take a break to wait for the stereo, but become impatient and resume their fête minus our boom box.

During the break Beatrice, in her bra and shorts, walks up to us and asks, "When is the music coming?" We tell her the volunteers are delayed by the rain, and she gives us this mournful look—influenced by alcohol, no doubt—and says, *On est fatigue parce qu'on a bu.* . . . . We are tired because we've been drinking. Shoshana and I decide we'll have to rename our celebration Get Our Daughters Drunk Day.

Of course the dancing continues—it *is* Africa—and when the girls start to feign sex with each other, they attract two male *functionaires*, who snack while watching the free show. I go home to the *maison* at this point. Next day Shoshana reports that later in the evening, the men offered the girls money so they would keep dancing. Apparently, some of the girls took the money, but Shoshana made them give it back.

꿈

René brings a stack of family pictures when he comes to my house tonight. On my bed, I flip through the stack while he lies next to me and listens to my CD player. I come across a photo of René with his wife; in the picture he hugs her, a huge smile on his face. My first instinct is to put the picture at the end of the pile and pretend I don't see it. But in Africa I'm trying to learn to open up the most intimate parts of myself, and I always learn from my relationship with René. So I force myself to look.

René is so obviously happy in the photo! When I tell him so, his face

121

lights up. He says the photo was taken "the Sunday before she left for France."

Then, I face what I have been sidestepping for weeks. René's wife will arrive next Friday, two weeks early, for an extended visit in Togo. Part of the time she will be here with René in Kougnohou. He has been very excited about her visit and, much to my chagrin, hasn't bothered to hide how eagerly he anticipates her arrival.

"You will be happy very soon." I have some trouble getting the words out.

Un peu (a little), he says quietly, as if indifferent. But a big smile fills his mouth and lights up his face, and he amends it to *Beaucoup!*

I want to feel happy for René because I care about him. I don't want to feel jealous—it's so ugly—or focus on feeling hurt. I tell myself that any man who truly loved me would not begrudge my love for Oded, something that to me is so pure and transcendent. So I hold tightly to that thought. (Still, there's only so much a woman can take!) I am further challenged when my newfound openness results in René's assuming it's okay for him to talk more about his wife's arrival. I must get a haircut! Do you have any medicine for *boutons*? (he is concerned about the pimples on his forehead). The bedroom is all nice for her, so don't come over. These comments tell me much more than I am ready to hear. I feel dismissed. I feel like the Other Woman. I *am* the other woman. How the hell do people do this?[2]

Still, I reach further. For the first time, I ask René for facts about his marriage. "Why is she living in France? Is she in training for a profession? Is she working?" As soon as I ask, I regret. I don't need to know anything else, I don't want to know, and I don't register René's answers.

When he finally leaves, I feel so unimportant, so very small. What a disconcerting feeling to be dismissed like this. It is a shock to my system, so strong that I have to stop what I am doing, lie down on the bed, and just feel it.

Even though I am full of disquiet, I cannot help smiling when I think about how René behaved tonight. Even now he can still manage to make me laugh. Earlier, when I was feeling jealous and resentful, René was studying his face in my two-sided mirror, talking to himself as if I weren't even there: *Je suis beau* . . . [he turns his head to better admire himself in the mirror] . . . *Je suis beau!* I am handsome! *J'étais né comme ça!* I was born this way!

René gazed at the mirror as if he was a stranger to himself, a confident man paying compliments to a handsome man. His vanity is charming and not at all annoying. But he is vain!

The next day, an idea awakens in my brain. That what to me is a break—my visit to a Third World, a different world—to them is their life. It's René's life. I have been envious of his business, his work, his life of church and friends. Now I think, Oh. This is his life. This is his whole life. This is not my whole life; it's my two years in the Third World, my break. We can't even dream the same dreams, can we?

On a day after his wife has arrived, René sneaks over to my house for a visit. I make him tell me—it is all my idea—what it feels like to have his wife around. I make him tell me: They'd made love. She is happy to be with him. She wants another child. He's enjoying their lovemaking. He is already thinking of his sadness at her coming departure. He likes that she is here.

I love his honesty, in spite of myself. How does he do it? Maybe I can learn something from him. So I ask.

"René, I am curious about how you do it. How do you manage having both of us?"

René responds only that I love him too much. He is more honest with me than I have been with myself. René is right, I love him. I am in love with the way he makes me feel. Good. Like a woman. I find this quality so attractive. I love how I feel when we play on the bed together—when I sit on him, punch him, and hug him while insisting he leave me alone—and how quickly he calls me on the inconsistency.

I love that René notices any and all contradictions between my words and deeds, and that he takes time to point them out to me, lovingly yet firmly. I learn so much from him, I laugh so much with him, and I adore this about him and our relationship. I never expected to find all this in a partner again, so soon after Oded—and certainly not in a partner who is a married Togelese. I love that his playful qualities are complemented by the seriousness with which he lives, works, and loves. I admire the way he balances these qualities.

Two days later, full of love and intense disquiet, I decide to break up with René. I hurt too much to be the Other Woman. I didn't really mind it when René's wife was in France. I could pretend she didn't exist. But now that she's here, in my village, in the house where I've spent so much time, forget it! I can't endure the awful feelings when I see him *en ville* and know that I cannot approach him, even to say hello. I hate that we have to hide our relationship. I especially hate that he is so completely unavailable to me. I didn't realize how much I depended on him. At my kitchen table, I tell René my decision.

"I do not accept this. I want to understand. You are right, you think I've forgotten you. But this will pass." René tries to convince me that things are hard for me merely because of bad timing.

"You are a husband, with a wife! This will never change."

René understands my upset. "You are alone! You need someone!" The understanding he conveys brings tears to my eyes.

René comes around the kitchen table to my chair and tries to comfort me. I lay my head gently on his shoulder, but I do not hold him, I do not touch him. I can feel his collarbone and his lovely attentiveness to me. But I feel so small. Not mad, not cold. Just sad, and small.

René walks out of the house, muttering *Merde, merde, merde*…. I stay somewhere inside myself, my hands clutching the back of the kitchen chair. To maintain my calm, I focus on my breathing. In, out, in, out. I tell myself to be strong, and I am strong. I don't go out, I don't give in to the urge to follow René. When I focus on myself, I lose the intense pull I usually feel to reach out to him.

Then René comes back into the kitchen and hugs me from behind. He puts his arms around my waist. He kisses my neck. He smells my hair. He wants so much to comfort me. He turns me around so that he can hug me from the front. My arms are limp, unable to move, my lips unable to kiss. I feel as if a part of me has withered away, rotted. René puts his hands on my waist, one hand inside my shirt, on my breastbone.

It is agonizing to not kiss him back, to not hold him.

"Don't cry, don't cry, *mon amour, ma petite, ne pleure pas, ne pleure pas.*" I look in his eyes and think he might cry.

René kisses me. His tongue is in my mouth, probing, as if he needs to reassure me he is there, that we are there together. It works. I kiss him back, our tongues twirling and sucking. He moans and I feel his hardening penis, and my moisture. My desire for René is still right under the surface, about to spill over on both of us.

He then stops, full of self-restraint, and announces, confidently, "I will find a time to return."

I tell him not to come back. He insists. I tell him not to do it.

He says, in very halting English, "I am coming back so I can show you that I love you."

I tell him in French, *C'est pas nécessaire.*

"I'm doing it because it's necessary for me. Not because you are upset, but to show you that I love you." In minutes, he is out the door and off on his motorcycle.

When René came to comfort me, in that moment he endeared himself to me forever.

René returns the same night, many hours later. We eat a late supper of rice in my kitchen, and stare at each other quietly. He looks at me, placating, hungry. Finally, he takes my plate, puts it aside and leads me to the bedroom.

We start as we usually do, by playfully touching each other, talking and chatting. But René is more determined than I tonight, and he takes the lead. He kisses the palms of my hands, he hugs me, he works hard to see my bare breast. When I reveal it, he stares at it like he has never seen one before, and I smile at his wonderful ability to emote about things I take for granted.

C'est la vie, c'est la vie là-bas. It's life," he says. "It's life there."

The awe in his face makes me feel powerful and earthy, as if I can perform magic, all because of a breast. He first seems to worship, then finally kisses, my breasts. Then he gets up to remove his clothing and tells me to do the same.

I wait.

He says it's an order.

I tell him I have not yet decided if I will fuck him. But I begin to remove my clothes, as if I do not control my own body.

"You've decided already?" he laughs. Realizing what I am doing, I laugh too.

We make sweaty love. I feel I am going to come, but he seems to come first, and I give up, tell him it's okay, I'm tired. But René knows I haven't come yet. He does all the work until I do. I have a cold, so he doesn't kiss me. But we do everything else—suck ears, necks, genitals. Finally, he comes on my thigh.

Afterward, we talk in bed. The conversation, at first general, eventually circles back to René's wife. He is the one who first mentions her, as if he were simply discussing the weather. I turn over. I want to stop, to close up, but I also want to stay open, to learn. Most of all, I want to learn what is in René's heart.

I have questions and he encourages me to ask. He is fearless about emotions. I love that quality so much. I want it for myself. So I ask my questions, and he answers.

"How do you feel love in your heart for two women? How hard is it? How do you make it less hard?"

"At some point I decided you should not come over because I would not be able to hide the fact that we are more than friends. I thought it is better if there is no clue at all. So I told you not to come."

This makes me happy.

"But it was not easy to forget you are here. I cannot even look at the pictures you took of my kids without thinking of you."

I am happy to hear this, too. But then René tells me things that hit me like a kick in the stomach. I swear it takes my breath away. Perhaps because he suspects his words are difficult for me to hear, René takes a didactic approach. He lectures me.

"In life, if you are with a man, with two men, the second man always knows that the other man is the priority. It doesn't mean he is not important. He is, but he is not the priority."

"Like us."

"Yes," he says, "like us." Like me.

René says he began to cut me off as his wife's arrival approached.

"Please explain," I ask. "I don't understand."

"I had to pull away because my wife was waiting for me. She emailed that she was counting the days until she saw me."

"What did you feel when you saw that?" I can't help the question—I want to know what René feels in his heart. A faraway look appears in his eyes; a serene smile comes over his face.

"I thought about love."

He has the same wondrous look on his face that he had when he admired my breast. He's so honest, he's brutal. Again I feel his words like a kick; he sees it and stops smiling.

Oh, it's lovely, love. But oh, it's awful! I don't know what to do with myself. I want to run away, I want to stay and be strong, I want to hide from the whole mess, I want to hold René, I want to hit René. I want to make him disappear.

It's May, and the rainy season has arrived in Togo. Now I know what it's like to live in a rainforest. It's misty. My hat smells of mold, and the purse I rarely use is covered with it. In fact, every piece of clothing I own smells like rain, as if it had never seen sunlight. I want to hibernate like a bear. I won't come out until the season in my heart has turned.

꒤ꖼ

Village authorities have been unable to repair my leaky roof or plug up the holes through which bats have entered since I arrived in Kougnohou last December. After two months of indoor rain, I decide to move. The village has been able to find me another house at a reasonable cost but, unbeknownst to me, authorities in the village of Djon located a house without a leaky roof and invited me to move there. The idea seemed crazy at first, but the more nights I spent with bats flying and roof leaks drenching my mattress, the more sensible I found it. After all, Djon is just a few kilometers from Kougnohou.

The clean, soundly built house in Djon is just one reason to move. Migrating to Djon is also the perfect way to expand my work. Djon has a great need for the GEE program and their people are progressive and motivated. Further, Djon is close enough so that I can continue my work in Kougnohou while expanding into the Akebou region.

When Sophie arrives in Kougnohou for a routine visit, I tell her about the opportunity to move to Djon. Sophie has always treated me with respect and confidence, and her response is no different.

"Laurie, you have great potentialities. What are you going to do? What do you need to accomplish your goals?"

"It's not just about the house." I tell her it's about expanding my reach through living and working in a village that seems ready for my project.

Sophie considers this, underscoring that it's a good idea that I'll come to Kougnohou from time to time to continue my work here. She wants to visit Djon right away so she can get a sense of the village. We jump in the Peace Corps Land Cruiser and are in Djon within half an hour. I direct the chauffeur to the house chosen for me, which I've only seen from the outside. We find the house locked up and the gate closed, so I suggest we drive *chez les soeurs*. I don't know who actually owns the house, but the nuns will know, and will help us find the *responsable*, the man with the house key.

Soeur Anne and I had a recent adventure in a bush taxi, and I am smitten with her contagious laugh and saucy manner. She knows the house and the man who has the key, and she goes with us to find him. Sophie, Soeur Anne, and I take a brief walk through the tiny village compounds, over creamy white and orange petrified rocks, among small mud huts and *concessions*, to find Monsieur Wiyao at home. His sister, who lives in Lomé, owns the house, and he is happy to show it to us.

The house is very private. It is right next to the CEG, but a cement wall encloses the front, and the rear opens onto a beautiful view of the plateau below. Heaps of dry brush serve as a fence around the back of the house, and the entire setting is spacious and quiet.

I can tell Sophie likes the house and the quaint village. She negotiates a rental price for the house with Monsiur Wiyao that is equivalent to ten dollars a month. However, she encourages him to consider donating the use of the house as a way for village to show its commitment to a partnership with Peace Corps in their region. Wiyao will have to talk to his sister.

This house is a compensation for my somewhat stagnant situation in Kougnohou. The first cycle of the class is nearly finished, but it's been difficult. I want to reach more girls, but I don't know how to do so in such a large town. I get the feeling that Kougnohou has had so many PCVs that its citizens have become somewhat apathetic, even jaded. Djon is smaller, quieter, than Kougnohou, and the milieu is similar because it's part of the same ethnic group, in the same (Akebou) region. If I move, I can start my next class cycle in two villages. Moving to Djon is a great opportunity, and I'll get to live in real village.

Now comes the hard part. I must tell the Kougnohou authorities that I am moving, and why. I don't anticipate the social ramifications of what is, for me, a personal decision. When Sophie and I return to Kougnohou, we stop for Bernadette and the three of us drive to Monsieur's Bénoît's house, where I tell all of them my plan to move to Djon. Bernadette indicates her support with the ubiquitous phrase I love to hear and use in Togo. She says, *C'est pas grave.* It's not terrible, it's not serious. But Bénoît taps his foot on the ground, looks angrily at me, and says nothing.

ꗏ

René is asleep in my bed. He arrives late at night, very sick with a fever, shivering. I dig out some medicine from my Peace Corps kit and start him on tea with whiskey and honey.

René squeaks out a revelation, the reason for his nocturnal visit: He is being relocated to Kpalimé. René says he is quitting his agro-economy company but will continue to work with them as a contractor.

"It is no problem that I will leave Kougnohou. We can still see each other a lot. You are moving to Djon soon, anyway." When I start to cry quietly, René pleads with me to not get upset.

He is alternately angry and reassuring: I shouldn't have told you! It's not now! I won't leave now! It's not Kara! (in the far north of Togo). You can still come to see me. If you were my wife, couldn't we live apart? We are still connected, even if we're not together. But it's for work! Shouldn't I do what's right for me?

Of course, all of his comments are rational and I could respond to them if I were in a rational state of mind. But not today.

René wants to give me a child before I go, he wants to get me pregnant, he wants to have "a beautiful child." I ignore him. I don't want to think about that right now. I don't want to deal with the feelings that will come if I think such a thought.

I tell René about the kiss between me and Antoine. We have not had much time to be together lately, with René's travel, his wife's presence, and my own travel to Atakpamé and Lomé. Now, because he is so sick and we are both upset, I skim over the details of the incident with

Antoine. Sensing correctly that I have not revealed the entire episode, René wants to know everything.

"Later."

When I finally tell René, that Antoine kissed me and touched my breast, he says, "Try to forget about it."

Silence.

"But he's a hypocrite." René adds, "And he'll try again."

Before he leaves, I give René a selection of my journal to read. He knows I write in my journal every day. He wants to read it as a way to learn more about himself and because "no one has ever written anything about me before."

A few weeks later, after updating Bernadette on my new house in Djon (the village is cleaning it and cutting down the brush), I tell her for the first time about what happened with Antoine. By now, I have talked to several volunteers about the incident; however, I have not discussed it with anyone Togolese except René.

Much to my surprise, Bernadette is not shocked.

"Antoine told me a long time ago that he liked you, and that he wanted to know your house. I told him I could not help him. Peace Corps asked me to make sure this does not happen." Bernadette adds, "That conversation was months ago."

Bernadette is actually surprised that I didn't anticipate Antoine's advance.

"All the priests have girlfriends here. They all have sex. What's forbidden is to have children. Priests cannot have *enfants*."

Her certainty makes me think the only thing the Catholic Church monitors among African priests is procreation, not sex. Hey wait a minute! In the Catholic Church, isn't that the same thing!

"All of this is forbidden *chez moi*," I try to explain.

"They don't do it?" She is skeptical. "They just hide it, don't they?"

How can I say to Bernadette that priests in the United States take their vows more seriously than the priests in Togo?[3] Is that really true?

"Even the white priests in Togo have taken women," Bernadette continues.

"That's because it's Africa."

Bernadette is offended.

"We aren't *chez blanches*," I try to explain myself. But when I hear my own words I sound completely ridiculous. Bernadette is absolutely right.

Interestingly, Bernadette is upset that I told other PCVs about Antoine's kiss, and now they will talk to others.

"Isn't there any confidentiality among volunteers?" She is very distressed by this, much more so than she is about Antoine's having kissed me. When I am silent, she changes the subject.

"Be careful of Antoine's jealousy, Laurie. He is a jealous man." She speaks with such conviction that I am taken aback. Slight, demure, fragile Antoine seems anything but a jealous man to me. He seems threatening in no way at all.

After this unsettling exchange with Bernadette, I am too upset to ride my bike, so I walk it home. Halfway to my bat-infested house, two little boys approach me, hesitantly, with a very serious question.

"Is your bike for sale?"

Ooouuuiii, I say, teasingly drawing out the word.

They look at me wide-eyed.

"One million dollars!" I yell.

"Keeeeeeee! Keeeeeeee!" They laugh. I crack up too.

The boys have not finished negotiating. One of them opens his hand to show me a palm full of gari, dry millet powder. He whispers to me, conspiratorially, *C'est de l'or!* It's gold! We laugh again, and the boys run home.

I stop at Honorine's house, because I have to let her go. I am firm when I do it, but I feel absolutely awful. Honorine takes the news badly; she loses substantial income because of my relocation.

As I walk away, Honorine runs to catch up. In a tone that sounds slightly sanctimonious (perhaps it's just my imagination?) she asks, "Did you know Akossiwa is pregnant?" Honorine whispers quietly, "They are saying her science teacher is the father."

René comes over tonight, still recovering from pneumonia. But that is not the only reason he is not himself; he misses his family very much. His wife and children have gone to Lomé without René, who must continue to work in Kougnohou while they vacation in the capital. René repeats several times that his 6-year-old son learned the word for goat in Ewé: egbo. René keeps calling me Egbo.

After René eats, we sit on the sofa and he kisses my neck and face, and then my breasts. When he begins to touch my abdomen, I tell him I'm on my period. As if to search for evidence, René cups my breasts in his hands, weighing them. He agrees with me, "Yes. They're heavier."

He lies on my bed while I read on the sofa. He asks me to join him on the bed and when I don't, he demands it. Like a dutiful soldier, I go.

René has already undressed. He has such a beautiful body, so smooth, not an ounce of fat on him. I lie near him, take off my *pagne*, and use it to cover us.

"If you had come the other day, we could have made love."

"I want to make love! It's a long time! You think I don't know that?" He seems playful as he admonishes me. "But I'll get sick and stay sick again and again."

I act as if I don't mind this. He looks at me in horror.

Tu ne m'aimes pas! You don't love me! We laugh at this.

"It's good for you to be distressed now and again."

I hate his little wisdoms.

"When I leave for Kpalimé, you will be happy!"

We laugh again, and then are quiet for a few minutes. René breaks the silence.

"We are going to have a child. I am going to make you pregnant."

"Why do you want to have a child with me?" This time I am ready to talk about it.

Je ne sais pas, he says, thoughtfully. Then he adds, "I would like us to gain something."

"Who will gain, you or me?"

Les deux, he says, simply. "You'll have our baby, and eventually send him to me."

"It's so simple, is it? We can send him back and forth like a pet!"

We are uncharacteristically silent.

"What are we going to do?" René asks.

"We're going to leave," I say. "That's it."

But I understand René's desire to have something that symbolizes what we've shared. I feel the same way.

We sleep very soundly. René has to travel to Kpalimé at 4 A.M. and I wake him up at 2 and again at 3 so he can go home, but I am not able to rouse him. He does get up once—and goes outside, but just to fart. When he comes back to bed, he spoons me. Only our feet, toes, and fingertips touch. He places his hand on my head, and leaves it there the rest of the night, as if to bless me.

Before René leaves, he remembers to return my journal (*cahier*). He mounts his motorcycle, ready to start the engine.

"You wrote about the *petites, petites choses*, the small, small things, unimportant things, but not when you wrote them—then they became important."

One day Antoine asks me to have fufu with him in Kougnohou at the priest's place. Because I miss our friendship, which has greatly diminished since the kiss, I agree. At the compound, I find Antoine in the outdoor kitchen. He is with a young CEG girl who I don't know. Apparently, Antoine asked the girl here to prepare our meal. Although the girl is the age of those in my class, I've never seen her before. She is one of many girls—hundreds, I'm sure—I have not been able to reach in Kougnohou. Antoine and I sit outside and watch her cook. I am surprised to feel awkward with him.

The girl works silently. She has already killed the chicken. He is in a *cuvette*, a large bowl, and still feathered. She has two mud stoves going, intensely hot; in one the *l'igname* boils, the other is for the chicken. She soaks the chicken in the hot water to make it easier to remove the feathers. She then cuts it open and guts it, taking out the intestines and the thinly lined stomach, still with about 20 or 30 pellets of corn in it.

The girl places the chicken's feet in the fire so it will be easier to pull them from the legs. She's cut the chicken's neck but left the head attached (Antoine says she will eat this herself). She puts the rest of the chicken in a pot and adds salt, a Maggi *poulet* cube, onion, crushed tomatoes, and garlic. She adds another seasoning that looks like caraway seed. She cuts up more onion and mixes it with *aubergine* (eggplant), then she pounds the fufu.

Antoine and I lunch alone, although Père Anselme, the other Kougno-hou priest, is in the house. A mist has started to fall, and the place seems very cozy, peaceful, and calm. The books scattered everywhere, the piles of paper and folders, all remind me of home and of my past life as a PhD student.

The food is delicious, but our silences are very loud. Although I've spent so much time with him, traveling to small villages for Mass, visiting with the Djon authorities to discuss girls' education in Akebou, meeting his family in Lomé when his brother the lawyer became a judge, I have never felt ill at ease. Finally, Antoine says what has been on his mind.

"I've been afraid to come see you. I am afraid you will think I am only coming to visit for one reason. I have thought for a whole month about what you said: '*Tu es prêtre.*'"

Oh. Good.

"When I kissed you, it was a sentiment of love," he continues.

I make a face at this.

"It won't happen again. I promise you," He adds hastily. He looks so earnest.

"I would like us still to work together."

He is having trouble sleeping. He asks again that I forgive him. I suggest, with some impatience, that maybe he needs to forgive himself. I feel sad because I see that this problem with Antoine is not over.

Père Anselme comes out of his room and sees us at the table. He says nothing as I wipe the unwanted tears from my eyes. I don't want this problem with Antoine.

After lunch, the young girl who cooked our lunch and ate hers outside walks me all the way home. On the way, we talk about the priests.

"The priests drink alcohol much more than they used to."

"When did you know you would have to come to prepare our lunch?"

"Today."

"What if you didn't want to do it. Could you say no?"

"I'd have to lie."

We are silent for a few moments before I say, with exasperation, "What would the men do without women in Africa?"

"I don't know!" We both laugh.

୯୬

On my last night in Kougnohou, I am summoned to dine at the house of the *sous-préfet*. Although I prefer not to go, I cannot refuse; the *sous-préfet*, who is the most prominent government authority in the village, is too important to risk offending. Nor can I be too friendly with him, or no one in the village will trust me. It's a bit of a bind. (As Maman would say, *En Afrique, c'est comme ça*.)

I try to get Bernadette or some young girls to come with me, but no one is interested. Instead, the girls want to know what sauce will be served with the fufu? What meat? (This commonplace question tells a person the sort of occasion it is—a party meal, a simple Sunday meal, a funeral meal.) Before I can say I don't know, one girl retorts, "Serpent!" We all laugh.

The driver picks me up at 6 o'clock, in the only SUV in town—in all of Akebou, most likely. Although the bright blue SUV always looks shiny and new when I spot it in the village, up close I can see it is cheaply made. Its interior smells like sweat. (The young chauffeur, however, is very cute, and that perks me right up!)

When the SUV passes Nyalewossi's boutique, I see her standing outside with some girlfriends. They all stare at me wide-eyed, as I give a small wave from the backseat. The SUV winds down a quiet village road on the far side of town before it arrives at the house of the *sous-préfet*, which is, miraculously, all lit up. How does he have electricity? The *sous-préfet* has the only generator in town.

The *sous-préfet* greets me, but does not introduce me to anyone else in his house, which is full of people. Only at the dinner table do I meet his other guests, including his big sister and his cousin (who cooked the meal), who are staying with him for several months. We all eat, at the table together, fufu with wild goat.

Afterward, everyone retires to another part of the house and I am left alone, a bit anxious, with the *sous-préfet*.

"Do you like music?"

"Of course."

The *sous-préfet* walks over to his entertainment center, which takes up an entire wall of the living room, and puts a tape in the VCR. He says he is a big fan of Phil Collins.

"I love Phil Collins!" We sit on the sofa together and watch a recording of a live Phil Collins concert. The television is large, nearly big-screen, with great resolution, and the sound system is excellent.

It is strange to talk to the *sous-préfet* as if he is a real person, but that is what I do. (Maybe he feels the same way about me!) Although we routinely pass each other in town (he always in the SUV, I always on foot or my bike), we have never exchanged more than a few words. Now, the *sous-préfet* wants to know all about me. He is impressed with my education. The fact that I have a doctorate always gets a man's attention here.

It is turning out to be a pleasant evening. But I am still nervous, because I suspect what is coming. I want to leave before it happens, but I don't know how to do it without being rude. We watch a little more of the concert, and I try to keep the conversation professional. I discuss my plans for Djon, and how I want to expand the girls' class further into Akebou.

The *sous-préfet* interrupts me to say there is another singer he likes a lot: Bonnie Tyler.

"Do you know her?" Yes, I say.

Repeating the singer's name, the *sous-préfet* squeezes imaginary breasts on his chest and smiles greedily at me. He repeats her name more loudly and makes the breast-squeezing motion again. I am laughing hysterically, but on the inside. This is too much!

Shortly after the fantasy breast squeezing, the *sous-préfet* surreptitiously touches my thigh. Okay, that's my cue. It has been an hour-and-a-half since I arrived. That is a gracious period of time and it is perfectly appropriate for me to leave now.

"I must get home. I must pack for my move tomorrow."

The *sous-préfet* offers to escort me. We are both in the backseat when we pass Nyalewossi's place, but she's gone inside. When the chauffeur stops at the path to my house, the *sous-préfet* says he will accompany me to my door.

If I refuse, the *sous-préfet* will lose face in front of his driver, and everyone will know I insulted him. I have to find a Togolese way to rebuff him. Personally, I do not care about the *sous-préfet* or about his face. However, he has great power over my stay in Akebou, and my work with the *jeunes filles*. He has the same power over my friends in the village, and I care about them. So I am cautious.

When we arrive at the door of my *clôture*, it comes.

"Madamoiselle Laurie, please, I would like to see your room. I want to know how you have arranged it for your move."

This is a modified version of the predictable Togolese sex come-on, "May I know your house?" It always sounds the same to me, no matter what words are used.

There is no audience now. No one can see or hear us. I am very firm.

"No. I do not want that. I am going to sleep." I look him in the eye when I speak; there is not even the hint of a Mona Lisa smile. My Togolese women friends say this is the best way to rebuff a Togolese man's advance.

"Of course, you are busy, you must pack." My rebuff deters him, and that is the end of it.

The next time I see the *sous-préfet* in public, we are in Djon at a funeral of a government official (who everyone suspects died of AIDS). When I greet him in the receiving line, the *sous-préfet* shakes my hand limply, barely acknowledging me.

ꙮ

Dear Mom,

I am writing you from Djon, my new village. Pascal, president of the CVD (Comité Villageoise de Développement), just came by to take me for a beer. We visited with the president of the Comité d'église *(church) and had a wonderful talk. To welcome me officially to the village, the elderly brother of the* Comité d'église *president prayed to the* anciens *(deceased elders of the village) for my* bonne santé *(good health).*

For dinner, I have cooked macaroni with sardines in tomato sauce but I think Dialo, the church president, is going to have his wife bring me a supper of pâte *(ground corn paste with sauce). So I'll leave the dinner I made until tomorrow.*

I love my new village, Mom. More than I could imagine. This village is of the same ethnic group as Kougnohou, and has same language, but it is much smaller (1700 people). They are much more pro-community. They also happen to be very idea-oriented and are extremely mobilized and aware.

I am so happy to be here! In October I'll start teaching the jeunes filles *class at the junior high in Djon as well as in Kougnohou, and maybe also at the new high school that Djon is building.*

I'm waiting for my water to be ready. To make drinking water, add two drops of chlorine to each liter of filtered water and wait 15 minutes. I'm told this method is as effective as boiling, which requires gas and is thus quite expensive. There is no pump for drinking water in Djon, only river water. It is a bit more primitive here, but I welcome it. A beautiful fog has settled around my house. I want to sit outside, but my furniture hasn't arrived so there's no place to sit. Soon!

I wish you were here, Mom. I think you'd love it, too.

Laurie

Chief Atododji sends for me my second day in Djon. I follow the messenger Kofi to the chief's house, deep in the heart of the village. When I see Chief Atododji for the first time, I understand why he did not come to meet me. He is ancient, blind in one eye, and bedridden. His good eye is yellow and his hair is completely white. He has four eggs on the small table next to his bed, still with tufts of feathers on them.

The chief doesn't speak French, so Kofi translates the Akebou for me. Gently, Kofi insists that I repeat the chief's name until I can pronounce it correctly.

After the greetings, the chief asks me all sorts of questions about my work: What will I be doing? How long will I stay? Will someone replace me when I leave? I am glad for his questions, and respond eagerly.

On the way home, Kofi tells me Chief Atododji is 115 years old, the oldest man in Akebou. The chief's reputation precedes him; I was told about him last year when I asked who was the oldest citizen in the area.

Lunchtime comes, and I have a taste for fufu again. My house is a mess, and although I have my stove set up I don't think I've done it correctly— the hose caught fire last night. In search of a free (and fire-free) lunch, I go *chez les soeurs.* They receive me graciously, and we lunch on fufu and wine, interspersed with snacks of roasted peanuts and corn kernels. The women delight me with stories of the challenges of being a nun in Togo.

"Everyone thinks we are rich, but we aren't."

The sisters are very funny together, and we have a lovely, intimate time. We eat lots of pimente with our fufu sauce. In fact, at the sisters' house I see for the first time a bowl of pimente (picante sauce) passed around like a condiment. This reminds me so much of Texas, of home, and I tell the women. The *soeurs* tell me they are very impressed that I can handle my pimente!

Walking home, I realize I can relax in Djon in a way I never relaxed in Kougnohou; it is such a different experience living in a rural community. My life is more isolated and I like this—I, who thought I preferred big cities and urban living. Part of me craves the peace and repose that is natural here. (Togo cities are much more challenging than the villages.) I also like the feeling I have here of being hard to reach. That no one but Peace Corps knows where I am or how to find me.

I am glad to have moved to a new village, and extremely grateful to be so much less naïve than I was a year ago. Djon is like both a new and an old Peace Corps experience. I feel rejuvenated. Maybe living here will provide something I didn't even know I needed.

I have to lock up quickly. Kofi just arrived to say everyone is already waiting for me at the chief's house. When I get there I see them sitting around the chief's *concession*, under a tree. (Kofi says the chief is watching from inside his room.) Villagers sit on benches made from old fufu mortars with a block of wood on top. The men sit nearby; the women stand in the back. Altogether I count about forty women and children, and twenty or thirty men, waiting for me to talk. Kofi stands ready to translate my French into Akebou.

This time, I introduce my project differently. I use the metaphor of religious faith, in God and church, to explain how to think about the value of girls' education to the village.

"You must have faith, be patient, and believe in the benefits—they will come to you. Even if you can't see them, hear them, or feel them. They will come. "

Here, of all places, my sensibilities as a family therapist come out. In a meeting of Akebou-speaking *anciens*, with the morning sun, the smell of cook fires, with nods from the audience and meandering children, my metaphors work. I pace around each time I stop speaking so Kofi can translate: What else do I need to say?

When I am finished, it is time for the village to speak to me. Dialo's brother blesses the ancestors, who in turn bless me through him.

"We used to be wary of you," he says to me. "We didn't know you, *les blanches*, but now you are here and you help us and we appreciate it and we know it is difficult for you. Please do not be deterred. Even if people don't understand, just keep going."

I think the Djon authorities understand exactly what I am going through. Kougnohou residents are angry that I have switched villages, even though I will continue to work in Kougnohou. By migrating here I've inadvertently stirred up old rivalries between the two villages. Some of my students have even refused to continue training with me unless I move back to Kougnohou.

"At first we were afraid of whites in Africa, but now we are used to them. We want you here to help us, and we look forward to your continued presence."

Our taxi leaks oil and seems to be gasping its last. During the ride, it dies a couple of times. I am always amazed by the ingenuity of Africans. A car that won't start is a minor thing to them. The worst result is our arrival in Djon after 8 P.M.

There are other reasons the ride took so long. The dirt mountain road from Kougnohou to Djon is almost impassable due to the rains. Taxis often get stuck in the road's big mud holes. Today, my front seat position allows me to see how narrowly we miss the huge holes. Racing against the nightfall, the chauffeur drives recklessly. Perhaps I need to ride my bike back and forth from Kougnohou to Djon? Biking up and down the mountain is probably safer—and may be faster—than a bush taxi.

When we arrive in Djon, under the third-quarter moon, I slowly make my way through the *concessions*, dodging both large and small petrified rocks. I pass through Kofi's compound and, although I can't see his wife and little girl, I can hear them; I can make out their shapes in the dark. I whip out my limited Akebou, which for some reason reminds me of Italian, to impress them.

Olokossosso! See you tomorrow! and feel that I am home.

Kofi's wife tells me he has traveled to a nearby village, but is expected back within the hour. Unfortunately, Kofi has the only key to my seven-foot front gate. After traveling four hours, all the way from Atakpamé, I don't want to wait to get into my house. With the help of two young boys, one with a flashlight, I climb through the thick brush behind my house.

I am not dirty enough to warrant a bucket bath, but I have one anyway, right there outside my kitchen door. The bath allows me to unwind, as I gaze at the stars and the Milky Way. *Milky* is not a bad way to describe it. I can imagine someone swishing a paintbrush, covered in midnight blues and creamy whites, across the sky directly above my head. I am in a star-gazing reverie when I hear Kofi pound on the metal door of my front gate.

"*Merci,* Kofi! I have entered the house! *Ça va!* See you tomorrow morning!"

Ça va bien! Bon nuit! he yells back.

When Kofi comes by the next day to leave me my key, I study his eyes carefully. He looks normal, so I think the secret of my bathing ritual is safe.

ॐ

I am on my way to Lomé, in yet another bush taxi. Today, I can't help staring at myself in the rearview mirror. Generally, I don't stare at myself in mirrors. Having been in West Africa for a year now, my experiences with mirrors are rare. I don't often see what I look like during the day.

Sometimes I only see myself after I've had pictures developed. My favorite one is of Grant and me, taken at his village, in Tchagritchakpa. We are in saggy flip flops with dirty feet, disheveled clothes, and full of dust. Grant wears a hat but my hair is wild, in desperate need of the salon.

Still, we look relaxed and at ease. Grant's arm is draped over me, and neither of us seems to care how we look. (I read somewhere that a woman can live anywhere in the world if she stops caring about how she looks and how she smells.) This picture with Grant is a perfect representation of how it feels to me to live here in West Africa—without pretense, without affectation.

Today, as I see my reflection in the bush taxi mirror, I look radiant. I don't recognize myself. This woman's skin is clear and tan, with new freckles on her cheeks. Her gaze is direct. Her neck is long, her jaw strong. Her hair, on the verge of wildness, is pulled back from her face with a scarf. Untamed curls escape in the windy bush taxi and look sexy. The truth is that I have never felt or looked more beautiful. The irony is that I've done so little to achieve it.

I think the raw physicality of Africa forces me to live in a way that is beneficial to my overall health and well-being. The walking, biking, climbing make such a rich contribution, inside and out. I am glowing.

Yesterday I biked to Kougnohou to work with the *Jeunes Filles* committee. Thirty girls and ten boys are now involved and yesterday they chose officers. They are working on a sketch about the importance of girls' education that they will present to the new *Jeunes Filles* classes in Djon. Nyalewossi, still the *presidente d'élèves*, and Imma, one of the girls I took to Atakpamé for TODTWD, are deeply involved in sustaining the group. I travel back and forth by bike between the two villages three times a week, consulting in Kougnohou while I teach in Djon.

Before I head home to Djon, I stop to see Akossiwa at her house. Akossiwa's breasts are huge, and she is obviously pregnant. Because she looks at me very timidly, and because she does not bring it up herself, I tell her I know she is pregnant. I ask her how she is doing. In reply, she says she's due in November.

"You are the first pregnant girl I know here."

"There are many at the CEG."

Where are these girls? Why am I not reaching them?

I am very sweaty on the ride home at dusk. I don't need my sunglasses except to keep the bugs away. The ride is so beautiful—I could smell the grass and forest in the morning when I left Djon, and now, when I return, at about 4:30, the hills are green and brown and red and the sky is blue and mauve and purple. I am sore from this morning's ride. I can feel the muscles in my thighs, my breathing is different. I feel great, even if I am a little bit *cassée* (broken).

Halfway home, my favorite gendarme gets out of his vehicle to greet me. When he sees a small gnat in my eye, without warning he puts his fingers right in my face to remove it. I love the way nobody's concerned about invading your personal space at times like this. Everyone understands it's more important to have good health.

The dusty road passes over two big streams. My nose runs and my snot is black. I inhale a gnat and try vainly to blow it out of my nose. I wipe the mucus on my T-shirt. I stop to drink water and notice the dirt under my nails and on my legs, feel sweat on my sweat, observe my flyaway afro hair with bits of grass in it, and see my tan, still obvious in the dusk.

I am the dirtiest I have ever been here in Africa. I am amazed by, and even a little proud of, the dirt; it's a test each time to see how much I can tolerate.

When I arrive in Djon an hour later, my bike and I are covered in red dust. Everyone in the road—kids, adults, men, women—greets me. Whether sitting in their *concessions* or walking by, they all yell, *Bonne arrivée!* They seem to know I've ridden my bike the whole way and are impressed that I make the effort. They respect *le sport* but perhaps it seems superfluous when so many daily tasks require physical strength. Also, they don't expect me to do sport because I am a woman and *blanche.* Even though I am not white, everyone I've met in Africa sees me that way.[3] Both whites and women are seen as weak and feeble, incapable of physical stamina or endurance. Today, when I arrive in Djon, I feel as if I've completed a marathon and the whole village is cheering me on.

I bathe as soon as I get home, a wonderful hot bucket bath. I like remembering how dirty I was and how good it felt. I'd much rather be dirty after a good bike ride than after riding in the bush taxi. I love how the bike puts me completely in charge of my own destiny. The dirt feels like a badge of honor.

In my bucket bath, reflecting tonight, I have a stark epiphany, so powerful it nearly brings me to tears: I am no longer counting the days in Africa. I am not marking time until the end of my service. Every single thing that I do during the day is something that I want to do, something that I choose to do. I don't long for anything I don't already have; I don't want to be anywhere else than where I am.

I finally feel worthy to live in Africa. I've earned her respect. I feel worthy of her because I can finally see her. Nothing blurs my vision; nothing is in the way. It took me nearly a year, but I can finally see this place, its glory and its intense disquiet. And still, I am at peace.

Africa's given me a nod too. I can sense it in the incredible will she inspires in me, and in the grace with which she's allowed my life here to unfold.

Sex, Love, and Other Demanding Parasites

I called Maxim last night to meet me for dinner, but he didn't return my call. So I had several gins and tonic and a lovely dinner *tout seul* at Da Claudio's, a fine Italian restaurant in Lomé. When Maxim calls early this morning, he apologizes.

"Will you see me after your medical appointment?" I am in Lomé for my yearly gynecological exam.

"Of course."

Several hours later, Maxim arrives at Mamy's, our PCV "hostel," and I take him back to my room (named Adam after a favorite volunteer) so we can talk. For the first time, we talk about our sexual relationships. I surprise myself by telling Maxim about Oded.

"I am in love with a man I haven't seen in two years," I say. I also reveal that I have a Togolese boyfriend in my village. Maxim confides in me as well.

"I have a young son. The mother is an ex-girlfriend with whom I don't get along." He is silent a moment before he adds, "We are only together because of the kid."

I had no idea that Maxim was a father. I am a little disturbed by the way he refers to his son, as "the kid."

Maxim then asks me what I want out of life, apart from my professional goals, which we've discussed before: Do you want children? When do you think you will have children? When do you think you will get married? Do you want to get married?

"I do want to have children, but I am afraid I am unable to get pregnant. I am already 35 years old, and I've never been pregnant."

"Maybe the time has not been right."

Oh. That's nice.

"You are not complicated. You are not a complicated woman." I think he means it as a compliment, but I don't take it that way.

"I am offended that you think I am uncomplicated!" He laughs.

"I don't know why, maybe it's your education, but you are not like other women."

"What drives you, Maxim?"

"Sometimes I want to change my life completely. I wish I could have nothing to deal with but the radio. I would like to just play music and sing and dance." Maxim continues, "There are so many things I want to do in my life. I feel I haven't even begun to choose my work."

But he has thought about it, in great detail. Maxim lists the advantages and disadvantages of various professions: As a journalist, you work as an idealist—you try to change the world in your own way—but because of that your work is very hard and you aren't always paid well. Lawyers are paid well, the work is good, it's a good profession. Policemen deal in strategies, analyzing, and thinking. I'd like that.

After we spend two hours talking, Maxim invites me to spend the rest of the day with him. Since I am free until tomorrow, I agree.

We take a cab to Maxim's neighborhood in Dekon, where he is meeting with the owner of an Internet business. In the cab, Maxim takes my hand. His touch feels different now; it's less platonic, more sexual. He plays with the bracelets on my wrist. He rests his arm comfortably on my thigh. We hold hands throughout the long ride, our fingers intermittently gripping, caressing, and flexing together. I let myself fall into his body, in the crook of his chest. I am completely relaxed, sitting so close to him.

We spend the whole day like this, at ease and in idle conversation, while we run Maxim's errands. We eat shawarma and share beer in the rain at Big Mak, Maxim's favorite Lebanese hamburger joint. We talk endlessly, all day. Two of Maxim's queries provoke wonderfully intimate conversation: Tell me your worst vice. Tell me a story to shock me.

Outside Big Mak, Maxim runs into a woman cousin, stylishly dressed and quite attractive, with whom he becomes affectionate and playful. When Maxim introduces me his cousin looks impressed and I imagine—fancifully, I know—that perhaps she's never met any of Maxim's "women" before.

After lunch, we visit Maxim's childhood friend Beti who, because of the name, I have assumed to be a woman. Instead, Beti is a male law student, born in Kenya, whose family now lives in Togo. At Beti's we drink the excellent Togolese beer, Awooyoo, eat snacks, and talk about politics in Togo and the United States.

Maxim and I debate the idea of foreign expatriates living in Africa. I say they take advantage of the remnants of colonialism, because they can jump a social class and live at a level they couldn't dream of at home. Maxim argues.

"It's good for the economy, so what harm can it do?"

Fueled by the strong beer, I heartily disagree, which allows Maxim to pronounce an *aha!*

"So! That means you can never live here!"

I don't know what to say. I *am* living here, what does that make me?

Leaving Beti's, we walk to a *veillée* for one of Maxim's distant relatives. It is 10 o'clock, but the *veillée* is still going strong. I recognize a woman I met at the Kougnohou taxi station about two months ago, with whom I'd had a lovely conversation. What a coincidence! The woman is also a friend of Maxim's deceased relative.

At midnight, Maxim and I walk for an hour-and-a-half, back to my room at Mamy's. The normally boisterous city streets of Lomé, full of honking taxis and motos, are blissfully quiet. As we pass through the center of town, Maxim points out his high school and his junior high. His family moved to a new neighborhood right before he started high school and he had to leave friends he'd known since childhood. In rebellion, Maxim ran away. Eventually, his father let him return to his old neighborhood to be with his friends.

Approaching the final two blocks, Maxim stops and looks down at me. He brings his great bald head down to meet my face and kisses me, hard.

I cannot reach Maxim's lips without getting on the very tips of my toes, because he is so much taller. I need something to stand on, or he, to sit on. We find a building with two shrubs by the front door, which is protected with steel bars. Maxim sits on the top step, his back against the bars, and I grab the bars and sit on his lap, with my knees supporting my weight.

Maxim holds and kisses me. He lifts my shirt, unhooks my bra, and buries his face in my breasts. When I arch my back, my head turns and I catch sight of a man walking quickly on the other side of the street. We don't care that we are in the middle of a road, in a public place, in the dead of night, behaving so indulgently. I don't care that my breasts are exposed, I don't care that anyone could see us. I have only one thought just now. I am a very lucky woman.

Months ago, I visualized myself straddled on Maxim's lap, kissing him. Just like this, I pictured myself fondling his large head, kissing his neck and his forehead, tasting his sweat, feeling his mouth and teeth on my breasts. Maxim's kisses are persistent but small and subtle, so that I almost don't feel them at all. I notice that Maxim likes me to suck his right ear. He hugs me harder each time and laughs when I tell him that's how I know he likes it.

I'm glad I'm wearing pants. If I was wearing a skirt. . . I can feel Maxim's erection underneath me.

Finally, I ask Maxim, "Where can we go?"

"A hotel?" Maxim offers.

Silence.

"The only other place is Agoe, where my office is." Unfortunately, Agoe is many miles away.

It is already 2:30 in the morning and I have to be at the Peace Corps bureau to catch a ride home at 6:30.

"I have an uncle who lives nearby," Maxim remembers. We actually consider showing up at Maxim's uncle's house at this hour of the morning, so that we can have sex. After a minute we become more rational, and I suggest Mamy's.

"Are you allowed to have visitors?"

"Of course."

"It's not good." Maxim doesn't like this idea. I tell him I don't have any condoms anyway.

"Me either."

"And I always carry condoms with me."

"Really?" Maxim is surprised.

We pass a pharmacy but, of course, it is closed. We walk silently to Mamy's, holding hands all the way.

I am glad it is not awkward to be with Maxim after such decadent behavior. I feel at home with him, as if we are a married couple—in love, in lust—happy and relaxed and uninhibited together. How wonderful it is to be openly loving with a man in Togo. I think I could stay in Africa for two, three, more years. Oh, Love.

❧

This year's *Journée de Réflexion* in Djon has sixty representatives present, three from each of the twenty neighboring farms of coffee and cocoa in Akebou. Every year, Djon sponsors this day of reflection to review the progress of the past year and plan for the next. I am here as a new Djon resident and as a guest; however, in a few moments I will speak on my GEE work and the Peace Corps. I will speak in French and someone will translate into Akebou.

When it is my turn to speak to the entire assembly, I am at ease despite the thunderous noise the rain makes hitting the metal roof. Using a microphone, I greet the audience in Akebou—it is so valuable to know even the few words I have—and they applaud my effort.

I switch to French and talk briefly about *Corps de la Paix*, then share some information about my educational and cultural background. Having been in Togo for a year, I discuss some of my observations to date and offer ideas about the way I want to work with the *jeunes filles*. When I am finished, the men applaud again. The first question is from a chief of another village. He wants to know if I can work in his village too.

After my talk, it is time for the pause—a short break, Togolese style. In a small building next door, each assembly participant is served a portion of rice, which we eat with sauce as we drink palm wine. Now the chief who asked if I could come to his village wants to know, "Will you take me to the States?"

He is smiling as are the others around him, and they all watch to see what I will say.

"I will take all the chiefs of Akebou!" This comment diffuses the chief's request and is met with great amusement.

After the morning session, sixteen of us go to Antoine's house for another village meeting, held entirely in Akebou. As before, I am the only woman. I get to drink more palm wine and eat fufu with *les autorités de Djon*. All these special invitations to join the *responsables* have made me an honorary man![1]

For the first time in Togo, I enjoy being an honorary man. I know this is partly due to what I have learned about the people of Djon. It seems that everyone, even the men, is serious about making Djon a fine place to live, for girls, for women, for businesses, for families, for each other. For me, even. I can't help responding to that.

It's Saturday, I don't know the date. I'm weak and cold with diarrhea. I drink hot tea and it soothes me a little. I feel so fragile—my shit is like water, I can't control it, it gets mixed in with the urge to pee and that's the end of it. All night I had that dry, hot feeling you get in your palate when you are dehydrated. That's what diarrhea does to your body.

At 6 P.M. I discover blood in my stool. All day it has been extremely watery and painful, but not bloody. Perhaps I need to go to Lomé? Maybe I can figure this out on my own. I take out *Where There Is No Doctor*, the health book given to each PCV,[2] and soon I am wondering if I have cholera? Whipworm? I imagine a big worm, or a big amoeba, is eating up my insides. I've never been doubled over with pain like this, never been unable to control my anal sphincter—never had shit just leak out of me, certainly never shit with blood. I decide to see if Kofi can help me get a ride to Kougnohou tomorrow morning. Sunday. I walk to Kofi's feeling very unstable.

"I will see about getting someone to take you by moto in the morning. Don't worry, we will find someone for you."

An hour or two later, after I bathe, Kofi arrives with Wialo—Wialo, in his evening *kenté*, and Kofi, in the stylish khaki trench coat (dead *yovo*) he always wears at night. Wialo will pick me up on his Vespa at 6 the next morning.

All night I fight any urge from my body to defecate or urinate. Instead, I try to pack, read, and sleep. I wake up at about 4:30 and am out of bed at 5. I have to shit, quickly, and I can't stop it this time. Carefully, I take a sample of my bloody stool for the lab tech in Lomé, who will need it to diagnose my problem. When Wialo arrives, we mount his Vespa and are on our way. We have to get off the Vespa several times to manage the mud because it rained all night long.

I call Beatrice from Kougnohou to tell her to expect me in Lomé. Wialo takes me a few more kilometers to Adapé, a small town on the main highway where I am most likely to find a taxi on Sunday. One comes within twenty minutes, and I thank Wialo for waiting with me. At the Atakpamé *maison*, I shit copiously again. What am I shitting? Hot tea? Water? I've eaten nothing for 24 hours.

I take a moto from the *maison* to the Lomé station and get another taxi. This time I nod off a bit, but hold my bag against my stomach to keep me from doubling over. Thank God for the Life Savers my sister Patricia sent me! I am afraid to take in anything more besides the juice of a hard candy, knowing it will have to come out, and there will be no shitting opportunities on a taxi in the African bush.

On the way to Lomé, I fantasize about going to El Emir, my favorite Lebanese grill. The thought of their hummus and shawarma, with a big Awooyoo, keeps me going. This is one of the worst things about diarrhea, you feel sick at the same time you feel hungry. It's torture. By the time I arrive in Lomé, I can't fathom the idea of putting anything in my mouth. Nausea comes in waves.

Dropped off on the outskirts of Lomé, I take my third and final ride, this time a private taxi, to the med unit. Once there, I immediately wolf down a bottle of water and an entire pitcher of Gatorade. While I wait for Beatrice, I give my sample to the lab tech, have a CBC drawn, and weigh myself: 125 pounds. I've lost 7 pounds in five days. When Beatrice sees me, she puts me on an IV to speed up my rehydration.

The diagnosis is amoeba histolytica, with a white t-cell count that indicates bacteria in my stool. I've likely had the amoebae for a while. Perhaps that hamburger I ate at the Roc Hotel in Atakpamé aggravated them? Somehow the bacteria were released, giving me an intestinal infection. I might not have known about the amoebae at all if the intestinal infection had not kicked in.

I am weak and tired, but I already feel better now that I am on medication. I felt so lost in my village. No one like Beatrice there, with a no-nonsense answer to everything; no Beatrice with a clear explanation of what's happening; no Beatrice with a plan for treatment. I feel terrible, but at least I see the light at the end of the tunnel.

Is this what happened to Bernadette's son Koffi that time he was so sick? Why do children have to get sick—die, even—from something that can be so easily treated? So easily prevented? How do the Togolese fight something as common as amoebae and dysentery? Where is *their* light at the end of the tunnel?

After four days in the medical unit, I am as good as new. I take a taxi to Maxim's new office in Agoe, on the outskirts of Lomé. I find the office easily enough, but Maxim is not in. The *guardien* leads me inside and I sit down to read and wait. I figure I'll wait an hour, two at the most, and then I'll leave for Djon. I hope Maxim shows up before then. An hour later, he does.

Maxim walks over to me and we kiss hello (cheeks only), smile, and look at each other, full of questions. Instead, we make small talk, and Maxim asks if I would like a drink, a beer perhaps? I can't drink alcohol for two weeks because of my medication.

"Oh, okay. I'll wait!" I think he is joking, but I can't tell. Maxim says he too has been sick recently.

"I had malaria. I was in the hospital several days." Malaria! I am horrified to hear this, but Maxim just laughs and says, "Everyone should have malaria at least once."

"When do you have to leave? In the afternoon? What time?" he peppers me with questions.

I felt reserved and withdrawn and hesitant the minute I saw Maxim, and I have no idea why. He greeted me, all teeth, and tried to touch me, kiss me, hug me. But I stayed in my chair. I felt nervous.

"I don't know," I say, answering Maxim's question. "When do you think is a good time to go?"

"Are you looking for a suggestion?"

"Yes."

Jamais, he says. Never.

Maxim has a way of saying things—charming things, unexpected things—that make me feel incredibly full in his presence. He constantly surprises me with this ability to make me hopeful. But then the hope mysteriously disappears as quickly as it came.

"I don't have to leave today."

Maxim arranges his bed for me to take *sieste. Chez toi,* he says. He makes me comfortable but doesn't let his day be interrupted, and I love that about him. He's independent, he's industrious. Left alone in his room, I still wonder, Will he nap too? What will he do?

When Maxim reenters the room, I feign sleep and watch him out of the corner of my eye. He opens the door to his armoire, accidentally bumps it against the wall, and quickly apologizes (*Excuse-moi*), then leaves quietly. When he returns the second time, I have given up on the nap and don't bother to hide it.

Maxim asks me about lunch. What do I want to eat? I am hungry but my interest in eating is severely curtailed because of my metallic-tasting medication. Also, part of me is still afraid to eat—to be feeding the amoebae. Nevertheless, Maxim sends his *guardien* out to get some food, and in the meantime we lie on the bed and chat.

Maxim makes the first move. He jumps on top of me. He showers my face with kisses, aggressively pushing me up against the wall. I am surprised at his ferocity—such a contrast from our platonic conversation a minute ago—and am remarkably disengaged. I am still not sure I want to do this. I didn't plan on it. I don't know what I had planned. Why did I come here, anyway?

Sensing my hesitation, Maxim stops kissing me and asks, "Are you sure you want to do this? You must be sure." It's not that I am unsure about what I want—I am sure—but I do not know if this is how I imagined it, if this is the moment and place and way I had expected. I keep romanticizing it.

"If we aren't going to do it, we should stop."

To myself, I think it makes no sense to wait. The perfect moment might never come. It will never be the way I imagined, right?

Although I say I am ready, I do not feel the wanton lust and abandonment I expect. It bothers me that I have expectations, but I do. I can't pretend they aren't there. Maxim laughs, perhaps sensing my hesitancy.

"Can you do this? Is it *interdit*?"

I am not sure if he is asking because of my amoebae, or because, for volunteers, so many things are *interdit*—forbidden. We are not supposed to travel at night, we are not supposed to leave the country without permission, we are not supposed to come to Lomé without a very good reason. But there are no rules about who we sleep with—except that Togolese Peace Corps trainers are instructed not to get involved with volunteers in training. (Interestingly, volunteers are told no such thing.) Still, that instruction applies only during the three-month training period.

"Are you sure you can do this yourself?" I tease him.

"I don't need permission."

He plants kisses on my stomach and the doorbell rings. Our food has arrived.

We eat in relative silence. The silence is heavy, full. What are those silences called? Oh yeah—pregnant. How appropriate. After the *guardien* takes the food and bottles away, Maxim closes the door and unbuttons his shirt.

"Are you going to take your clothes off?"

"It's hot." Maxim stretches out on the bed in his t-shirt and pants, and we continue to talk. He pulls me close and I think at this very moment I want to see his chest, his body.

"If I come any closer, you are going to take your t-shirt off." Maxim laughs, stands, and pulls off his shirt.

"You must, also," he demands. When I don't do it, he says I must be shy. Maxim removes the rest of his clothes, except his boxer shorts, of worn cotton. I sense his slight embarrassment. I say I think he is the one who is shy.

Maxim kisses me then, and soon our activity works up a sweat. The middle of the day is hot, and Maxim's fan is not working. I look up and see sweat dripping in rivulets from his scalp. I can hear the sweat as our chests and bodies slap together. I can smell him, and us.

When night comes, I put on my pajamas and read while Maxim works at his desk. He looks at me on his bed as if I have always been here, as if I belong here. He soon joins me on the bed with his own book (about finance), and we begin a whole new kind of intimacy. We are both at our best in bed, talking, cuddling, kissing. Maxim is a cuddler, he likes it almost as much as I do.

I jump on Maxim's back while he reads, and caress him as we talk. We passionately disagree about money.

"I want money to do things," Maxim insists. "I want to own things, buildings, export, import. I want to fund universities and institutes. I want to make money so I can do the things I want to do."

"Money is not in my plan at all. First is doing what I love. If money follows, great," I counter. "Money is not necessary to be happy."

I insist on this, partly because I believe it but also because I know Maxim doesn't, and I like it when he disagrees with me.

"Do you really think money is unnecessary?" Maxim still doesn't believe me. I love watching his face change with his emotions; in the span of five minutes I see him confounded, mad, frustrated, curious. Maxim wears all his emotions on his face.

"It's necessary, but it is not enough."

"You are an *idealiste*," Maxim replies. "You do not understand how the world works. Nothing works without money. You need money for everything you do or want to do." Maxim turns around to face me and I adjust, now sitting on his pelvis.

"You are a pessimist," I tell Maxim. He holds my hands and flexes our fingers together.

"No. *Je suis un réalist.* You have seen a lot, yes, but you do not know how the world works."

"What about your boyfriend?" He changes the subject.

"It's over," I say, surprised by the conviction in my voice. René has moved to Kpalimé, and I've moved to Djon. I have not seen him in weeks and don't know if or when I will see him again. "I cannot make love to more than one man at the same time."

I ask Maxim about the mother of his child. "Have you always had girlfriends at the same time you were with her?"

"Yes, sometimes two or three. But I didn't care about them, so it was nothing."

"Then why did you do it?" The question comes out more accusatory than I intend. "No, forget it. I'm sorry."

"No, it's okay, really," he says. "Ask me whatever you want."

I do have questions for Maxim: Have you ever been with a volunteer? *No.* Another African (non-Togolese)? *No.* Not even when you lived in France? *No.*

"Why?" I ask, not sure if I believe him.

"It was never my aim."

Maxim makes me laugh when he turns the tables on me: Have you ever had a *formateur*? How many Togolese have you been with? This question makes me feel uncomfortable, more sexually promiscuous than I like. I tell him two. I have included Maxim, but I am not sure he knows that.

Maxim confides that he is concerned about his relationship with Peace Corps. Although we are not breaking any rules, Maxim says his reputation as a "lover" of volunteers concerns him. I ask why he thinks he has such a reputation.

"I am nice to everyone, but I am not necessarily close to all of them." He sounds professional, mysterious, and charming, all at the same time.

"Yes. Everyone likes you."

Maxim's response is fierce and immediate. "They don't even know me!"

I didn't expect him to be so animated and expressive. He's completely unlike the image he projects, the image most volunteers—including me—had of him during training.

"You seem very different to me than the *formateur* I knew last year—and now I don't think of you as a *formateur* at all."

"Me either. Now I just see you as 'Laurie.'"

I like the discussion but I don't want to talk anymore. Our touches have become more aggressive throughout the conversation, as if our bodies want time to get to know each other. Our kisses are very sensual, very heated, and when they reach a crescendo, I pull off my shirt. Maxim tugs at my pajama pants, so I remove them too.

Maxim, his broad face and hands nearly twice the size of mine, is quiet as we make love. He has a peculiar habit of burying his face in my neck when he is thrusting, as if he wants to watch me but doesn't want to be watched. The penetration reminds me of our sex play on the street corner in Lomé—I can't really feel anything. He's aggressive, but the effect is so subtle that I almost miss it. While we make love, Maxim steers clear of my pubic area, neither touching nor kissing me there, and I never get a good look at his penis, even though I want to. He doesn't make it easy. Nevertheless, I feel so close to Maxim that I tell him so. He laughs.

"You *are* close to me."

In the middle of sex, Maxim pauses to put the mattress on the floor.

"It makes too much noise." I didn't even notice. Maybe he's thinking about the *guardien*, who will sit in a chair on the front porch, inside the concrete walls of Maxim's office compound, all night long.

On the floor, I cover myself with my *pagne*, but Maxim throws it off. He mounts me, thrusting so hard that he develops abdominal cramps. When he is ready to start again, I have to pee. It's almost comical, our awkward sexual mechanics. Still, there isn't any pressure to perform, or succeed, or to come, and that is nice.

I am surprised by how sex changes our intimacy. We use English a lot more. We become pensive and contemplative. I just clam up; I am full of thoughts. Maxim becomes self-conscious, hesitant, shy. It's as if we've entered a realm about which we cannot speak.

Being in bed with him, cuddling, is exactly as I have imagined it. We hold hands all night, in one fashion or another. Our fingers touch, our palms cup, our feet are entwined. During the night I feel his hand cup my breast and fondle it. Even our cheeks find each other in the night. We breathe on each other. All night, I hear his faint but consistent snore. In the early morning I find my face so close to his that all I have to do is purse my lips and I will kiss his cheek, so I do. A second later, he surprises me by doing the same. I had thought he was asleep.

I hate that the night has to end. I can kiss Maxim all night; his lips are so big it takes two or three kisses to cover them. I feel so natural it's as if we've been together for years.

I don't know how to explain my other feelings. I did not expect sexual incompatibility. I am surprised by Maxim's lack of proficiency as a lover. (He has had more partners than I, but I suspect his experience is not as versatile as mine.) I am also confused by my own timidity, the lack of sexual assertiveness that I routinely practice with René. What's wrong with me?

Maxim makes love the way I had initially expected, before René, that a Togolese man would. I had been told by volunteers that African men make love mechanically, only in a missionary position, and absolutely do not have any kind of oral sex. René had proved them wrong. However, Maxim's lovemaking fits the description I had heard. During sex he is rote, linear, unimaginative.

The addition of sex to the equation makes things extremely complicated. Maybe we need time to develop compatibility. My contrasting sexual assessments of Maxim—one wonderful and the other not—force me to ask myself some very hard questions: What am I seeking here? What are my expectations?

If I saw René right now, as I sit writing about Maxim in my journal, I would have sex with him just to get the satisfaction that was sorely lacking with Maxim. Maybe I can be with two men at the same time! Well. What a demanding woman I've become.

༄

Back home in Djon, not more than a week after my night with Maxim, a young boy delivers a handwritten note to me. *Can we get together to talk?* The message is from Antoine, who is in Djon for the weekend and wants to see me. Wanting to see him, and still hungry after a pathetic supper of instant oatmeal, I go to Antoine's to eat *la pâte*.

When I see the look on his face I know Antoine wants to tell me something. Nevertheless, I am unprepared to hear it.

"I have changed my mind," Antoine says. "I have not stopped thinking about making love to you. I have decided not to give up on you."

What?

"The fact that I am a priest should not stop us."

I try to control my emotions, which seems increasingly difficult around Antoine, because I want to explain how I feel. I want him to understand what it's like for me to hear this. Maybe then he'll stop.

"I love you only as a friend, and I do think of you as a priest." I can see by the look on his face that my perspective does not make sense to

Antoine. He looks confused. "If you insist on this, Antoine, knowing how I feel, you will jeopardize our friendship. I will no longer be your friend."

But Antoine does not respond to my questions the way I want him to. Instead, he tries to convince me of the logic of his decision.

"I have only once had a friend like you, someone that I could confide in. It is natural to want to make love."

I understand how he has made this leap from friendship to romance. However, the fact that he refuses to try to see things from my perspective makes me angry.

"You have made a big mistake if you think that. You do not know anything about love. There is more to love than that!"

Antoine and I may as well be speaking different languages. His view of love is a polygamous one; it involves inclusion, not exclusion. His view of the priesthood includes fucking, but not bearing children, which is forbidden. Does he practice safe sex, I wonder? In his mind, what's to stop us? Surely not some colonialist idea of priestly celibacy.

How ironic this is! If Antoine had more experience in romantic and sexual intimacy, he might be able to deal with my refusal, we might be able to get past it. However, he's not supposed to have this experience, he's a priest. Neither the fact that he is a priest nor that I don't want him matters to him at all.

I try to appeal to Antoine's ethical sensibilities, and suggest that he may need help from priests he trusts.

"You are wrong to come to me about this," I tell him. "If you need to talk to someone to alleviate your suffering, then please do. But, must you do it with me? Is it appropriate?" We talk in circles, and I become frustrated, tired, and bored.

Antoine tries to appeal to *my* ethical nature by telling me that he is suffering. "People are talking in Kougnohou, saying you are my wife, my woman. They think you moved to Djon because of me, so we could be together. So it makes no difference if we make love. That is what they think anyway."

"I don't understand you," I retort. "You are trying to manipulate me."

"But I am being slandered," Antoine insists. Then, in the slightly ingratiating tone I've heard from so many Togolese men, he says, "I only tell you this because of concern for you. I want to protect you."

At this, I disengage. I pull myself inward. Outwardly, I prepare to leave. Then Antoine asks me directly, for the first time, about what I am sure he has suspected for months.

"Do you have a boyfriend in Togo?"

I remember Bernadette telling me that Antoine was a jealous man. My love life is none of his business, but I want to say something that will shut him up. I don't care if I hurt him. I breathe in deeply before I speak.

"Your question is unfair to me and, by asking it, you risk our friendship. I do have a private life, Antoine, but I am not comfortable telling you about it."

And with that I walk out the door. Antoine insists I wait so he can walk me home, but I ignore him. He hurries to walk alongside me. On the road, we are silent until he asks, "Can I hold your hand?" Antoine and I have never held hands before. I don't know why he suggests it, except to continue with his harassment.

"No," I say. Antoine does not like this, but he does not ask again.

Antoine follows me inside the gate to my house. In Djon, I rarely use my front door; I always enter through the side door, which opens into a hallway right off my kitchen. When I unlock the side door, Antoine tries to push himself into the house behind me. He's so close I can feel his breath.

"Do not close the door behind you," I tell him. "I do not want you to come in my house."

"Why can't I come in? Are you afraid? I think you are afraid of me." Antoine's statements indicate hurt, but his tone is hostile. He then says, with just a bit of self-pity in his voice, "I am angry that you are afraid of me."

Oh, God. Please.

Antoine steps back outside the door. When he begins to plead with me once more, I shut the door in his face.

The next day I am on a mission. I bike to Kougnohou, specifically to talk to Bernadette about Antoine. Bernadette is my counterpart, my co-worker, my confidante; she is my consultant on all things Togolese. I trust her implicitly, and I need her advice. Instead of useful advice however, Bernadette brings me more upsetting news.

"Laurie, sit down." I sit on the bench outside Bernadette's door.

"Several weeks ago," she says, "Antoine asked me to talk to you. He told me he wants to have you as a girlfriend. He told me you said no, and now he has asked me to talk to you again. He would like me to find out why. He thinks you will not be with him because you already have a boyfriend."

When I realize that Antoine has tried to enlist Bernadette as an accomplice, I lose it. Only my anger keeps me from crying in front of Bernadette.

"I did not ask you this, of course," Bernadette says. I am not sure if I am glad or upset that Bernadette did not tell me what Antoine had asked her to do. What is the appropriate reaction here?

Il me dérange, I tell Bernadette. He is bothering me.

Bernadette has no advice for me. She is out of her league on this one. Père Antoine is not the coarse, bumbling *sous-préfet,* nor is he a stranger with a *coupe-coupe* in hand. He is the village priest. He is *her* Catholic priest.

Recalling Maxim's promise to visit me in Djon, I ask Bernadette, "What if Antoine sees me with another man?"

Il va mourir, she says. He will die.

I hope Bernadette is joking, but she doesn't smile.

The moment I am on the road to the seaside village of Aného, I am calm. In Aného just before sunset I see a star right above the burnt orange-and-blue sky and feel the swift ocean breeze in my face. The beach in front of the hotel looks completely different than the last time I was here. A whole section is now underwater. Ah, how I love Aného!

On my way I made a pit stop at Geyser, a quaint hotel in Kpalimé with a beautiful, well-maintained swimming pool. When I arrive several volunteers, including Shoshana and a woman named Beth, are already enjoying the Geyser pool. All women, we spend the afternoon swimming and eating, ordering our pleasures from the nifty pool restaurant—hummus and baba ganoush, vegetables and bread, and lots of cheese and wine.

In the pool, we talk about (what else?) sex. I relate some of my sexual adventures of the previous two years. When I say them aloud, my confessions surprise even me: I had sex at the FBI Academy. I've been a phone sex operator. Doesn't everyone have anal sex? One lover liked to watch me shit. I had an affair with a married man. Another lover needed a horse video to get it up! Beth and Shoshana are enthralled and shocked.

"You're such a vixen!" Beth says.

"You are a stud," Shoshana adds.

I'm not sure what to make of their comments. I've never been told such things before! Until today, I had not thought of myself as a sexually confident woman to be reckoned with. As I look back, my range of experience is unusual, though my partners have been few. I decide I like the comments. I am grateful for the sexual choices I've made; I've learned a lot from them.

When I tell the women I must leave early to make it to Aného by dark, Beth pays me another lovely compliment, the value of which I recognize immediately.

"I gotta hand it to you, Laurie! You do what you need to and you don't feel guilty about it, or pretend, or make excuses that it's all about work."

I needed to hear that right now. I need to hear things that validate who I am. Despite my laundry list of sexual adventures, my recent experience with Antoine has made me feel very insecure about myself as a woman.

Before I leave, I update Shoshana about Antoine. Several months ago, Shoshana and many other GEE volunteers met Antoine at one of our training seminars. Shoshana liked Antoine, but Miriam, one of the other volunteers at the conference, who is half-African herself, thought Antoine was "creepy" because he was too quiet, didn't say much, and observed everyone rather than participating in the discussions. Interesting that it was only Miriam (who was partly raised in West Africa), who saw something beyond Antoine's priestly demeanor.

At Geyser, Shoshana, who knows about the kiss, asks questions about Antoine that give me pause: Why do you think he is not listening to you? Why is he so insistent? Have you told Bernadette about this? How is she helping you deal with this? Shoshana's sharp questions make me think I need to tell Sophie, or someone else (but who?), about Antoine's behavior.

In Kpalimé, I begin a self-destructive phase of drinking gins and tonic, smoking Gauloise cigarettes, and taking Valium to sleep—habits I never had in the United States, but which I will continue with great relish throughout the rest of my time in Togo. And for some time afterward.[3]

ֆֆ

I am meandering around Djon one day in October, on my way to the *dispensaire*, when I see Soeur Bénédicte on the road a few hundred yards from the clinic.

"We had a very serious case this morning," says the *soeur*. "A woman from a small village arrived on foot, pregnant, and in the midst of delivery. The baby's arm had exited the birth canal, but he was stuck."

As Bénédicte tells the story, the woman walks out of the *dispensaire*. Dressed in several layers of *pagnes*, her condition is impossible to assess; however, it is not impossible to imagine. The woman still looks pregnant, and she walks as if bow-legged. The woman passes me and Bénédicte on the road, and we all nod in the African way.

"She is going to look for money to get a taxi to Atakpamé. We can do nothing for her," whispers Bénédicte.

We both knew, but did not say, that the woman's baby had to be dead. The baby was probably dead even before the woman arrived in Djon.

On another day, I go to the *dispensaire* to help with the polio vaccination campaign. Soeur Anne invited me to help and I eagerly agreed. I like being around Soeur Anne. Open, kind, and loving, she has a perfect soul for a nun.

"An infant died this morning, just a few minutes ago," she says as I arrive.

"How?"

"The baby arrived with an infection last night, a bloated stomach, and died just now." This doesn't make sense to me. Soeur Anne, seeing my puzzlement, invites me to come in and see for myself.

I follow her into a large room with about a dozen beds. All the beds are empty except two. A man sits on one bed, and facing him on an opposite bed is a woman, her head hanging down. I see no child anywhere. Maybe someone has taken the baby away? But then Anne says something to the mother in Akebou. Slowly, the mother raises her head, then reaches around her back, to pull forward the *pagne* she has wrapped around her waist. The baby is on the mother's back, wrapped in her *pagne*. The mother lifts the dead baby, only 8 days old, to her chest. The baby's mouth is slack. Anne closes it repeatedly with her fingers as the mother weeps, but the baby's mouth won't stay closed.

ቶ

Each Monday in Djon, beginning at 7 A.M., I teach my girls' classes for five hours straight, working with a different class each hour. Although I find it mentally exhausting to repeat the lesson, the intimacy of each class makes it worthwhile. I can more easily talk with the girls in small groups of fifteen or twenty, rather than addressing a group of fifty girls at one time, which is what I did in Kougnohou. Although my new method is tiring, I am better able to express the course content, having already taught one cycle in Kougnohou.

At a quarter to 10, during the pause, I sit on the terrace while adolescents snack on bananas and peanuts and teachers eat bowls of rice brought from home. The CEG director asks if I will help teach English at the school. I decline, at least for now, remembering Père Didier's comment—how important it is that girls know I am here for one thing only, for *les jeunes filles*. The director understands and is very accommodating. He even finds yet another free hour for me to work with the girls in *4ème*. The *4ème* girls have a tougher school curriculum and are not as available to me as I'd like—so the director's gesture is welcome.

The *4ème* girls are also much more mature and serious than the younger girls, and their French is much better, more at the level of the *lycée* girls in Kougnohou. Working with the *4ème* girls, I sense a very different vibe. These are not girls; they are young women. They already know the bind they are in as African females; they live it every day. They are a challenge for me, and I am intimidated by them.

"Do you think black Americans are different from black Africans?" I ask a *4ème* student one day during a discussion on the construction of gender roles across cultures.

"Of course!" She says, as if the question is silly.

"How do you know?"

"Their behavior," she says. "They behave like you."

Confused, I ask for specifics.

"They wear what they want, they don't care what people think. If I was one of them, I'd wear this (points to a sexy outfit in the *In Style* magazine my aunt Jani bought me in Paris), and no one would say anything. We can't do that here."

Although this girl is candid, most of the other girls remain silent. The girls' silence doesn't seem like nervousness, it seems like seriousness, as if they have a lot on their minds.

After work, I walk to the *dispensaire* to leave copies of a handout for one of my classes with the nuns. I run into Bénédicte and leave the papers with her. Glancing at a list I've compiled of obstacles to girls' education in Togo, Bénédicte tells me of an incident at the clinic yesterday afternoon.

"A young girl in *5ème* (7th grade) arrived at the birth center after taking medicine to induce labor, so she could return to school."

In Togo it is illegal for girls to attend school if they are pregnant (except at university). Abortions are also illegal.

I want to see the girl, but I am hesitant to invite myself. I ask Bénédicte, "Can I help in any way?"

"I've completed everything. But you may come in to see her."

I park my bike and go back inside. Bénédicte points the girl out to me. I saw her here earlier, but I did not notice a baby. The girl had been visiting with some students I taught earlier in the day. Now, the girl is alone.

The baby is lying next to her, in a *pagne*, so very tiny. Two months premature, his heart pumps rapidly. Bénédicte does not expect either one of them to live. The girl is vomiting, and she looks weak. Bénédicte tries to find out what medicine the girl took but the girl won't say.

Bénédicte, engaged in sweeping the large room, moves off to one corner.

"Soeur Bénédicte threatened to beat me," the girl whispers.

I sit down near her bed, so I can see her eyes. I have so many questions for the girl! But which question to choose? What to say?

"Do you know how you became pregnant? Did you use a condom?"

In Togo, a referent for the word for condom is the French word *produit*. Bénédicte hears me say *produit*, and rushes back to the girl's bed.

"What *produits*?" she snaps. Before either the girl or I can respond, Bénédicte continues, "Condoms only work 40 percent of the time, and why not be abstinent?"

Bénédicte's accusatory tone and inflammatory statement completely shut the girl down and absolutely stun me.

When Bénédicte walks away, I manage to tell the girl, "I'll be back tomorrow. We can talk more then."

Walking my bike home, I am still dumbstruck by Bénédicte's remarks. I did not expect to have to educate the *soeurs* about condoms. No wonder the girls don't talk to anyone about their sexual activity. They're afraid. They're demeaned.

The next day, I head over to the *dispensaire* after *sieste*, to see the young student who gave birth. She is gone, her bed empty. I go inside and see the short guy who is always visiting people at the clinic; he is reading the Bible. He tells me the girl left, but that Soeur Marie-Claire, a new sister just dispatched to Djon, is inside the pharmacy. I go in to see Marie-Claire and ask about the girl.

Marie-Claire says, "The girl has returned home. Her baby died this morning."

I am shocked but I don't know why. I saw the baby. I knew he would die.

"That's what she wanted, isn't it?" Marie-Claire says. "She took the medicine to have an abortion and now she has no baby."

The lack of openheartedness, of generosity, was stark. Bénédicte seems so jaded and cynical, and Marie-Claire is just the same. Don't they see how their manner encourages the girls' secretiveness?

Nyalewossi travels to Djon today specifically to tell me that Sophie has been trying to reach me. Nyalewossi bursts with excitement and enthusiasm as she says that Sophie wants me to come to Lomé for a meeting with the new Peace Corps trainees. Sophie has also invited Nyalewossi to attend a girls' education conference next month, in Côte d'Ivoire.

We walk around the village of Djon, visiting with each other and buying fufu for lunch, and when I introduce Nyalewossi to Kofi as *notre presidente d'élèves,* she acts the part beautifully, not at all passive or timid.

On the way to Lomé for the meeting, I stop in Kpalimé to see René. His wife left months ago, but I have not seen René since he moved. The office manager at ERSA tells me René lives in the house across from the Hotel Geyser. When I find his new home, he is surprised to see me, but very welcoming. I watch him give his young son a school lesson; I eat dinner with them. I can see how happy René is to have his children close to him, and how at home he is here in Kpalimé.

After the kids go to bed, I announce to René that, as I now have a boyfriend in Lomé, René and I can no longer make love. René's skepticism is evident in his one simple question.

Il fait bien l'amour avec toi? Does he satisfy you in bed? No, I say.

Fueled by our desire, and my need for satisfaction mingled with a bit of curiosity, René and I have sex. Although I miss being kissed the way Maxim kisses me, the sex with René is very good, *comme d'habitude.* As usual.

I can't ignore that René and I know each other much better than Maxim and I do, and we are much more transparent with each other. We share more intimacies, both in bed and out.

After the sex, René and I talk. I am not confused, but rather stymied, by all René's questions.

"What can he give you? What does he do for you?"

I don't say anything.

"What do you want?"

"Good sex, love, and companionship. I don't want to choose among them. Why should I have to?"

René laughs, but then he says more seriously, "You don't know what you want. You're only thinking of yourself. Enough for you is never enough."

Perhaps René is right. Maxim told me recently, "You are too impatient. You can't have everything you want. You are passionate, but too impatient." I hated hearing Maxim's statements, but I will never forget them, either, especially, this one: "You can't have everything you want." René seems to be telling me the same thing.

This whole thing confuses me. The sex is better with René, but with Maxim, love is involved. Right? I have no future with René, yet with him I feel like a whole person. I am more likely to have a future with Maxim, but I don't know where I stand with him. I don't know who to choose, or what to do. I feel as if I am floating; I could land anywhere.

"You must make a choice about what you want," René says. "but I will make love with you again if you come back here."

Weeks later, I spend my second Christmas Eve in Togo. I've been in the country for a year and three months and consider myself a connoisseur of the local cuisine. I have grown to love African food. Tonight I am in search of fufu, but have to settle for *la pâte* and a nice place to sit and drink. This Christmas Eve I am in Aného, relaxed, reflective. Tomorrow I go to Benin to meet Shoshana and Grant for a short vacation. I chat with a guy at the *buvette* and find myself completely undisturbed by his come-ons or the children passing by who stare at me. Christmas spirit, perhaps? A group of women dressed in yellow skirts and white shirts, with flowers on their heads, pass by on their way to the hospital to greet the sick. A young girl smiles winningly at me as I sit.

I return to the Hotel l'Oasis, but only after stopping by the beach. I want to have a gin and tonic but I can't; I am coming down with a cold. I start to doze off on the hotel deck when the waiter comes by to take my dinner order. I choose spaghetti and a carafe of wine. The rest of Christmas Eve I spend on my hotel bed, listening to CDs—Abba, Counting Crows, and 'Til Tuesday. I feel so tired. Although I had a three-hour nap at *sieste*, I am still exhausted, depleted. From the year, perhaps.

I've achieved a milestone in my sexual evolution by doing what I thought I could never do—sleep with two men in the same week. Last week, actually. I spent Monday—or Tuesday, I don't even remember—at Maxim's home in Lomé. For the first time, he came between my breasts and, although I would have preferred intercourse, I loved that he did it.

Conscientious as he is, Maxim suggested we take a bath immediately afterward. Although we shower at the same time, we do it separately, not together. Maxim is somewhat . . . prudish? Proper? Serious? I don't know.

Four days later, in search of sexual satisfaction, I make an impulsive trip to Kpalimé. There, René and I fuck for real, with condoms, and it's wonderful to feel him inside me again, to kiss his nipples and feel his ass. He fucks me from behind and then I am on top and he thumps me playfully twice on the head when I scream a little too loudly. When we shower afterward, it's the absolute opposite experience I had with Maxim. René soaps me up and down three times and then announces, "Now—you are clean!"

I had forgotten what it is like to sleep with René. During the night, he has his legs all over the place. I spoon him and grab his ass and penis in the night. René laughs at me the next day and says, "I know you could make love every day. Every day."

"Once a week," I say. "Two or three times."

He laughs, unbelieving. "You want it every day!"

It feels great to finally have sex, to have real, lusty, passionate sex. Two men in the same week. What a demanding woman I've become.

Diplomacy au Village

The U.S. Ambassador to Togo is coming to Djon next week. Newly assigned to the country, he will visit two volunteers, chosen from the eighty PCVs in Togo, to witness us "in action." Sophie told me the news two weeks ago, and the village has been hopping with anticipation ever since. I have planned a couple of activities with the girl's class, and tonight Kofi and Pascal stop by to fill me in on the various committees' preparations for the visit.

On the appointed day, late in the morning, a black SUV with tinted windows pulls up in front of my house, which is adjacent to the CEG. A crowd has gathered, headed by the village authorities, dressed either in colorful *kenté* or Western clothes. The crowd inadvertently blocks the road, and the SUV is forced to stop.

The ambassador is easy to spot as the group exits the vehicle. Tall and confident, he immediately identifies me, the only *yovo* in the throng of villagers. The ambassador is accompanied by two staff members, one male and one female, plus the driver. I am glad to see they are informally dressed. They seem surprised to see the crowd of colorfully dressed Africans.

I approach the ambassador to introduce myself and, when I offer my hand, he smiles and says, conspiratorially, "Stick next to me!" I should feel free to take charge of him: "I'll follow you; just tell me what to do." He is open, and observant, as when he notices my purple batik African blouse and says, "I like that shirt!"

And he is funny. When I inquire how long he will be staying, to make sure we have enough time for everything the village has planned, he tells me he has about three hours.

"You'll be here longer than I expected."

"I can leave earlier if you want!" he smiles.

We walk together to meet the waiting authorities. As we close the gap, I feel as if I'm in the midst of a summit of two great countries. There I am with the U.S. ambassador and his staff, and we are approaching the Akebou authorities of Djon, who have become my dear friends. Pascal steps forward and, in Akebou, does a traditional ceremony, pouring tchouk on the ground for the *anciens*. He thanks the *anciens* for the ambassador's visit and asks them to bless the ambassador with a good sojourn and good health in Togo.

I bring the ambassador through my gate so he can observe a brief skit by the girls while the village prepares the luncheon. On my porch, the girls demonstrate what *mariage forcé* looks like, as a way to show how hard it is to keep girls in school. The ambassador listens closely and the skit goes well. The girls are fearlessly dramatic, and they don't mind being watched, either by the ambassador or by all the kids who are sitting on the concrete wall surrounding my house. Later, on the short walk to the school, the ambassador asks me some questions about myself:

"How long have you been here?"

"A year and four months."

"What do you do for fun?"

"I've been biking a lot lately."

"How often do you get to Lomé?"

"More often than you'd think!"

"What did you do before you came to Togo?"

"I just earned my PhD in family therapy."

"What's your dissertation on?"

"A hostage incident at a high school."

The ambassador and I sit together under the patio in front of the principal's office while the villagers perform traditional dancing, drumming, and singing in the CEG courtyard. Then, there are official words of welcome for the ambassador from Pascal, the CVD president:[1]

"Excellence, Monsieur l'Ambassadeur: In the name of the chief canton of Djon, I have the honor of welcoming you here today. We present to you our sincere thanks that you have come to Akebou to visit the volunteer charged with the project, *La Promotion de la Jeune Fille*.

"The problem of educating young girls touches a very sensitive development issue in Akebou. In effect, the young girls of Akebou have been left behind, without support. This situation has received the attention of our parish in Djon; our Père Didier recently organized a *Jubilée 2000*, which was a delightful and productive meeting at which young girls representing all of the villages of Akebou came to debate this problem. The presence among of us of Mlle Laurie, who we consider as a sister to us, has helped us to continue the undertaking of Père Didier.

"We appreciate the value of the program. . . . We are aware that the health, nutrition, and education of young girls contribute to the well-being of our society, one which is harmonious, permanent, and strong. In this way, each of us here can ponder the adage that says, 'If you educate a woman, you educate a nation.' On our part, we say simply that women are the hope for tomorrow.

Vive la cooperation Americaine/Togolaise!"

Luncheon is in the principal's office, where a few small tables are set up. Of course, fufu is served. I am not sure if the ambassador has seen fufu before.

"Do you eat African food?" I ask him.

"I can," he says confidently.

The ambassador is a little tentative with the fufu, but he's only been in Togo for three months. I remember what it is like to be new. You are afraid of everything you don't cook yourself. I explain how to eat the fufu and he is very gracious when he tries to do so in the African way, without utensils. Any *yovo* who dares on the first try to eat fufu with fingers earns my immediate respect. The ambassador is a diplomat in the truest sense!

The best moment for me is when we go to visit the chief. This visit is not on the agenda; the village committee didn't plan it.

"The chief of Djon is very old and frail, and does not leave his home," I tell the ambassador. But the ambassador wants to meet him, and assures me it is okay for us to walk there. So we trek through the village, a small diplomatic unit on our way to the meet the chief.

Kofi goes ahead to tell the chief we are coming and when we arrive the ambassador takes the initiative. Samuel, a villager who speaks perfect English, translates his words into Akebou for the chief. The ambassador gives a simple yet heartfelt speech to the chief acknowledging how earnest and hardworking the villagers are in Djon. He thanks the chief for hosting a volunteer in his village, then bows to him graciously. Then the two members of the ambassador's delegation go down on their haunches and thank the chief in their own words, holding his hands while they talk quietly.

Now it is Chief Atododji's turn. Although he can barely sit up and is virtually blind, Atotdodji manages to outdo all of us in the diplomacy department. When he is finished, he thanks the ambassador and his delegation for his journey to Djon, "our humble and modest village."

It is my turn to say a few words. I speak in Akebou, and when I am done the applause feels grand. All I say is, "Good afternoon to all of you," and "Thank you very much for coming," but it is enough. It is more than enough.

As we walk back to the SUV, the ambassador tells me, "You've obviously had an impact here." I tell him that Djon was already a progressive and mobilized community before I arrived.

"They've obviously got their stuff together, and you do too. That's how it's supposed to be," the ambassador responds.

The village has been very high ever since. Pascal and Kofi joke that they are going to name a street after me in Djon. (There are no streets in Djon!)

Today I got an email from my sister Patricia.

January, 2001

Hey Sis,

I have some not so great news to tell you. Sorry it's an email. I debated whether to tell you, but then realized I would want to know. Mom was in the hospital last week for six days. She had difficulty breathing late Saturday night so they called an ambulance to take to her the hospital. After sitting around there all night, they decided to admit her to do some tests, supply her with oxygen and drain some fluid built up around her lungs.

By the second day she was feeling much better, not so tired, and by the third she was antsy and ready to go home. When she went through some tests months ago, there was one they didn't perform. I forget the full name, but basically they inject her blood with a dye to detect blockage of the arteries, which they did last week. They found she had some blockage.

Rather than perform any invasive surgery they placed a shunt/stent in her vein/artery to open it up a bit. A common procedure with a local anesthetic. She has to go back for a follow-up in a month. I was there from Sun to Tues. She had the shunt placed on Thursday and went home on Friday. She's fine now. Don't worry—I'll keep in touch.

Love, Patricia

Dearest Laurie,

I know this letter seems overdue. I know Patricia emailed you that I was sick. Well I'm better now. Got out of the hospital on Friday, a week ago. For some reason I was retaining liquids, which hampered my breathing. While I was in there a cath was done that showed a blocked artery so the doctors went ahead and did an angioplasty (balloon) with a stent. That's something to keep the artery from closing. I think my allergies triggered the shortness of breath. I've lost count of the number of doctors I have to see now. I have become my mother. The one thing I swore I wouldn't. I am dependent on medication. But if it makes me feel better or almost normal I'm okay with it.

I am going to try to finish this letter ASAP so David can mail a package we've been trying to get in the mail for a while. Everyone wanted to put something in the package but I think we needed a larger envelope. The wind chime is from Paul and Mercy. The jerky is from David. We had too much so we had to eat some. Sorry. We are also sending the pictures we had developed for you. I kept two of them with you in them. I wanted to tell you that you really look good in your pictures. Happy and healthy. I hope that's true.

The weather's been really bad, raining every week and really cold. Right now the sun is out temporarily. Tomorrow the rain comes. This is the first time in years that I have been chilled to the bone.

Honey, I'll close, since this mail is getting ready to hit the road to Africa. We love you and miss you tremendously. Try not to worry too much about things here. If necessary we'll get in touch with you, but for now and hopefully for a while we're doing fine. I am in good hands, okay? Let us know what we can send, okay? We love you and miss you.

All my love,
Mom

My mother's abrupt diagnosis and quick deterioration make my life in Togo very uncomfortable and, eventually, impossible to continue. Although I do not want to leave, I feel terribly irresponsible being a Peace Corps volunteer in Africa while my mother is in such poor health. After weeks of vacillating, I finally decide I will leave Togo six months before my expected close of service. I advise Peace Corps that I will remain in Togo only six more weeks to wrap up my work. It's barely enough time—there is so much to do.

One afternoon, I make a trip to see Père Antoine, who has been relocated to another village, near Kpalimé. I have not seen him since he told me he was trying to protect me by suggesting we sleep together because the village thought we were lovers anyway. With my departure pending, I want to tell Antoine I am leaving Togo. I want us to put our differences aside.

I also want him to continue a project we recently started in Djon. The Djon CVD, headed by Pascal, its president, has been promised funds by a U.S. church to build a high school. Père Antoine and I have been the main contacts for the project, which was initiated before the kiss and its aftermath.

Arriving at Antoine's new village, I walk immediately to the Catholic church. It's a beautiful church with lovely stained glass windows and an open, airy feel. In a compound behind the chapel, surrounded by leafy green trees, I locate Antoine's living quarters. A young man tending the chicken coop goes to fetch him for me. Sympathetic when I tell him about my mother, Antoine says, "I will pray for her, and for you." Antoine comforts me further with his understanding.

"Things will be fine if you leave Djon. Nothing has to end because you are leaving."

I am so grateful for his words, which remind me what our friendship used to be. I decide to stay for lunch instead of leaving immediately for Atakpamé. Antoine and I share fufu, and our conversation further recalls the old days.

I explain to Antoine how to deal with the U.S. community in order to complete the project. Djon authorities need to establish a bank account for the transfer of funds to avoid the possibility of anyone stealing the money. They need to take pictures of the building before, during, and after the renovation, so that the U.S. church can see where their money went. Thus the church will be more likely to donate money in the future.

After our working lunch, I tell Antoine I have to leave if I am to get home before dark. But Antoine wants to show me the chicken coop be-hind the church. As we walk under the shady trees, Antoine whispers, out of earshot of the young man cleaning the coop, "I have the urge to hold you. I want to kiss you right now."

No! Not again! A huge wave of emotion washes over me and I want to scream. I look at Antoine and see what appears to be mischief on his face—I can't tell if he is joking or he is serious. Later he will say, "I only wanted to tease you." But how could he want this after all I've said to him? I am angry at myself. How could I have been so naïve?

"*Vous êtes malade.* You are ill. Do you know I am so angry I feel I could hit you right now? Why are you doing this? Are you trying to make me angry?"

"Yes, I am just playing with you. That is all." Antoine's sounds smug, self-satisfied. Heat floods my face.

"You do not have the spirit of a priest, Antoine."

He just laughs.

Shortly after this incident, I travel to Okou, the village where Pascal lives. I have told no one in Akebou about Antoine's behavior except Bernadette; I did not want to risk hurting Antoine's reputation. Now I decide to tell Pascal, because I cannot continue the project if I must continue to work with Antoine. I just can't deal with him anymore. I will tell Pascal what has transpired between me and Antoine, and I will also explain why I am leaving Togo.

Pascal is surprised, shocked even, at Antoine's behavior; the men have known each other for years.

"Didn't you explain to him he can't do that?"

"Is that my job? To tell him his obligations as a priest?"

Pascal shakes his head, perhaps thinking of his beautiful wife and five lovely daughters.

"That is why I didn't become a priest. Exactly."

I feel validated by Pascal's comments, but my mind is on my departure. My thoughts race and I am very distracted. I do not think what it would be like for Pascal to hear that I will leave Togo six months early. Pascal is the man who found my house in Djon. He is the man who first suggested I move to Djon. In a way, Pascal is directly responsible for the second wind I experienced in Togo. So preoccupied am I that I almost don't hear what Pascal says next. He looks at me with a direct gaze that pulls me out of my thoughts.

"Laurie. When you go home, when you see your dear mother again, you must bring with you all the goodwill of the people of Africa."

My eyes fill with tears.

Maxim visits me in Djon for the first and only time. When I tell him about the incident with Antoine at the chicken coop, Maxim kisses and caresses me and, best of all, listens to me. We speak in English, and he asks good questions.

"Why did you trust Antoine would stop? Knowing him as you do? Why did you go back to see him?"

Because I thought Antoine would stop, I thought I could trust him again, but now, "I am considering reporting Antoine to his superiors." Maxim agrees.

"Yes, you must report him. Go to the Catholic bishop in Atakpamé. But what will you do if the bishop won't help you?" I don't have an answer to this.

I tell Maxim I am worried about us, about our relationship. I also say I think our sexual relationship is not very good. Maxim, to my surprise, is not upset. Instead, he is curious about my point of view.

"When did you think the sexual chemistry between us wasn't good?"

Because he does not seem upset or offended, I decide to confess further. I tell Maxim that I have continued to sleep with René intermittently while he and I have been together. Surprising me again, he understands.

"When we met, I knew you had a man in your village. I knew you also had a man in Israel. I knew the other men were there before me, and you would have to work that out for yourself."

This speech reminds me of René's comment when his wife was here and he tried to explain "first" and "second" lovers. Now it's me who's explaining. Only Maxim doesn't need the explanation, he's African. He already knows the rules.

Changing the subject, Maxim says, "Oh! I almost forgot—I brought something to show you." Maxim brings out pictures of his recent birthday celebration. He tells me the party was impromptu. He bought his own wine and beer and invited a few friends over to celebrate. Someone gave him a CD of the "Thong Song" for his birthday and Maxim is holding it up in one of the photos. I can't help noticing that in every picture Maxim looks deliriously happy. I have never seen him like this, and when I tell him so he challenges me, "Make me happy, then!"

"But you didn't invite me to your party!"

"You live too far away," Maxim says. "You need a mobile phone." As if I do not live in a tiny village in the African bush.

"Why?"

"So I can call you," he says. Silence. "But you are leaving Togo anyway, so forget it."

I come across a photo of Maxim dancing happily by himself, his friends watching. I tell him he looks so young and carefree.

"I am young."

"Yes, I know." (But I remember that during our first dinner together, Maxim told me he thought he was old.)

"You've only seen me this way," he says. "You've never seen me mad, you've never seen me manage the men who work for me, you've never seen me teach, nothing."

"It's the same for me."

"I know, we don't know each other." Maxim adds quickly, "But I can discover you."

I love Maxim for saying this. He makes me feel hopeful, as if our future is completely open.

"I am coming with you to the States. I will spend a month with you."

"Why are you coming? To be with me? To stay with me?" I hear fear in my voice.

"Yes," he says. "And to see. To see."

I am shocked at Maxim's plan. He never even hinted at it before, and I've never considered it a real possibility. Maxim asks me if I am ready to be with one man.

"You think you are," but he seems skeptical. "You are the problem, I cannot be sure about you. I don't know what your plans are. Where will you go? What will you do?"

I don't have any answers for Maxim. I just want to be in San Antonio with my mother. But I am worried about being separated from Maxim at what seems to be the beginning of our relationship. I tell him things change between people when oceans separate them. It will be different between us after I leave.

"How?" he asks. "It won't be."

"Something could happen."

"What's going to happen?"

"I don't know." (I don't want to find out.) "I'm not patient."

Il faut avoir de la patience, he says, laughing. You must have patience.

But I've just come out of the transcontinental relationship with Oded. I promised myself I wouldn't do it again. It's not good for me. I can't put my heart on hold anymore.

Maxim tells me he's been planning this. Being practical, he asks, "Can you look for a job from here? Can you live in Togo?"

"No."

"Then I must go to United States," he says, clearly and firmly.

"What will you do there?" I hear worry in my voice.

"I don't know yet. I have to see first what's there. Then I'll know. There are those less than me who have gone and lived there for years." He seems so sure of himself. "I know myself. I believe if I'd been there already I would be rich by now."

Maxim says he is not at all bothered by a separation, or the fact that we will be so far away. He says it does not matter.

"Tell me why." I want some of his confidence.

"It doesn't matter. It is no thing to go back and forth. Paris is even better if I can live there."

"After a while I could live in Europe," I pipe in. "There are family therapy programs in Europe, Germany, even Italy. But I don't speak *l'Italienne*."

"You can always learn." Like I can do anything.

It's time for me to visit Kpalimé and meet with the Diore family, who know nothing of my mother's illness or my impending departure. I arrive at the house midmorning and find no one at home. So, I walk to Marguerite's *lycée* and, in a fit of maternal confidence and Western arrogance, decide to pull her out of school. I have an urgent situation, I tell Marguerite's teacher.

Marguerite's look when I interrupt her class is priceless. I apologize profusely to the teacher as Marguerite gathers her things and hurries out of the room.

Marguerite and I walk to a nearby *buvette* for a *sucrerie*, so we can have a talk, woman to woman. I feel a need to confide in Marguerite; so many serious things are happening in my life right now. Marguerite is older now, and she is wise beyond her years. I know she wants the best for me.

Without hesitancy, I tell Marguerite about my relationship with Maxim (she giggles with glee), the incidents with Antoine (she is upset), and my mother's illness (she is sad).

I fear Marguerite's disappointment when I tell her I am leaving Togo early, but when she says, "You've almost done two years! And you must go!" her endorsement lifts a heavy weight off my shoulders.

Even about Antoine, Marguerite is supportive, alternately shocked and upset.

"He has behaved badly! Why is he even a priest? Who does he think he is!" I tell her I plan to write a letter of complaint to the bishop, but I need some help with my official French correspondence. Will she correct and proofread the letter once I've finished it?

"*Bien sûr*, I will help you," she says without a second's hesitation.

Marguerite's reaction is nothing like Bernadette's. Occasionally I have to remind myself that, although Marguerite is Togolese, she lives in a modern city with an educated family who watches CNN. She is very different from many people in my village. (The one time Marguerite came to visit me in Djon—with her contemporary clothes, fashionable hairstyle, and confident manner—she was as foreign to Djon as it was to her.)

I am grateful Marguerite understands my wish to report Antoine for another reason—because she is a devout Catholic. Her Togolese outrage at Antoine makes me feel validated. I have so often wondered if I am wrong, if I misinterpreted Antoine's behavior, if I provoked it. Marguerite reminds me that Antoine is the one who acted inappropriately. I tell Marguerite, "I will come back to Kpalimé once more, after I've written the letter, to have you review it before I take it to the bishop."

Having said goodbye to Marguerite, I walk to René's new office in Kpalimé to tell him I am leaving. René is busy but he makes time for me, calling me into his office as soon as he has a break.

"I want to ask you a question," René says, looking very serious. "Has anything happened between you and Antoine?"

"Yes!" I exclaim, and proceed to tell him the events that have transpired since the first kiss: how Antoine first apologized, then took it back and said he wanted us to sleep together; how I told Bernadette and she was not surprised; how I found out Antoine tried to get Bernadette to convince me to be with him; and how in his village just the other day he said he wanted to kiss me. To my surprise, I become upset and teary and angry as I recount the details to René. It sounds worse when I put the whole story together.

Blowing my nose with my handkerchief, I tell René of my plans to speak to the bishop. As I sit in the chair, sniffling, René kneels in front of me, placing his hands on my knees.

"Laurie, Nyalewossi said everyone in Kougnohou thinks you are sleeping with Antoine. Is it true?"

What? Tears fill my throat and I try to talk but cannot. I stand up to leave. Finally, between sobs, I accuse him.

"I can understand the villagers thinking this, but you? How could you believe it?"

René finally calms me down.

"I knew it could not be true! I told Nyalewossi you would never do that. You could never go with Antoine. But I had to verify it," René says. "Please allow me to present my excuses to you."

How has it come to this? That even my friends who know me well have to ask if I sleep with Antoine? Even René has had his doubts. I get angry all over again and start to leave, but when René asks a third and a fourth time to present his excuses, I smile in spite of myself.

"Okay! Present them!"

René smiles too, and puts out his hand, which I accept half-heartedly. He kneels on the floor in front of the chair where I sit.

"If no one was here I'd show you how much I am sorry." René cups his hands on my cheeks, wipes my tears away, and kisses the bridge of my nose. I relax immediately. As René repeats how sorry he is, a tear falls down my cheek, and René kisses it away.

"Please excuse me. I knew it, but I had to ask you. You must know that this is something Antoine is encouraging people to believe."

"Yes, I know," I say. "He wants it."

Voilà! René says, slapping my knee, sitting at my feet.

René helps me find a taxi to Atakpamé. I take the front seat, next to the driver because two male passengers are already in the back seat. We are on the road about fifteen minutes when a brand new, dark blue pickup truck passes in the opposite direction. I recognize the truck as Antoine's; it's the gift he received from his Italian friends several months ago. Antoine, who does not know how to drive, is in the front seat with a man he's hired as his personal chauffeur at the wheel.

One of the men in the back seat also recognizes the truck. In towns the size of Atakpamé and Kpalimé, a brand new 4×4 truck stands out. The man says simply, *C'est le prêtre,* as the truck passes by. I say nothing.

Just when the tension in my body starts to subside, the chauffeur says, "The truck is following us." The truck rides our bumper before it swings over to the other lane and races alongside us, risking an accident by traveling on the wrong lane of the highway.

The men in the car don't understand why the car has followed us, but I do. I'm afraid. When did I become afraid of Antoine?

I am sure Antoine saw me in the front seat of the taxi. I know he wants to talk to me, perhaps to apologize for what happened at the chicken coop a month ago. Perhaps he's talked to Pascal? The taxi and truck are speeding down the road, side by side. In my peripheral vision, I see Antoine motion for us to get off the road.

I look straight ahead, paralyzed with a fear I don't understand.

"The man in this truck is bothering me. He wants to talk to me, but I do not want to see him."

The men listen to me with interest. I doubt they expected this turn of events. But the driver says he must stop even if I don't want to, because it's too dangerous to drive this way.

Both vehicles pull over on the side of the road. Antoine's chauffeur parks the truck behind us, and for a few minutes no one moves. I realize Antoine expects me to get out of the taxi and walk over to his truck. I have no intention of doing so. Finally, Antoine's chauffeur exits the truck and approaches our passenger-side window.

"Père Antoine would like to see you."

"No, I do not want to see him." Confused, Antoine's chauffeur walks back to the truck. I sit in the car, nervous, shaking, afraid.

"This priest is bothering me. He has sexually harassed me and I plan to report him to his superiors. I do not know why he is following me. I do not want to see him."

The men respond to me in that lovely Togolese way, with comments that convey shock and surprise, worry and caring, all at the same time.

Kuh! Kuh! C'est grave! C'est grave ça! Kuh! Il est prêtre! Kuh! I feel the men's support immediately. How I have hated keeping this secret!

Antoine is at my window. Later he will say that, when he saw the look on my face that day, he knew I was going to report him. However, what he says to me at the window is fairly innocuous.

"I have received an email from the church in the United States about our project in Djon. They have raised the money. The project will go ahead." Antoine does not know I have already spoken to Pascal about having the U.S. church work exclusively with Pascal from now on, and not Antoine.

Although I glance briefly at Antoine as he speaks, I say nothing. Confused just as the chauffeur was, yet likely much more cognizant of the reasons for my behavior, Antoine walks away.

"We can leave now," I tell the driver. As we pull back onto the road, the passengers in back make a few more *Kuh!* remarks and clucks of the tongue.

Today, for the first time, I experience the cumulative effect of three individual incidents with Antoine in one emotion—fear. My God! How could a Togolese girl deal with such an experience? I have barely been able to deal with it myself. What recourse do they have? How can they say no? Who can they trust to support what they say? How do you change a problem of *mentalité*, as Maman once said, a mentality that permits such behavior?

Recently I talked to one of the new volunteers, Shelley, about how conflicted I felt in reporting Antoine. Shelley is a woman of color in her thirties, like me; she's had experience as a professional woman in the workplace; she's seen sexual harassment cases up close in the United States. I told Shelley I was conflicted about reporting Antoine because "he isn't aggressive." Shelley responded immediately, with two words: "Not yet." Only now, as I feel my own fear in the form of clammy skin, quickened heartbeat, and goose bumps, do I believe her.

Today I had another email from my sister Patricia.

Dear Laurie,

I still can't believe you're going to be here in less than two weeks. We need to have a beer together. Maybe you can help me with my work while you're here? I just finished sanding several canvases and I'm on my way up to DiverseWorks to put in a couple of hours sanding and painting walls for the next show.

Believe it or not, I've not been eating cheese. Maybe I'll indulge while you're here. I feel better without it. I'm inching my way toward being vegan.

You sound incredibly busy during your last couple of weeks in Togo. Will you sleep for days when you arrive? Maybe I'll teach you how to use my sander while you're here. Ooh, isn't that exciting?

There are a few of my friends I'd like you to meet, but I promise not to parade you around too much. Well, good luck with all your shit. There's a big box of mail waiting for you here. Gotta run, e-mail me again as soon as you can.

Love, Patricia
P.S. I'm glad you are reporting the priest. To think of these things as isolated situations denies the likelihood that they are part of a pattern of behavior.

A week before I leave Togo, I go to the office of the bishop in Atakpamé to deliver my letter of complaint. A secretary tells me the bishop is indisposed and sends me to see the vicar. I explain to the vicar that I am a *Corps de la Paix* volunteer who lives in Djon, in Akebou. Familiar with Akebou, the vicar names off the priests we both know: Didier, Anselme, Hugues, Michel. The vicar is pleasant, he doesn't know why I am here. He chats easily with me about his local diocese. Then I clarify the purpose of my visit.

"I have a problem with a priest. I am not here to ask about a project. I have a personal issue to discuss with the bishop." The vicar looks confused, but I continue.

"What is the procedure to meet with the bishop? Do I need an appointment? Can I see him now?"

The vicar does not answer my questions. Instead, he sends me to the bishop's secretary, where I explain myself all over again. The secretary says the best thing for me to do is to tell the vicar my problem, as if the vicar were the bishop.

"The vicar is the second in command."

So I return to the vicar, explain what the secretary said, and finally tell him I am here about an issue of *harcèlement sexuel* by a priest.

"Oh," he says.

I give him the letter Marguerite helped me write, and the vicar reads it for many long minutes. When he is finished, he says he understands everything in it.

"May we talk a little bit?" I say yes.

"Why did Antoine insist? I know him, we're brothers. This is hard to believe." The vicar seems genuinely surprised. I say that I would not have believed it of Antoine either.

"Antoine seemed to insist because he thought he loved me and we could truly be together." But it is Antoine who should be asked this question. Later I am upset with myself for trying to explain his behavior. The vicar apologizes for Antoine and describes what will happen next.

"Père Antoine will be called in to the *evêque*." The bishop. He will be reprimanded, so hopefully he will not do this again. The vicar says Antoine's behavior clearly reflects badly on the Church, but he intimates it would have been better if I'd talked to them first, rather than Peace Corps. He seems miffed that I cc'd my letter to Sophie and to Rafael, the Peace Corps Togo director, who is a U.S. citizen. Interestingly, both Sophie and Rafael suggested I not bother with the report because "It will do nothing."

The vicar then asks me a few more questions, "for clarification."

"So you lived in Kougnohou and went to Djon." Yes. And then, hesitantly, "Can I ask . . . are you married?" No.

"How old are you?" What does that have to do with anything? But, I tell him.

"Are you Catholic?"

I finally acknowledge my discomfort and stand up to leave.

"Yes, I am Catholic." With that, I gather my belongings and thank the vicar for his time. He says the *evêque* will hear me out.

"He will phone you at your Peace Corps volunteer house—your *maison*—here in Atakpamé."

As I leave, I realize the vicar didn't seem surprised by anything I wrote, except that my allegations involved Antoine. At the same time, he clearly wasn't used to receiving a written complaint; he didn't know what to do with the letter. His surprise at the form, but not the content, of the letter was disturbing.

A few hours later, I am back at the Atakpamé *maison* with Shoshana and her boyfriend, an environment volunteer from Pittsburgh named Eddie. Someone knocks at the door, and it's the bishop's chauffeur and *secrétaire*, who have arrived in a black Mercedes-Benz. Eddie calls me to the door and the men deliver the following message: "The bishop is ready to meet with you now."

Now? No way. We've already had half a bottle of gin, and I am not inclined to go over the whole Antoine thing again today. I say that I can meet the bishop in two days.

Rather than agree to the meeting, the chauffeur writes the bishop's cell phone number on a scrap of paper and suggests I contact him myself. Before I drink any more gin, I call the bishop on his cell phone. We arrange to meet at 4:30 the day after tomorrow.

I arrive at the appointed time and am led to the bishop's private office. The bishop is in informal robes and wears thick glasses. He is tall, with a substantial build, a commanding presence. The bishop greets me and immediately says he has read the letter and understands it. He is informal but serious.

"Is there anything else you would like to tell me? Is there anything else that is not addressed in the letter?"

"There is nothing more to add."

The bishop then ushers me into a large formal meeting room full of ornate furniture, with a 20-foot ceiling. Several priests—maybe six or seven—are seated in a circle of small armchairs. Antoine is among them. The bishop says quietly, "We will wait for a few more people before we start." Apparently, the official meeting will not begin until 5 o'clock.

The bishop and I remain at the door of the intimidating room. I am grateful for this, because I am not ready to go inside. Standing in the door together, I have an idea. Why didn't I didn't think of it before?

S'il vous plaît, Evêque, I have a question, may I ask you outside?"

"Of course," he says, and we step into the courtyard.

"I think it is better for me to have someone here at this meeting. May we call a volunteer at the *maison?*"

"Absolutely," the bishop responds. "It is right that you have someone here with you. We are all priests and we know each other. You should have your support here too."

The bishop hands me his cell phone and I step a few yards away to call the *maison.* I find Shoshana.

"Get over here!" I blurt, laughing nervously. "The bishop has called Antoine and some others to the meeting! It's going to be full of people. I need support, I need an ally."

I use the term Peace Corps trained us to use as a metaphor for ways to support each other during our service. It was always a joke to me until today. I ask Shoshana, completely serious now, "Will you come?"

Shoshana agrees immediately. When I tell the bishop, with Shoshana still on the line, he instructs his chauffeur to retrieve her from the *maison*. I tell Shoshana to watch for the bishop's black Mercedes-Benz.

Bernadette is the last to arrive at the meeting, even after Shoshana, and I am very surprised to see her, but I shouldn't be. I stated in my letter that Antoine had repeatedly sought out Bernadette in an effort to convince me to be his girlfriend. When the bishop's staff contacted her in Kougnohou, unbeknownst to me, she was obligated to come.

Although I am glad to see her, I am upset that she has had to travel here. Bernadette rarely leaves the village; she can't do it easily as a single, working mother. Bernadette does not look at me as she walks to her seat diagonal from mine. Although she is civil to all, I can tell she is unhappy to be here. I don't blame her. I just wish she'd look at me.

The bishop officially starts the meeting by introducing everyone except me and himself. He introduces Shoshana as my "*Corps de la Paix* colleague," and he makes Bernadette smile when he tries to pronounce her family name, Dionené. She corrects his pronunciation with deference. I realize again what a difficult position she is in, a position for which I became responsible when I named her in my letter.

Then, without any other comments, the bishop reads my letter aloud. When he has finished, he pauses for what seems a very long time. Then, he makes a personal statement about his view of my letter, and I find his words both touching and painful to hear. The bishop looks directly into my eyes.

"Because of this incident you have been caused pain and you were right to write a letter and tell the story." Then he looks Antoine in the eyes and publicly chastises him for his behavior. For the next two hours, I am peppered with interesting and unexpected questions from the priests. The questions make me curious and, at times, extremely uncomfortable.

"What do you suggest we do to Antoine? What punishment do you think best? What will please you?"

"It is my job to inform you. I cannot pretend to know your milieu, or suggest what you should do. I now present this to you. It is for you to decide what to do, not me."

"What about Peace Corps? Why did you inform them first? Will it hurt the work in Akebou?"

"Peace Corps is like our parents here, it is our duty to inform them. They are responsible for us, and we have a responsibility to keep them informed about anything that happens to us."

Shoshana then adds, "It is not uncommon for volunteers to have problems and it is necessary to report any incident to Peace Corps immediately. Volunteers have been killed."

I am asked three different times, by three different priests, "Why didn't you go to Antoine and tell him you were going to make a report?" This question, and that it is asked repeatedly, upsets me. Isn't that what I already did? Why don't the priests see this? Why aren't they listening? I make an effort to remain calm.

"Please allow me to explain to you again—for I notice I have been asked this question three times. I did talk to Antoine about the inappropriateness of his behavior. I told him several times, over the course of nine months, that his behavior was a problem. The reason I didn't go to Antoine before reporting this is because I had already talked to him many times about stopping his behavior."

"Why didn't you report this immediately after the first incident?"

This question is harder to answer, and my French falters as I try to explain. Why didn't I report it? In hindsight, my explanation seems unbelievable, even to me. But the truth is I didn't report it the first time because I believed it wouldn't happen again and I didn't want to hurt Antoine; I felt more concerned about hurting him than about possible unpleasant repercussions. I never considered reporting him until many months after the kiss, which I now consider "the first incident."

"I did not want to realize, or could not realize, how serious it was. I thought Antoine would stop. Then, when he didn't, I was unsure what would happen if I reported him. I asked advice from friends and colleagues, Togolese and American. What helped me decide was hearing a volunteer say, when I told her my dilemma because Antoine's manner was not aggressive: 'Not yet!'"

I see Shoshana nodding her head as I explain, and I am so glad I asked her to be here.

"After that, I thought more about the girls or women who might come after me, and I felt obligated to report what happened. I could not leave Togo without doing something."

The bishop repeats my statements, all of them, and he agrees.

"You did the right thing."

A priest asks, "How do you feel about Antoine now? What are your feelings for him?" This question upsets the bishop, who is seated next to me. He looks at me as if to say, "Do not speak." Then, he directs his response to the priest. With his right arm raised, the palm of his hand facing the priest who spoke, the bishop declares in a booming voice, "That is a personal question that is not relevant."

The bishop is really moderating this very well. His actions make me feel protected and honored.

Antoine, a small heap slumped in his chair, does not participate much. I caught him staring at me more than once. I try to avoid his eyes, but I can't. I'm very uncomfortable that he is here and I'm not sure why. At one point, Antoine raises himself out of his chair, to address me.

"Laurie," his voice pleads, "Laurie, please, I ask you if we can have a reconciliation." He speaks in a very personal way, as he has always done, as if no one else is around. He sounds *faible*, weak. The bishop reprimands Antoine.

"You do not ask that question here. That is not a question you can ask anymore." Antoine slumps back in his chair.

Now, it is Bernadette's turn to ask a question. She has not looked at me during the entire meeting. Now, she does. She addresses me directly, with her dignified face and her sharp eyes.

"Laurie," she too uses a personal tone with me, and I feel my heart reach out to her, "Laurie, you contradict yourself by believing now what people in the village said and before, not."

Bernadette's right. For a time, I didn't care what the villagers thought, not until the day René asked me himself whether what they said was true. In the meeting, one priest had already asked me, "How could you believe

Antoine would want people in the village to know he has a girlfriend? Why would he want to hurt his own reputation in that way? Do you really think a priest would tell others in his parish such a thing?"

Perhaps not every priest would do that, I conceded, but I'm certain now that Antoine led others in the village to believe we had a romantic relationship. I'm certain he did nothing to correct people's misperceptions; on the contrary, I think he liked having the villagers think we were a couple.

In response to Bernadette's observation, I try, but ultimately fail, to explain in French that Antoine could have encouraged people's beliefs about us without saying anything directly—and that this, too, is inappropriate. I have plenty of words to describe this concept in English, but in French, a language I've only spoken for eighteen months? It's terribly frustrating.

Bernadette's question makes me feel defensive. She's chosen her side, and it's not mine. But isn't that her only choice? What else can she do in this situation? Bernadette lives here, she is a Catholic, this is her bishop. She is the only Togolese layperson at this meeting, and the only Togolese woman. She has no power here. In fact, Bernadette is the most vulnerable person in the room, even more than Antoine, who will go on being a priest, with the Church behind him, even when he behaves badly.

Bernadette is doing what she needs to do. Me? I will leave Togo. I will not be here to help her manage any fallout from being involved in this episode. She has no choice but to discount me, and she must do it in front of this audience. She must reaffirm her status as a good Catholic, a respectable woman, a Peace Corps homologue. I understand what Bernadette has done, but I still feel betrayed. I wonder if she feels betrayed too. Maybe that's why she won't look at me. My heart is so heavy right now.

"Is it possible that Antoine can write a letter stating we have had this meeting, and you can take it to Peace Corps?" one of the priests asks. His request surprises me. It is not deflected by the bishop.

"Of course he can write a letter, but I will not take it for him. He can send it himself."

After this question, the meeting finally winds down. Two hours have passed. The bishop looks at me.

"Is there anything you would like to say?" It is the first time I have the floor; the first time I talk of my own accord and not in response to a question. Until now, my letter has spoken for me.

"Thank you, *Evêque*, for taking this so seriously. I thank Shoshana and Bernadette especially for attending the meeting. I know it is difficult for you and an inconvenience. I very much appreciate the opportunity to have this meeting." I pause, thinking. "That is all I have to say."

The room is silent. Shoshana whispers to me, "I think they are waiting for an apology by Antoine."

Just as she predicts, Antoine makes an apology for his behavior. I pity him as he speaks. The meeting put him in the hot seat, and although he was honest and denied nothing, he does not carry himself well. He looks guilty, and somewhat pathetic. At one point the bishop tells him, as if to shore him up, "What you did was weak, but you are not weak."

After Antoine speaks, the room grows quiet.

Shoshana whispers to me, "They are waiting for you to forgive him."

I whisper back, "I don't want to say anything more."

"Then don't." And I don't.

I have done what I came to do. Silently, I make a small speech to Bernadette and Antoine: "I am so sorry it is like this. I am sorry for the three of us. We are not at peace, and won't be for some time. We were friends, but we can't go back to the way it was before."

Out loud, in front of the group, I say only that "I am finished speaking at this meeting."

Shoshana and are waiting a few minutes for bishop's Benz to take us back to the *maison*. When I see Bernadette, alone in the bishop's courtyard, I approach her with some determination. Bernadette looks right at me and smiles slightly. She is aware I will leave Togo in a matter of days. We both realize this is the last time we will see each other.

"It is not over between us," I tell Bernadette. "I am your friend and I will always be your friend. I am now Togolese, like you. I am now African, like you. I will always be your sister. Even when I am far away, when you do not hear from me, when you do not see me, I will be near. You will always be my friend, Bernadette. Nothing will change that."

Bernadette smiles her mysterious, knowing smile, and holds my hands. She communicates to me with her eyes, with the mischievous expression in her face that I love so much. But her mouth is silent.

The impromptu speech did not sound like me. It sounds like Bernadette. Perhaps I spoke for both of us? I can see Antoine watching us, but I do not approach him.

When Grant and I arrive at Geyser it is nearly 11 P.M., and we find we are the only guests. It is too late for me to see René, even though his house is just across the street. If I go over there now I will wake the entire household so I decide to stop by in the morning. Grant and I order shrimp avocado and a *salade niçoise* for dinner, and because it is dark, hot, and very late, we decide to go for a nude swim while waiting for our food.

I turn my head while Grant disrobes and gets in the pool, then he does the same for me. We have the whole pool to ourselves, and we are completely comfortable. We have had a lovely platonic yet affectionate friendship for over a year and it's no problem for us to be naked together. The only person who has difficulty with our nakedness is the chef, who can't stop staring at us while he prepares our dinner. The swim is lovely; the food, delicious. I drink gin and tonic, and eventually Grant and I somehow stumble off to bed, exhausted and happy.

I wake up in the night and through sleepy eyes see René at my bedside. I feel his kisses on my face and neck, and wonder, Am I dreaming? How did he get in here? (It turns out that the owner of the hotel, a friend of René's, let him in our room. René can be very persuasive.) René coos in my ear as he caresses me. I am more awake now, but still out of sorts, drunk. Yet I am happy to see him.

René has no mercy. He takes advantage of my disoriented state, not caring that Grant is in a bed next to mine, awake and aware of us. René sucks on my neck, then explores my backpack to find my cosmetics bag, where he knows I keep my condoms. Not finding one, he comes back to the bed and tries to insert his penis inside me anyway. His pants are already off. When did he take his pants off?

"Go to sleep!" René tells Grant wickedly.

I refuse to have sex with Grant in the room! I force myself to get out of bed and throw some clothes on so we can go across the street to René's house. In the bathroom, I realize I must be insane. I am getting a cold, my throat hurts, and my hair is still wet from my swim. I feel miserable.

I want to get rid of René, but I also want to be with him one more time before I leave Togo.

Still in a daze, I walk to René's house, and we talk as we eat mayonnaise sandwiches on his bed. René's pants are off again, and I realize I have carried his underwear across the street!

René and I note that it is one year we've known each other. He pats himself on the back, *Je suis un bon homme!*

Me too, I say. I am a good woman, *n'est-ce pas?*

"No," he says. "I am honest. You had sex with another, whereas I have not."

"What about your wife?" Apparently I have to remind him he has one.

"Yes," he admits.

As we sit on the bed reflecting on our time together, I tell René, "I am sorry that you are married, otherwise I would keep you." I am surprised by this statement, but right now, I absolutely mean it.

When I ask René if he loves me, he says, "Yes. You know it. Why do you ask?"

So I can hear it, I say.

Silence.

René thanks me for my friendship and companionship and then, finally, we make love. We have great sex and afterward I fall asleep immediately. I am sore from it the next morning.

I wake up at 4 when I hear René's sleepy 6-year-old son crow with the roosters. I dress to leave and René walks me part of the way to Geyser. He promises to stop by for coffee before I go.

The Geyser gate is locked, and I contemplate scaling the concrete fence. Fortunately, I find an unlocked door at the back of the hotel. I sneak into the grounds, walk to the room I share with Grant, and go straight to bed, chlorine in my hair and spermicide all over me. I still have a terrible sore throat.

Unable to sleep, I get out of bed and shower. René stops by for coffee and the three of us chat as if it is any other day. René says he will take me to the gas station on the outskirts of Kpalimé so I can more easily catch a taxi back to Djon. I have to go there one last time for a village meeting, and to pick up my things and close my house.

In Kpalimé, I repeatedly hug and kiss Grant goodbye. I say goodbye to the Diores. I bid goodbye to Marguerite yet again when she stops by the Geyser on her way to school. At the gas station, it is time for René's goodbye. I can't believe I will never see him again.

René doesn't cry. It's not his style. Even though it *is* mine, I don't cry either. In fact, I can't even speak. René is one of my most true companions in Togo. He is one of the few Togolese I have met who treats me like a peer— emotionally, intellectually, and sexually. We are nearly the same age; we are both passionate about our work; we both demand honesty of each other about our relationship, its limitations as well as its glories. I don't know how I would have managed Togo without René. René's goodbye feels different from everybody else's, even Maxim's. I do not want to say this goodbye.

As the taxi arrives, René has the composure to tell me, "You must let me know if you get married, if you have a baby, when you find work. You must call me to tell me."

I cannot put my own feelings into words. So I say nothing.

My last day in Djon there is a meeting at the chief's house for all of the village authorities. Formally, I explain what many of them already know— that I am leaving Togo six months early and going home to Texas because of my mother's illness. My announcement sounds somber, because I feel terrible about what I am doing. I only arrived in Djon six months ago. However justifiable my reason for leaving, I feel I have let the village down, have disappointed them. Nevertheless, the authorities offer supportive comments.

"We thank you very much for what you've done and we are clear that the reason you are leaving has to do with your mother," Monsieur Wialo says.

"I will recommend that you have another volunteer, but there are things you can do as a village to ensure Peace Corps will replace me without hesitation. You must put together a letter and send a delegation to the capital. Monsieur Pascal knows what to put in the letter." The authorities promise to do whatever is necessary. Still, it will be a year before I am replaced.

I am so glad for the meeting. It's important to make a public state-ment, to openly voice my reasons for leaving, to make transparent what everyone already knows. When we finish, I suggest we take a photo to commemorate my time in Djon. Pascal's black-and-white film is finished, so I run to my house for my camera. I grab the rest of my backpacks and close up my big, beautiful house in the African bush.

We take the photo by setting my camera on top of two chairs and us-ing the timer. The authorities pose with me at the chief's front door, about twenty of us all together. When I develop the picture a few weeks later in the States, I will think it is one of the most poignant photos of my entire Africa experience.

After the picture, Kofi, Pascal, Didier, and I walk to Pascal's small room. I've named Pascal's room "New York," because of its bohemian feel, its interesting surprises around every corner. When I go there, I feel as if I am in Greenwich village, rather than a small village in West Africa.

Pascal has arranged for us to have a box of wine, and my favorite meal, fufu with chicken. (Pascal eats a mushroom-based version, how-ever, because he is vegetarian.) I eat slowly, savoring the moment.

Pascal surprises me again when he presents me with a wooden carv-ing to hang on my wall back home; it's an impression of a young girl, reading a book, with a palm tree over her head and mud hut nearby. Pascal explains that the CVD bought the work from a local artisan "so you can remember your work here with us. The key you see on the book means that the girl's education is the key to her future."

Pascal then wants to say some things to me, on behalf of the village, for my mother. He makes me promise to carry this message to her in Texas. After I promise, Pascal clears his throat, and states in a formal, dip-lomatic tone (perhaps the ambassador's visit influenced him):

"We've lived in harmony and joy together, and we understand your obligation to your mother and appreciate it. Please tell your dear mother we are all praying for her health and her recovery, just as if we are you. Please know that because your mother is sick, we understand you cannot be happy here, and so we cannot be happy either. Therefore, you must leave, and go with our blessings."

The sentiment in this brief speech takes my breath away. I don't know how the village can be thinking about my mother right now, about how happy she will be at our reunion, but they are. I expect them to think about themselves, and their loss of a volunteer, but they don't.

Fighting back tears, I announce, "I will return one day, and with my mother!" I don't say this because I believe it, I say it because I know it will make the men happy, and right now, all I want to do is make them happy.

The men clap loudly and yell, *C'est bon! C'est bon!*

My final moments in Djon are reserved for a private meeting with Chief Atododji, who recently returned home from the hospital. Kofi, Didier, and Pascal accompany me into the chief's quarters, and Pascal announces me. I get down on my knees before the chief, so very tiny in his bed now, so he can see my face. Taking his hands, I thank him for everything he and the village have done for me. The chief, no longer able to speak, smiles at me.

Translating Chief Atododji's unspoken sentiments to me, his secretary says: "Chief Atododji would like to thank you for your work with the *jeunes filles* of Akebou. He wishes you to take back to America all the greetings of the village. And you must please thank your family and your loved ones for allowing you to come to Africa and to leave them for so long."

When I hear this, I feel satisfied, proud, and humble—all at the same time. How can I explain to the chief how grateful I am? How can I explain the eyes Africa has given me?

I take Chief Atododji's hand and say, simply, "I will thank them."

Togo Postscript, Five Years Later

The first time I had to stay overnight in the Peace Corps medical unit at Lomé, I had been in Togo about six months. I cut short my work on the Take Our Daughters to Work Day so Beatrice could treat a massive rash that mysteriously appeared on my back. The rash itched painfully, making it difficult to wear shirts, much less a bra. Beatrice was confounded: Shingles? A heat rash? Insect bite? Because nobody could figure it out, I was kept in the med unit, out of the heat, for nearly five days.

Alone in the artificial, air-conditioned, hospital-like room, I wrote the following journal entry.

Journal entry
I dread the thought of going back to the United States. I dread it! I fear that I will become so bored and complacent and unstimulated and unhappy . . . I miss things about home. But here, I have so much. I don't think I will ever be the same after Africa, but I'm afraid I may be wrong. It's so easy to forget village life in this air-conditioned haven. Who knows what will happen in the States?"

Writing this book is one way I chose to remember my village life. I wrote it to counter the dread that permeated the journal entry, which I still feel today. I did write my story to memorialize my own experience, but I also wrote it to bring other people along for the ride, and to shine some light on a place, on a people, and on certain phenomena that are otherwise hidden, ignored, or romanticized.

I have focused my attention—in both form and content—on demands of the head, heart, and body that are typically relegated to the margins in Peace Corps memoirs (as well as ethnographic research). In the next chapter I will discuss more fully the decisions made in the process of constructing this book. This chapter provides a brief postscript to my experience, an update on some of the threads left hanging when I departed from Togo.

⅋

I left Togo on March 23, 2001, six months before my official "close of service." I traveled first to Houston, to sort out my mail and my post-doctoral life, which my sister Patricia had handled by proxy while I was gone. After a week in Houston, I traveled to San Antonio, where I stayed with my mother, and often, my friend Jessie, for nearly six months while I looked for an academic job.

During that time, I reconnected to friends in Florida and Texas, took sporadic phone calls from Maxim, and drank lots of gin and tonic—usually while watching *Globetrekker* on Jessie's satellite TV. I liked comparing the experiences of the host travelers with my experience in Togo. I missed Africa terribly.

I had great difficulty readjusting to life in the United States, to put it mildly. Peace Corps literature states readjustment takes a minimum of two years and I needed every single day of it! I found I was disgusted with the consumerism I saw in the developed world, and I floundered in a struggle to maintain the simplicity I had lived in Africa. Witness some of my journal entries, post-Togo.

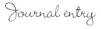

Two days after leaving Togo

I feel fine, no serious revelations. I have sporadic and strong bouts of thirst, hunger, and a need to defecate. I am somewhat dazed and stunned, by everything. It's too much. Too much. I just want to hibernate. I passed a group of women while walking Patricia's dog and fought the urge to yell *Bonsoir!* at them. I didn't. I still feel as if I'm being watched. I can't even concentrate to write.

After three days

I'm feeling fine. We went out to Taco Cabana last night and had beer and nachos—yum! Patricia hugged me and told she was very glad I am here. I am too. I can't do much, it seems; I am on sensory overload. I keep losing my footing, and find myself avoiding a lot. No Border's, not yet. No museums, not yet. Not a lot, not yet.

First observations: Everyone has nice cars ("Houston is a big phat car town," my sister says). You have to drive everywhere. Credit cards. You can hide out from the world; no one can stop you from hiding. Food everywhere. All kinds. Everyone here has so much free time. To work! That's what they use it for, working.

Patricia says being with me is like being with Tom Hanks in that movie, *Big*.

After ten days

Douglas, my dissertation chair, said he was surprised I wasn't depressed. I told him I am avoiding talking to people and I am staying indoors. I told him I miss reading, I miss the stars, and I miss my village. "You need to guard your privacy," he says.

I am noticing frustration/audacity/complete *astoundment* (Is that a word? As I told Douglas, "My English is all screwy") at the following.

Everyone thinks it is so hot! But if I don't have to worry about putting sunscreen on at 7 in the morning because my face is burning, it's not hot.

The things people talk about! Nothing! Time is spent discussing nothing, and yet everyone is in such a hurry because there is no time.

Of course, too much TV. Stupid waste of time, just watching nothing. Nothing of any significance.

How tame the partying is! Last night, at the club with my friend Jessie, the "crazy" dancing was so tame. It's as if everybody's life factor is at 70 percent. No one is at 100 percent, no one is really all here. Everyone is holding back . . . something. All the time. It is so weenie.

I have this curious fascination with black people—couples, women, men. I can't stop watching them. I'm so curious. I want to see them, to know them. They look like strangers to me and at the same time, they don't. As if I knew them before they became black! Silly, huh?

After twenty-three days

Signs I've adjusted to the developed world: I channel surf. I don't notice not exercising. I've gained weight. No more *franglais*.

And signs that I haven't: I still get too excited when I see food. I still hate TV, would rather read or talk. I still want to say *Bonjour!* to people on the street. I still lapse into French when emotional.

After 6 weeks

All white people look alike. Everyone wears the same kinds of clothes, shoes, hairstyles.

Everyone watches the same shows on TV. I can count on one hand the number of good talks I've had since I've been back. I couldn't keep track in Peace Corps.

I am no longer able to get up at 6 A.M., *sans problèmes*. It's all about work, and money, and it's all oh-so-superficial. Nobody (strangers) seems to care about anyone else. Example: I tucked in a woman's dress label for her one night in a San Antonio club. A week later, I saw the same situation at another event, Taste of New Orleans, and no one had told the girl or, better yet, fixed it for her. Never would happen in Africa.

I can't live here!!!

✢

As I finish this book, it has been five years since I left Togo. Some of the changes I experienced immediately post Africa persist: I still wear sweaters and long sleeves when it is 75 degrees outside; my bowels continue to be a health gauge; I am still overwhelmed by restaurant menus; I still bike fifty miles at a time.

I find it interesting that Africa made me more tolerant of certain things, such as not having electricity or running water, or eating with my fingers, but less tolerant of others, such as superficiality, or spending money frivolously. Living in Africa disoriented me into wakefulness. The Third World gave me new eyes with which to view my life in the First World. I have tried to convey a sense of that disorientation, that double vision, in this book. How disorienting it all was for me! And how very necessary.

✢

Maxim arrived in the United States three months after I had left Togo, on a tourist visa (we had planned for a fiancé visa if he couldn't get the tourist visa). The visa allowed him to stay for three months. The visit was terrible. When Maxim arrived, my mother's heart had stabilized. I had no money, no car, and I had spent three months job hunting and dealing with my readjustment to the First World. I had missed Maxim and Africa enormously. I looked forward to Maxim's upcoming visit, and I was eager to start my first academic job.

Maxim stayed with me and my family for a few days, then traveled with me as I began my first academic job in another state. During my trip for the job interview, which took place before Maxim's arrival, I had found a house to rent in the town's historic district. It was gorgeous—over 100 years old, with 7 rooms and 16-foot ceilings, hardwood floors, a gas fireplace, wallpaper, a new kitchen, and it was very affordable at my new salary. I loved the house immediately. But when Maxim saw it in the cold light of day after we arrived via Amtrak, he was not so enthusiastic. "It's old," he said.

At my new university, they were very appreciative of my Peace Corps service. They knew I had come directly to them without furniture, a car, or even my books. To show their support, the faculty, staff, and students threw me (and Maxim) a surprise housewarming, with a roomful of gifts, kitchen and cleaning supplies, a toaster oven, and canned food. It was an amazing gesture. Yet, at home with our stash of gifts, Maxim was upset. He wanted to know why my university colleagues had decided to shower me with gifts. "What did you tell them!" he cried, embarrassed.

I was glad to be in a new town, with a new job. But without money in the bank or transportation, it was stressful. During the weeks of Maxim's stay, he and I had to walk to the library and the grocery store or rely on rides from neighbors or new university acquaintances. It was a small town; these inconveniences seemed very slight to me. Also, stress didn't mean the same thing to me after Togo: *Ça va aller*, it'll pass, I thought. I knew money would come with time, and I didn't worry about what I was lacking.

I was keenly aware of the things I did have: A house to live in, a place to sleep, food to eat (so much food I couldn't believe it). I could telephone my mother anytime I wanted. I had meaningful employment. According to my journal, I had "lots of open questions! No fixed end in sight!" I felt satisfied, and was content.

But Maxim had a completely different view of my post–Peace Corps life. He seemed ashamed. In his view, I had "a lot of problems." Possibly he had expected me to have all the things he had heard North Americans and Europeans are supposed to have, and of course I had none of them. I was taken aback by his reaction to my situation; he didn't seem like the Togolese people among whom I lived in Djon. And then I remembered that Maxim was raised in the capital, and had studied for a time in France. He did not relate to my village life in Togo, nor could he appreciate the village mentality I had acquired.

Two pivotal incidents illuminated the cultural gap between us. I learned that Maxim was a religious fundamentalist; he had never revealed how often he attended church and church study groups. The first pivotal moment involved a dinner invitation we'd received in San Antonio from a gay couple who are mutual friends of mine and Jessie's. Maxim was gracious, as always, about the dinner plans, but he made sure to tell me his view about the men, who he'd never met, with these words: "Homosexuality is civilized decadence and an abomination."

We had never discussed same-sex relationships in Togo. However, we'd always had wonderfully intellectual discussions, and so I figured we'd have one now. Instead, Maxim pulled out his Bible to show me what he said was true. He'd never done this in Togo (neither had any other Togolese person I knew, despite their religious views), and I was mortified.

I knew that, despite his beliefs, Maxim would go to the dinner and charm the male couple with his *politesse*—just as he effortlessly charmed everyone he met—and no one would be the wiser. I cancelled the dinner. I loathe duplicity among intimates, and I am even less tolerant of it after living in West Africa. I didn't talk to Maxim for hours after the Bible incident, and I didn't tell my friends the real reason I'd cancelled the dinner. I tried not to let the incident get in our way, but the moment stuck with me.

A second pivotal moment occurred when Maxim neglected to tell me he was in the midst of a religious fast at the time he arrived in the United States. This meant he could not eat until after 5 P.M. (which I knew was part of the fast), and it also meant that we could not have sex (which I didn't know was part of the fast). Although Maxim had started the fast in Togo, he didn't tell me about it for two weeks. I had attributed our lack of sex to our disjointed connection, our travel from New York City to San Antonio, and his newness in the country. When I learned about the sexual aspect of the fast, I told Maxim, "If you're fasting, that means I must fast too. I wish you had told me." Maxim did not see it that way, and I was more confused than ever.

When Maxim left after a month to visit an uncle in Atlanta, he took all his things with him. He wouldn't give me a date of return. "I can't," he said. When I spoke to him on the phone a week later (it took that long before he returned my calls), he told me clearly, "Laurie, I will not make plans with you. You have too many problems." I was devastated.

Fortunately, human hearts are resilient, and eventually I healed. I did not hear from Maxim again for years. Then he sent me an email in which he apologized for the way he had treated me, saying he would come to the United States one day soon, and "make it up to me." By this time, I was involved with the man whom I would later marry. I told Maxim not to worry about making anything up to me. "It isn't necessary," I said, and meant it. We didn't correspond again until I contacted him about this book, which I will discuss in the next chapter.

It was not the loss of the relationship with Maxim that was so hard to accept; rather, I had to deal with the loss of what he represented to me. Maxim represented Togo, and my ongoing belief that people can cross cultural barriers in matters of love, despite geography. In Togo, I romanticized my relationship with Maxim. I did not deal with him as I'd want someone to deal with me, honestly and forthrightly—as I'd dealt with René, for example.

I thought that Maxim and I had crossed many barriers in Togo and, there, our lives seemed full of possibility. But now, I am not so sure; perhaps the gaps between us would have simply taken longer to surface in Togo. In my experience, dinner invitations from openly gay couples were not as common in Togo as they are in the States. Religious fasts in Togo didn't stand out for me there the way Maxim's stood out here. Still, it is curious to me that Maxim did not reveal how important his religion was to him. He chose not to tell me about what was most important to him. I chose to believe he was secular.

Maxim was very unhappy with my set of "problems" in the First World: he didn't expect them, he didn't want to deal with them, he couldn't respect that they had value to me, how much they related to my emerging identity. Not having been to this country before, Maxim could not see my "problems" as I did. He could not believe deprivations would pass; he could not understand that the things I was lacking did not affect who I am or what I am made of. That's why I went to Togo in the first place—to sort those things out.

Ironically, back here, it was as if I had become the resigned *Africaine*, and Maxim the materialistic American.

René and I kept in touch intermittently by email for several years. He has moved to Europe and is doing very well. Nyalewossi moved to Lomé and finished school; I have lost touch with her, unfortunately. I have not had any contact with Antoine.

The bishop who facilitated the *harcèlement sexuel* meeting retired, Chief Atododji passed away, and Togo has a new president (although he is the former president's son, who many think gained office illegally). Since I left Togo, the village of Djon has had a second, and then a third, Peace Corps GEE volunteer.

My mother continues to adjust to her new life of leisure as an early retiree. I am deeply grateful for her stable health and steady heart. Each time I speak to or hear from one of my Togolese (or Peace Corps) friends, I have the opportunity to say how grateful I am, because they always ask about her. My mother acquired a sort of fame among the people I knew in Togo.

Marguerite now lives and works in Lomé. She updates me regularly on her life, by email, as does Pascal. I think Marguerite was greatly relieved when I married. One of her recent questions has been, playfully, *Laurie, quand vas-tu faire le premier bébé?* Laurie, when will you make your first baby? Marguerite is like a sister/daughter to me; our relationship continues to be one of the lights in my life. Sophie, the Togolese GEE program director occasionally emails from Lomé, and I remain close to Shoshana, who now lives in Europe.

Bernadette is the Togolese person I miss the most, the one whose company I still long for, someone I think about often. She wrote me a brief letter, which I received shortly after I returned home. In it, she told me she had moved to Aného to be with her son's father, because her son had been quite ill. She asked me to pray for her, to think about her. She said she hoped to be back at her stand in Kougnohou soon.

Before she signed the letter, Bernadette wrote: "Laurie, I need you to come back to Togo." I imagine Bernadette's serious, dignified face, barely hiding mischief. "Laurie, I need to have you here, so that we can go eat fufu with agouti sauce, your favorite."

I look forward to that day.

Constructing an Intimate Text

I have always felt that truth is prophetic, that if you describe precisely what you see and give it life with your imagination, then what you write ought to have lasting value, no matter the mood of your prose.

Paul Theroux, *Fresh Air Fiend*[1]

[T]o observe [or interview] others is to colonize them. To write their experiences in your book or article is to use them. It is to place yourself, as author, in a superior relationship to the persons you are observing, hearing, and analyzing.

Goodall, as cited in Nick Trujillo
In Search of Nauny's Grave[2]

Language can never contain a whole person, so every act of writing a person's life is inevitably a violation.

Josselson, as cited in Carolyn Ellis
Telling Secrets, Revealing Lives[3]

In Togo, we volunteers had a lovely book-lending system, built up over Peace Corps' long presence in the country. Over the years, books have been sent by family and friends to volunteers, or brought to the country by the volunteers themselves, and then left, supplying future volunteers with several well-stocked libraries that are scattered at volunteer houses throughout Togo. Peace Corps memoirs are well represented in the collection.

I had not read any Peace Corps memoirs prior to Togo; however, I read quite a number of them while I was there. What struck me about many of them was the tendency of the authors to paint rosy pictures of their lives as volunteers. It was ironic to read these memoirs as a PCV in Togo, because most of them did not seem to fit the experience I was having, nor that of my volunteer friends.

Rarely were we privy to the emotional, embodied vulnerability of the author.[4] In a sense, many of the Peace Corps' memoirs I read were very much in the tradition of modernist, realist ethnographies. Some focused on rigor, others on imagination,[5] but rarely did a memoir achieve both. Also, most of the memoirs tended to focus primarily on the "other," ignoring the wealth of subjectivities and assumptions inherent in the author's gaze.

I liked the informal, rich detail of these memoirs, but I was hungry for stories that were more like the experience I was having in Togo: messy, full of unanswered questions, surprising discoveries, and unpleasant revelations. Similarly, so much of the experience was tied up in emotions and bodily sensations; it is hard to intellectualize parasites, intense heat, or romantic/sexual complexities. For me, dealing with the multiple facets of living in the Third World required incredible emotional engagement and exquisite attention to the body. I promised myself that if I ever wrote a book about my time in Togo, I would make such things transparent in the text; I would not shy away from the roses or the thorns.

In Togo, I wrote my experience from multiple perspectives. I was a Peace Corps volunteer, but I was also a single woman in my thirties, a U.S. citizen assigned to a project on girls' education in a developing country, a recent PhD thrust into the role of ex-pat *fonctionnaire*. Each of these roles brought unique experiences with Togolese people, which in turn revealed unusual emotional, embodied, and intellectual reactions in me. It was an extremely disorienting but also fascinating experience.

To cope with the disorientation, to understand the experiences I was having, I wrote. I wrote to make sense of my strange new world; I wrote to think my way through all I was seeing and hearing and feeling; I wrote to remind myself of the person I was before I arrived in Togo and to understand the person I was becoming. I wrote to survive the experience,[6] head, heart, and body intact.

Getting Down the Details

In Togo, I kept two different types of journals. I had a daily *cahier* (French notebook) journal, in which I documented interactions, conversations, and observations, and I had a slim hardcover notebook in which I wrote longer reflections, usually several times a week. In the hardcover notebooks, I tended to write essay-style observations on phenomena about which I wanted to ponder, such as my early flirtations with Maxim, or how it felt to hire a woman, Honorine, to do my laundry for me. By the end of my service, I had twelve volumes of the *cahiers* (about 100 pages each) and two notebooks of essays (about 200 pages each).

I kept my *cahier* journal in my *sac de secrets*, as Bernadette called it, and consistently wrote down things I heard or saw throughout the day. I often wrote in my journal while sitting at Bernadette's stand, or at Nyalewossi's, or in the *marché*. My journal writing was fairly public; you may remember that René once asked to read sections of my journal, and that Maxim, who often found me writing in my journal during training, surmised that I would write a book in five years' time. (As I write this, it has been five years since I left Togo.)

A third documentation method I used was letter writing. My third month in Togo, I began to carbon copy all my letters home. I decided to archive my letters because my early letters felt like good writing to me; my family commented on how descriptive and detailed the letters were. To document the letters, I bought large French notebooks the size of legal pads and three pieces of carbon paper, which I used to copy each letter I wrote. I had accumulated five volumes of letters by the end of my service. Many of my fellow volunteers approved of my carbon copying strategy; several told me they planned to ask family and friends for copies of their letters upon their return to the United States. However, my research background made me less sanguine about that method. It seemed wiser to "get the data down," right in the moment, than to wait for a future moment that might never come.

At the time, I did not know what the final product of all this writing would be. I don't think I even had a final product in mind, although since I had already written a book based on a qualitative research project (a doctoral dissertation), another did not seem out of the question. However, I did not think of my documentation methods as the raw material for a book. Rather, I thought of my journals, essays, and letters as a useful method to document the experience, for myself, and my family and friends. Several years would pass before I could see how strongly an inductive rigor had informed my writing methods in Togo. Nearly the entire content of this book originates with the journals, essays, and letters I wrote while I was in Togo.

Weaving a Story Out of Details

After I returned from Togo, I kept my Togolese journals, essays, and archived letters in a box along with other Peace Corps Togo memorabilia. In the back of my mind, I wondered if I had a story in all those journals. Was there a book in there? A scholarly paper? A memoir? A novel? I wasn't sure.

My journals and other "data" sat neatly in a cardboard box for months, then an entire year, before I was ready to deal with them. But what to do? I knew the story of my experience was in the everyday details of my journals and letters. So, I decided to start there. A year after I returned from Togo, I began the process of transcribing the contents of my twelve *cahier* journals. I remember this early process as very insular, personal, and exciting. Going over every paragraph in my journals brought back many memories of Togo, and allowed me travel vicariously in a way that was very satisfying at a time when I was undergoing major personal and professional transitions.

Next, I transcribed my two hardback volumes of essays, and the five "volumes" of letters. I also transcribed field notes from conferences (such as the WILDAF women's conference in Lomé), and trainings I attended. I transcribed these latter materials for two years. In the meantime, I changed academic positions, moved across the country, and wrote other scholarly pieces that now seem precursor to this book.[7]

Overall, my transcribing process lasted for three years. At first, I did my transcribing at my leisure, when I had time, when I wanted to reminisce about Togo. However, in the second and third year of transcribing, I began to get more excited and organized about it, because I could see a story forming. I did not know exactly what story would emerge from the details of my documentation, but I recognized this uncertainty from previous qualitative projects. I wouldn't know what the data had to say until I began to analyze their patterns.

When I had a combined document of all the journal, letters, and essays, I focused on recognizing patterns in the material. I decided to do this in a visually dramatic way, because the document was extremely long, nearly five hundred pages, and overwhelming to look at. To size it down, I color-coded text to indicate themes, ideas, or experiences that emerged repeatedly. For example, many passages referred to religious/animist themes and experiences with priests; for those, I chose the color brown. Purple went to my experiences in the work with young girls, pink to represent the romantic/sexual experiences with Maxim and René, blue to represent any incident or narrative chunk that seemed especially moving or profound but didn't fit anywhere else. I also assigned certain colors to the "characters" who appeared most often: Bernadette, Odette, Nyalewossi, Marguerite, and others.

I continued with the color coding, which was a kind of editing process, until I had very little text left that was black. Then I deleted details that did not seem to contribute to a coherent narrative.[8] This was difficult to do at first—every detail seemed important. But I was determined that the document not read like a journal but a story, one that could appeal to an audience wider than me, my friends, and my family. I wanted the story to be personal, but I did not want readers to feel as if they were reading a diary. So I took out what seemed to me solely diary material that did not contribute to the overall narrative. Eventually, I began to think of my writing process as constructing a story, rather than transcribing a journal.

Shifting to the role of storyteller, I made many other choices. I changed the tense from past to present. I made the people I wrote about "speak" the dialogue I had heard them say (and fortunately written down, many times verbatim, in my journals). I removed dates preceding each journal entry; instead, I labeled passages according to a theme that emerged from something in the passage (A Question of *Mentalité*, The Little Things That Matter). As I wrote and edited, I changed the names of the themes many times. Eventually, these themes evolved into chapters, with a discernible chronological order.

Later, as stories began to emerge out of the many details, I read passages out loud to hear whether they rang true. When they didn't, which was often, I went back to the passage and looked for the reason. Usually, I had not made something transparent enough. Then, I focused more precisely on writing a careful and meticulous lead-in to the complex interaction I was trying to portray. When I had difficult judging my success with this, which was also often, I read passages out loud to my husband, to a close female friend, and to my sister.

By reading passages out loud, I was able to witness my first audience reactions to the material and experience firsthand the emotion certain passages might evoke in readers. (It was fascinating that my micro-audiences routinely reacted differently to the same bit of text—making me more conscious of another goal in the book, which I will address in a moment.)

Reading passages out loud also changed my point of reference about the book: I began to think of the work as public. As I experienced the diverse comments, I was compelled to think more critically about ways in which the listener's reaction could actually help me expand my ideas about the book's form and content, and thus improve the text. This was in marked contrast to my earlier view, which was more about defending my version as the story that was most "true."[9] Gradually, I surrendered the idea that I had any control over how readers might respond to the book.[10] At first this was scary; eventually I found it liberating.

Increasing the Story's Literary Coherence

Soon after this, I felt ready to send the work for review to a colleague, a writer familiar with autoethnography and autobiography. As a result of her suggestions, I made significant changes to the book, all of which focused on managing the story for the reader.

I collapsed the female Peace Corps volunteers into one person, who I named Shoshana (initially I had had four female PCVs in the story). I forced myself to delete stories about my travels to the West African countries of Benin and Ghana, as well as to France and the United States, during my time in Togo. I abbreviated information about my mother's poor health and the manner in which I found out about it, collapsing many months of contacts and indecision into several weeks and a few sentences. I removed vignettes about the U.S. presidential election of 2000. Each of these decisions was designed to streamline the story for the reader.

Additionally, I addressed my numerous letters home to fewer people, focusing on my mother, sister, and Oded. (I had written letters to nearly twenty different people while in Togo—too many to put in the book.) Letters I wrote to several female friends back home are addressed in the text only to one person—my sister, Patricia. In some cases, when a letter was particularly compelling but did not work well as a letter in the overall story, I made it a bit of narrative in the text. For example, some of the stories on bush taxi travel were written in letters to my brother David; my brother Paul was the recipient of a letter about "The Little Things that Matter," some of the content of which appears in Chapter 2. For the book, I edited these letters, shortening them a great deal.

Another literary strategy I used was to focus more intently on character development. In the first draft, René's character came across most fully. This was in stark contrast to Maxim, who did not come across well in early drafts. In hindsight, I think that René was easier for me to represent because I had spent so much time with him, while Maxim had lived hundreds of miles away. Also, I had many interactions with René in which I learned something meaningful about myself. This was precisely the kind of thing I tended to write down.

I had many meaningful interactions with Maxim, of course, but many of those occurred in the context of his work life in Lomé. Also, I wrote less in my journal during my Lomé visits than I typically did in Djon, where I had so much free time. Further, I knew much less about Maxim than I did about René—although I did not think so at the time. It was a writing challenge for me to leave the reader with this contrary impression of Maxim, while developing Maxim's character more fully in the overall story.

To add depth to Maxim's character, I collapsed several conversations I had with him into one interaction, rather than relating multiple conversations that occurred over 18 months' time. I also inserted some of our conversations in geographic "places" and chronological "times" where they did not actually occur.

I focused on adding depth to Antoine and Bernadette's characters. To do this, I went back through my journals, pictures, letters, and emails (to my sister Patricia, with whom I discussed Maxim and Antoine at length), as well as the letter I'd written to the bishop. These materials helped me to both remember and reconstruct[11] interactions that I had with each person.

To build Bernadette's character more fully, I added the story of her experience with the police officer who tried to build his house on her land, and in it, described details about her personality and her facial expressions (evident in the many pictures I have). I also added details about the way I felt when I was around Bernadette, to more fully illustrate her persona to the reader.

To build Antoine's character more fully, I included the story about his visit to Italy, some details on the numerous brief working trips we'd taken together, and also the story of how his truck followed my taxi. As a bonus, the latter episode also helped to explain the unpleasant culmination of our relationship, which had been unclear in early drafts. Later, I realized I had not included the story in the initial drafts because, unbelievably, I had not written about it in any of my journals or in any letter home.

To reconstruct my memory of that event, I borrowed Ellis' evocation method.[12] I focused on re-imagining the experience, and on how I felt being chased in the taxi; in so doing, I remembered how afraid I had been. Tellingly, re-feeling the fear also helped me recall subtle details of the event.

Bringing Heart and Body Out of the Closet

When I began to read excerpts of the work to others, I reached an important turning point in constructing the text—the end of my private story and the beginning of the public one. Shelley Green described autoethnography as an outing process.[13] Her description fit my experience writing this book. When I began to think of the book as my "outing," I was able to make a more widely informed set of decisions in the writing process. These decisions were prompted by questions about potential audience reactions to the text. Who will the audience see? Who do I want them to see? Am I ready to be seen in ways that may be uncomfortable? By asking these questions, I also began to think more about the kinds of relationships readers would have with each of the characters in the book (not just my character), and the decisions I could make about how to represent them.

In Togo, I felt I lived so many different identities, some of which I embraced and many of which I rejected, and most of which were contrary to nearly every way I'd identified myself back home. I wanted the complexity of the stories to elicit a cacophony of reactions. To me, this is the very nature of the Peace Corps experience—it's entirely unique, individual, and surprising in the effect it has on the volunteer. I wanted readers to experience that too—so I focused on presenting the details of interactions, rather than on tying up all the loose ends. I provided in-depth glimpses of the multiple roles I lived during my time in Togo, with details that illustrated the complexity of my everyday life there, so as to evoke multiple and varied reactions for the reader and thus engage them in my experience.

Although I have attempted to be varied and inclusive in accounting for readers' different experience of the text, I wrote the book with specific intentions in mind. I bring particular identities out of the closet. In this book, I out the restless 30-something woman with a PhD. I out the ambivalent Peace Corps volunteer. I out the woman who used and was used by Togolese men for sex, love, and companionship. I out the feminist ensnared in a postcolonial, patriarchal Third World. I out the Latina absent her cultural identity, which emerged only after, and as a result of, my Togo experience.

By constructing this book along the lines of narrative ethnography, I also out myself as a certain type of researcher—she who appreciates lived experience as a worthy academic endeavor, values personal vulnerability over self-certainty in scholarly writing, and strives for qualitative rigor alongside—but not at the expense of—qualitative imagination.[14] That's my broad daylight.[15] That's the person I see in this book.

Writing About Friends and Enemies from a Relational Perspective

Unlike traditional ethnographic research, autoethnography is not necessarily done with those "whom we have no prior relationships and plan no future interaction."[16] Autoethnographic research is unique in that it illuminates methodological practices that acknowledge and expand understandings of how phenomena exist in relationship. Because relationships change in the course of research,[17] the strategies autoethnographers choose to manage the ethics of writing about these relationships need to be equally fluid. In this research, I discussed relationships with friends as well as "ex-friends." To write about both sets of these "others," I was impelled to devise specific ethical strategies to guide my representation, in writing, of the people I portray in this book.

I described here many intimate friendships that helped me further my understanding of life with the Togolese. The "involvement, compassion, giving, and vulnerability"[18] I experienced with the people who appear in this book was extremely productive for me epistemologically, both in the living of the experience and the writing of it. Information I gleaned from these relationships greatly contributed to my understanding of the "other," and also, necessarily, of myself as an "other."

However, I had also experienced "authentic engagement" and relational knowing that occurred in "meaningful and sustained ways"[19] with people in this book who I no longer identify as friends. Indeed, my relationships shifted in unpredictable ways throughout my time in Togo; friendships went awry, became out of kilter, or reverted to something that felt marginal and oppressive. Could I be honest about how I felt toward the people of whom I'd written, despite our terminated friendships? Could I incorporate and acknowledge in my analysis and text construction both the desire and repulsion I felt for them?[20] How was I to write such unpleasant relational "data"?

I wanted to engage readers "intellectually, aesthetically, emotionally, ethically, and politically" with all of the characters in the book, but I knew I could not do so by relying solely on the rubric of friendship, because I was no longer in friendship with several key persons in the text.[21] Even more significant, I had learned a great deal from the intimacies with the "ex-friends" as well as the "friends." In fact, pivotal moments in my experience came directly from the unpleasantness I shared with people who are now "ex-friends." To write about these intimate relationships, I had to come up with a more expansive metaphor. Rather than suppress my upset or disapproval at some of the interactions with ex-friends,[22] I wanted to discuss how I dealt with those feelings as they occurred.

In this book, I strived to be accountable to the text in a way that was true to my character, and to keep in mind the consequences this would have for others. I continue to feel engaged with Togo; I expect to return there someday; I wanted to write about everyone in a way that was as fair and just as I could manage. If and when I return to Togo, I will likely see most of the people I portray in this book. So, I asked myself: How could I be humane, even with those I am no longer close to? Was I willing to be responsible for my actions and their potential effects? Could I remain true to my story, to my version of the world I inhabited in Togo? Could I do this in a way that did not come at the expense of the village where I lived and worked?

Carolyn Ellis has suggested that researchers engaged in these dilemmas not focus on what they are *supposed* to do, but rather, constantly ask the question, "What should I do now?"[23] Ellis advocated a relational ethical stance, which allows researchers to act from both "heart and mind," acknowledge the "interpersonal bonds" to others, and display a willingness to take "responsibility for actions and consequences" of their work.[24]

In a sense, a relational ethical decision-making process was one I lived every day in Togo. I often thought about how I could behave in a way that would maintain my own integrity but still allow me to be considerate of the community and village mores. I wanted to meet my own needs, varied as they were, but I also tried to do so in a way that was respectful of the cultural context I had joined.[25] For example, René and I never openly acknowledged our affair in public, and we took great pains to keep our relationship a secret.

History is always revisionist. When I suspected that my version of history, as constructed in this book, would likely collide with that of the character I was writing about, I asked myself Ellis' question: "What should I do now?" I also considered "my characters' " reactions to "my text" as I wrote. I imagined myself, book in hand, a year or two from now: Could I present all of the passages with confidence? What reactions did I think my stories would invite? Would I be willing to embrace the consequences?

Now that I was writing the text about the lived experience, I thought a good strategy was to be consistent with how I had participated in the lived experience. Could I consider both the context in which I lived and the context in which I wrote? Could I maintain a double-description, a bi-nocular vision,[26] that acknowledged both contexts, U.S. and Togolese? I asked myself, "Am I writing anything that would be an unpleasant surprise to the character? Can I look him or her in the eye and read this?"[27] These questions provided a useful template for me to evaluate my ethical decision-making process as I wrote.[28]

With this template in hand, I chose to conduct follow-up interviews with some of the people described in the book. In some cases, I had no trouble incorporating the person's feedback into the text. In other cases, my re-contacting efforts resulted in new strategies I could use to introduce further reflexivity into my project. However, I did not contact everyone, for reasons I shall discuss in a moment.

I was often faced with the "What should I do now?" question when I felt my U.S. worldview too strongly collided with a Togolese worldview. If I did not know what to do, if I felt truly confounded about how to proceed (a sensation I often felt in Togo as well), I did what I had done in Togo: I consulted with a Togolese citizen. In this case, the person was Marguerite. Marguerite became a very useful consultant on ways to deal with the Togolese "ex-friends" during the writing of this book. She also became an important editorial resource, a process I will describe in more detail later.

Introducing a Relational, Ethical Reflexivity in the Writing Process

I wrote to Maxim and René first, by email, to tell them I had signed a book contract to publish the story of my experience in Togo and to tell them they were both characters in the book. In my introductory salutations, I told each of them I was a newlywed. I chose to say this up front because I did not want either man to misconstrue my email as a romantic invitation. Both Maxim and René had written me emails in the recent past that implied or suggested a reunion.

Boundaries set forth, I told each something about the book. I told them that, in the book, I discussed my experiences as a GEE volunteer, my observations of Africa, and my relationships with Togolese people. I explained that since each had been part of my life in Togo, each was portrayed in the book. I told them that while I'd changed their names and other identifying details, it might still be possible for someone to identify them.

René immediately congratulated me on my recent marriage, and suggested I telephone him, giving me his cell phone number. He was forthright and clear in his response to me about my concerns: "I think it is fine you changed my name and the name of my workplace. Please do not use any pictures of me—I don't see how that can help me at all."

Maxim told me he was "surprised but happy" to hear from me. He stated he was worried about what I had written in the book. In another email, I explained that I had written about how we met, fell in love, had a relationship, and parted. I told him, while I did intend to publish the book, I did not want to disturb his life in any way; I was willing to hear his point of view. What did he think about the fact that I had written a book?

Maxim did not contact me for several days. When he next wrote, he did not reveal any thoughts regarding the book. Curious about the omission, I prompted Maxim for an answer. I was beginning to feel frustrated. Maxim seemed cagey and guarded; I was reminded too vividly of our experiences when he had visited me in the United States.

I prompted Maxim by reminding him of some things he'd said to me during his disastrous visit: "I tell everyone the minimum they need to know"; "It's not good to tell everything to everyone"; and, "You talk too much." (I thought the last one was quite prophetic, given the nature of the book I had written.) In the next email, Maxim agreed that he still preferred to tell people only the minimum they needed to know. As far as my book was concerned, he said he could not comment on it without reading it first.

I took this as a sign Maxim wanted approval of what I wrote; he was concerned about how I had portrayed him. Privately, I was glad to hear this: maybe Maxim knew he had behaved badly with me when he was in the States; maybe he was regretful about his actions. Recall that Maxim had apologized to me for his behavior, in an email, about three years after he left here. "I'll make it up to you," he said. I had begged off, explaining it was not necessary because I had forgiven him. But had I? Was my book a way to seek justice for a wrong done to me?

I gave this question much thought. I had felt wronged by Maxim. But I also knew the book was about so much more than my relationship with him. Still, our experience together greatly informed my understandings about relations between men and women in Togo. Although I wanted more information from Maxim, I did not want to rehash old issues with him. But how to avoid it? How could I listen to Maxim's opinion, how could I share what I'd written, without losing myself in our old history? Weighing my welfare alongside his,[29] I made a compromise with myself. I would not give Maxim any drafts or pages of the book to review, because I could not figure out a way to do it without revisiting our relationship, an idea that made me acutely uncomfortable. However, I did feel comfortable sharing small chunks (via written messages) about some of the stories I'd reconstructed. Specifically, I wanted to be explicit with him about how I had depicted our sexual relationship.

Maxim and I agreed to discuss the book's content via Internet chat, and arranged a time to meet. I was careful to choose a time I thought optimal both for me in the United States and Maxim in Togo. Early afternoon and evening seemed best, so I arranged for a chat at 7 P.M. Togo time, 1 P.M. my time. Our first attempts to chat via Internet failed due to technological problems. Feeling bad about the failed attempts, I wrote an email to Maxim and apologized. In the next email, by now our sixth or seventh, Maxim reassured me: "Don't worry, we will find a time. I am here in the United States, so we can do it easily."

I was shocked to hear Maxim say he was in this country. I had been arranging times to speak with him based on my assumption that he was in Togo. Maxim, typically not wanting to share much of his life with anyone, never bothered to correct my assumption. I wanted to discuss how he viewed my transparency about our relationship and Maxim neglected to be transparent about being in the same time zone—a detail salient to when we'd have any discussion at all.

I realized in that moment that it didn't matter what story I told in the book—Maxim would not like any of it. How could I expect otherwise?

He'd hate my sharing so many personal details of our time together. Of course he wouldn't be happy, or accepting of it, and why should he be? That is his worldview—just as it was when I knew him. Why should I expect that my lived experience with him would be any different from my writing about the lived experience with him?[30] Extrapolating my thoughts easily after this episode, I recognized that, of course, Antoine would not like this book, either.

Focusing on *Othering* the Author

When I realized that Maxim (and very likely Bernadette, definitely Antoine, and perhaps even Sophie) would disagree with my decision to publish my personal Peace Corps memoir as an autoethnographic work on my Togo experience, I stopped trying to find ways to make the idea more palatable to them. Instead, I tried to be impeccable about the way I represented each of the characters in the book—including my own. I stopped trying to portray everyone in a flattering light so as not to risk offending them. Instead, I focused more precisely on portraying my character in as equally unforgiving a light as I had everyone else.

The epiphany I had after Maxim's email was another pivotal moment in the construction of this text. I was now challenged to evaluate whether I'd been as successful in portraying my own shortcomings as I had everyone else's. Had I inadvertently made myself look better? Had I really shown readers my "perceived warts and bruises" as well as my "accolades and successes?"[31] Had I "othered" myself in the same way I had "othered" the Togolese? Had I put us all on the same playing field, at least in terms of the text? Had I treated us both as knowing subjects, equally vulnerable in our relationships together?[32]

Expanding on this idea with regard to the other characters, I wondered, Can I make Antoine as appealing as I found him in my early time in Togo, and as frustratingly dense as I found him at the end? Can I depict Maxim so that the reader saw him as bewitching as I had early on, and as bewildering as I did at the end? Can I evoke in the reader a portrait of the Bernadette I so admired, the Bernadette I felt betrayed by, and the Bernadette whose choices were so obviously limited at the bishop's meeting? Even more significant, can I depict myself and my relationships with each of these people in a way that their behavior toward me made sense? Can I be honest and imaginative enough to portray my own character with the lenses through which Antoine, Maxim, and Bernadette may have seen me?

I challenged myself to depict each character so that each could inspire divergent feelings in the reader. My goal became to compel the reader to have diverse feelings about all the characters in the book—to love and hate everyone in it, at least once, while reading it. For this is how it felt to live the overall experience—I loved it and hated it, I was confused and charmed by it, I was frustrated and at peace with it. Could I convey that sense to the reader, and still maintain the narrative's coherence? I had not focused on this goal so intensely before contacting Maxim. Nor had I challenged myself to write my character in such a way that I might be fearful, like Maxim was, of how I was being portrayed.

Consulting a Togolese Woman for Editorial Advice

At this point, I had yet to have any critical reflections about the book from anyone Togolese, from anyone outside of my Euro-American worldview. In writing this book, I have inevitably "othered" the Togolese, despite my best intentions. However, was my book likely to harm the Togolese in ways I did not want? My most pressing ethical concern was to do with the village of Djon. Would my book hurt them in some way? How could I write my story, including the story with Antoine, who is from the village of Djon, and still feel I could return to the village, head held high, without regret? To figure this out, I took the same steps I'd often taken in Togo when stymied over a cultural morass—I consulted a Togolese woman for advice.

In this case, the most appropriate (and easily contacted) person was Marguerite. I had written Marguerite an email about the book (*C'est trés cool!* she said), and telephoned her in Togo one Sunday afternoon. I asked Marguerite for her advice. I told her I was wondering what she thought of being in the story, if she thought it was sufficient to change names, and if she thought my story about Antoine would be detrimental to the village of Djon. I paraphrase Marguerite's response here:

I think it is okay that you changed names, that you changed my name and my family's name. In my view, you don't need to worry about the village because the village has already had two volunteers since you left. Your report of Antoine has not adversely affected the village.

Oh. Why hadn't I thought of that? Marguerite continued, with confidence and clarity:

In my view, changing names is good but it won't protect him [Antoine] from knowing himself in the book—he'll know—but others won't necessarily know. There is nothing wrong with that—he did it, didn't he?

Marguerite's words lessened many of my concerns about the Antoine-Djon dilemma.[33]

They also reminded me I'd already made the story of Antoine's sexual harassment public knowledge—in Togo, anyway. I publicized the story in the form of the letter I gave to the bishop, which I'd copied to Peace Corps and to Sophie. In fact, I struggled mightily the first time around over whether to make my experience with Antoine public. The issues I was confronting in the writing process were not dissimilar from the ethical relational decision making I had done before.

Interestingly, if I had not already made the story public during my lived experience in Togo, I think I would have had more difficulty with writing the story for this book; I would have difficulty looking Antoine "in the eye."[34] However, Marguerite reminded me that I had already outed myself as a target of Antoine's sexual advances; I had already publicly discussed the behavior and feelings between us that resulted in my report to the bishop.

Duneier noted that "being a social scientist does not preclude having strong opinions, values, or feelings. But it demands a willingness to be public about the way they affect one's standards and the claims one makes."[35] In Togo, by reporting Antoine, I had already decided that the benefits of telling that story outweighed its potentially negative consequences.[36] By including these episodes in the book, I make the same claim, but to a wider, non-Togolese audience of social scientists, and I do so because of the potential value of this story toward better understanding the complexities between men and women in Togo.

I still have many questions about my experience with Antoine. One interesting idea I can't shake is that I am not sure how I would have handled my report to the bishop had I not left Togo early. I would like to believe I would have still made the report, but I have wondered how my imminent departure from Togo may have influenced my decision. I remember how torn I was—and how it felt so "American" to make a report like that. Also, I remember thinking about the girls I worked with, and how I wanted to be a model for them. But was I? I left Togo; I have no idea what the *jeunes filles* of Akebou know about my report. I also find it interesting that I had not written more about my decision-making process in my journals or letters; it's as if I had stopped reflecting on the complexities of my everyday life in Togo once I knew I was going "home."

I do think my story with Antoine reveals information about what can happen when values from one set of cultural beliefs (such as those to do with Catholicism) travel across continents and settle in with values from another set of cultural beliefs (such as those to do with polygamy in West Africa). I think the story raises interesting questions, and it's compelling to me today, even after five years. I am not sure my story provides any answers to such complex dilemmas. However, I do hope the story can lead to more informed questions about the existence of such phenomena in the first place.

Marguerite turned out to be a bigger help to me than I ever expected—just as she had been while I was in Togo. Marguerite edited the entire text, corrected my French[37] (and some of my English), and answered numerous questions about Togolese food, history, and phrases. When Marguerite didn't know the answer she took it upon herself to find out, with a research ingenuity I didn't know she had. Our numerous emails, in French, English, and lots of *Franglais*, became an important secondary data source for me.

I am embarrassed to admit I had not thought earlier to ask Marguerite to review the book; the idea did not occur to me until I wanted to ask her opinion about leaving Antoine's story in the book. I am appreciative of the emergent nature of qualitative work, and the reflexive nature of autoethnographic writing process in particular, both of which promoted my recognition (late as it was) of this now obvious strategy.

As for her opinion of the book, Marguerite assured me she would give me an honest opinion of its content, I needn't worry. After she read a few chapters, she told me, "The story is good because—I think—people need to know what goes on here." Later, when she finished the book and gave me my final list of corrections, she said (in poignant words that do not translate well in English, I'm afraid): "I find that you have really written what is at the bottom of your heart! It's good that Africa did so much for you—Africa revealed your true humanity, your real self, and this is very good, my sister!" I am greatly indebted to Marguerite for her many readings of the text, the chapters of which she downloaded at her office in Lomé, one at a time.

ꬽ

> At first, Africa assailed my senses. I smelled and tasted ethnographic things and was both repelled by and attracted to a new spectrum of odors, flavors, sights, and sounds.
>
> Paul Stoller
> *The Taste of Ethnographic Things"*[38]

Dead or Alive? Writing the Heart and Body into Autoethnography

In this book, the characters fuck, shit, have periods, sweat, get dirty, puke, and blow snot rockets.[39] They fall in love, disappoint each other, share affection, giggle together, romance, offend, and disturb each other. In this book, I illustrated my experiences in the country by using my head, heart, and body as resources for understanding. In Togo, I used my body and emotions as instruments both to help me survive and to make sense of the intensity of my life there. In concert with my intellect, each instrument revealed to me interesting patterns of information about phenomena that were new and unfamiliar to me.

This book illustrates how my emotional, embodied subjectivity was epistemologically productive.[40] The intense nature of my interactions in Togo engaged my senses in a way that promoted an extremely generative method for learning, evident in the quality of relationships I developed in Togo.[41] The emotional and embodied aspects of experience I have discussed in this book are not applicable solely to a small group of scholars. Rather, they are "relevant . . . and salient for all of us who engage in qualitative research."[42]

It wasn't just a sexual embodiment I experienced in Togo, my body was alive in so many other ways as well—whether sick or well, on my bike or sound asleep, in its fluctuations of weight or well-being. I have not focused on sharing or revealing aspects of my embodied experience solely to shock or titillate, but more important, because it was the only way I felt I could illustrate a coherent and rich account of the experience. Many of the bodily experiences I described in the book provided a template for me to ask more informed questions about the Togolese people's experiences of the same phenomena.

When I became ill with parasites, I had a unique understanding of how deadly such a treatable problem could be for a Togolese child. When I began to rely on my bike as a mode of transportation (instead of the bush taxi), I emulated the Togolese' incredible reserve of resourcefulness and ingenuity at problem-solving transportation dilemmas. I also, unexpectedly, gained many Djon villagers' respect for *le sport*, and, as a bonus, I earned a body that began to look less "U.S. American" (with extra pounds on it) and more "Togolese African" (with just enough pounds on it to get by).

In Africa, I experienced life at a heightened level of intensity. Giardia, diarrhea, muscles on 9-year-olds, insects in eyes, rain pounding on tin roofs, and, especially, sexual relations, were intense. I could not have written this account of my life there had I not been willing to immerse myself, to engage myself, to make myself vulnerable in the midst of that intensity, and to do so with a "critical, analytical, self-conscious awareness."[43] In my view, one cannot live honestly, productively, or fully in the Third World by any other means.[44]

Some of most the compelling stories in this book come from the characters' sexually embodied interactions—encounters that were desired and rejected, awkward and fulfilling, oppressive and liberating. As the "character" in this book who is also its author, I could not have told my story about Togo without including what I learned from those episodes, both where I was participant and where I was witness. I wrote the stories in an evocative and vivid format, reflecting upon them "critically and honestly," to better illustrate how they helped me locate myself and my beliefs within the context in which I was living.[45]

Typically, researchers' stories about sexual identity in the field have been on the margins of most social science literature. The unspoken assumption inherent in this literature was captured by anthropologist Esther Newton, who stated, "[W]hen a fieldworker writes in the first person, she or he thinks and sometimes feels but never actually lusts or loves."[46]

Newton pointed out that researchers' sexual identity hangs out on the margins of the literature because the sexual politics in the field of anthropology—a discipline that has greatly informed autoethnography—came of age at a time the New World was busy colonizing what is now the Third World. Because most anthropologists at that time (typically males) did not "problematize" their own sexuality, they inadvertently made male gender and heterosexuality a "norm," thus excluding the ways their sexual identity affected their "perspective, privilege, and power in the field." This oversight has made it very risky for women, people of color, and sexual minority writers to introduce their sexual identity in research texts later on.[47]

Citing Clifford Geertz, Newton also pointed out that, just as it is impossible for researchers to evade the burden of authorship, neither can the researcher avoid the burden of being seen as an erotic creature when in the field.[48] This is precisely how I felt many times in Togo. There were times I wanted to be seen as—and identified myself as—an erotic creature; however, there were many times I did not. The most poignant example of this for me is my experience with Antoine. I became accustomed to rejecting others' views of me as an "erotic creature," on a routine basis—not unlike the experience I witnessed among many of the Togolese adolescents with whom I worked.

Understanding Eroticized Knowledge

My sexual experiences in Togo strengthened, rather than threatened, my identity as a woman, a feminist, and an academic.[49] The intimate relationships with René and Maxim dramatized my life in Togo and symbolized "a very fundamental type of belonging."[50] Although I rejected Antoine's identification of me as a sexual partner, in the experience with him I was able to increase my sensitivity about the positions and roles of each in the situation.[51] Examining our relationship as it unfolded, despite its increasing unpleasantness and my growing confusion, increased my awareness of how Antoine saw himself as a man and a priest (and a friend). It also increased my awareness about how I wanted to be seen—as well as how I didn't—in Togo, an awareness that serves me well to this day.

My sexual intimacies in Togo, platonic and romantic, desired and rejected, brought into "theoretical and political focus" for me the "asymmetrically ordered conditions" that allowed for their occurrence in the first place.[52] In particular, my sexual relationship with René, a married man, replicated notions of polygamy still common in certain social and religious circles in Togo. I had witnessed the lives of openly polygamous men (such as Nyalewossi's father), and I'd discussed with Togolese girls the relational dynamics between first, second, and third wives. However, it was one thing to witness or discuss such phenomena, entirely another to live it.

My relationship with René compelled me to examine more critically the social conditions in Togo that allowed such relationships between men and women to exist. As René's sexual partner, I learned that he'd had numerous lovers, many times European; in fact, he had a girlfriend when I first met him (a young Togolese woman in the capital). René told me once that his wife did not like but accepted his extramarital behavior, given their long-distance marriage. Her only caveat (that René told me about) was that he use condoms.

I can apply the same polygamy principle to my relationship with Maxim, and one episode in particular comes to mind: Maxim pardoned me immediately when he learned I'd had sex with René. Similarly, Antoine did not see any contradiction between his priestly vows and his hope to include me in his life as a lover. It was as if he was married to the church (a metaphor my U.S. priest friend Jimmy also uses) but had girl-friends "on the side"—a practice I learned was not uncommon in Togo.

Villagers accepted and knew of these practices among priests, as Berna-dette explained to me: "What is forbidden is having children." I would not have learned this—nor believed it—had I not had the experience with An-toine. Further, that experience compelled me to try to understand the dif-ferences between the way Antoine (and Bernadette) framed the experience and the way I (and my fellow U.S. friends and volunteers) framed it. How could we see it so differently? What does that say about "us" and "them"?

My intimate relationships with Antoine, Maxim, and René were richly productive epistemologically, providing vivid information about relationships between men and women in Togo. In particular, my sexual affair with René, the person I was most intimate with, made me "privy to backstage thoughts and opinions" to which I would not otherwise have had access.[53]

Furthermore, in hindsight, I can see how my sexual expression in Togo put me in the same position of many Togolese women, despite my U.S. other-ness. In Togo, I found myself mired in the sexual dynamics between men and women in the same way many of my GEE students were—hiding my sexual activity and cultivating relationships in secret. Although I taught my girls' classes from the worldview that each of us has individual agency, I too was caught up in the web of hiding my own sexual agency so as to maintain credibility in the village. In Togo, and in many other parts of the world, women invite criticism and judgment when they overtly express their sexual freedom in ways that men do not. I did not escape that in Togo, nor do I think I will escape it in the United States now that my story is public.

My intimate relationships in Togo, both platonic and romantic, were a way I made myself vulnerable and curious about what I experienced in the country, and the way I positioned myself in it. My participation in these meaningful relationships was the most valuable way in which I put myself at stake, in order to "be with the other."[54] In putting myself at stake, I learned about myself, and about Togo. I also learned a great deal first-hand about how sexuality "varies widely . . . between individuals in any culture," something I don't think I could have learned as profoundly any other way.[55]

ço

The sexual experiences I described in this book provided a great deal of information to me about relationships between men and women in Togo. Ironically, they also gave me incredible insight about the problem I was focused on as a Peace Corps' volunteer. I had watched adolescent Togolese girls deal with sexual desire, and been compelled and confused by what I witnessed. Odette seemed more an adult lover to her teacher/partner than she did a student; I think the relationship worked for her in many ways. Initially, it was very hard for me to accept or believe this. I watched Nyalewossi effectively reject the gendarme who wanted to father her baby—but at one point Nyalewossi did have a boyfriend; although I did not approve of it, I did not tell her so directly. I was glad when she broke it off with him, but I kept silent about that too. In hindsight, I think my experience with Odette informed my reserve with Nyalewossi about this issue.

Watching these two young women, and many others I met, navigate their sexual identities generated enormous information for me about the lives of young women in Togo. I doubt I would be able to ask the questions I ask now about their sexual embodiment and sexual identity, here at my computer, had I not been provoked to do so by my own sexually embodied experience in Togo.[56] In fact, I am sure I'd be much more judgmental of these young women's experiences, just as I suspect some readers may judge my sexual embodiment when they read this book. The eroticized identity I could not escape in Togo mirrored very closely what many Togolese women experience—whether girls, adolescents, or grown women. Like them, I too had to deal with persistent, unwanted sexual advances, figure out how to embrace my sexuality while not losing credibility, and experienced firsthand the pervasive difficulty of reporting incidents of harassment to authorities.

In this book, I wrote about the experiences of my head, heart, and body in a small country in West Africa. My focus on those elements granted me a window into the lives of young Togolese women. In my classes with the girls, we talked about how the demands of their heads, hearts, and bodies were dismissed or discouraged; as a result, I learned a great deal about how Togolese girls find agency in what might seem to be impossible circumstances. When the girls created skits and presentations on issues that provoked debate and discussion in the community, such as *mariage forcé*, I learned about the ways they try to confound societal expectation, sometimes successfully. As we explored the reasons parents preferred to send their sons to school rather than their daughters, I learned from the girls how they hope to gain the respect of others in their country, so that such a *mentalité* will one day become the exception, not the norm.

It is important to remember that despite their complex circumstances these young women live, work, and love from a powerful sense of agency about their lives. This sense of agency is no less profound, worthy, or productive than my own, which drove the impulse to write this book. I am humbled by what I learned from the Togolese young women among whom I lived and worked. I am grateful that I had the opportunity to bear witness to their lives, even for a brief time.

So much of what I learned about why girls don't go to school revisited me as I considered whether—and then how—I would write my own heart and body into this text. For women academics, confessing one's emotional and embodied life, particularly the sexual embodiment or activity, is risky; its consequences are markedly different from those for a male academic.[57] Yet, illuminating such experiences, and documenting them in rigorous, thoughtful, reflexive ways can provoke important debate and discussion about "power, privilege and perspective" in auto-ethnographic fieldwork and writing.[58]

In a sense then, in constructing this text I have mirrored my experience in trying to understand, amplify, then publicize the voices of the young girls I worked with in Kougnohou and Djon. In my attempt to write a story about them and my life in their village, I have tried to understand, amplify, and then re-present my own voice—the voice of my head, heart and body. In this chapter, I have positioned myself as the "other" striving for liberation outside the margins.

When I think about what I saw young girls experience in Togo—how pervasively and persistently their unique and powerful voices are marginalized—a scholarly discussion about the pros and cons of writing my sexual identity into this text pales by comparison.

Come to think of it, not everyone in Togo would find this book objectionable. I think the young girls I worked with would like it very much.

Notes

Introduction

1. Hoeg, 1996, p. 169. Note: Title is correct for the UK version that I read: page number from that edition was recorded in my notes years ago.
2. Kundera, 1984, p. 75.
3. Boyd, 1994, p. 24.
4. *Pax per conloquium*, or "resolution through dialogue," is the motto of the FBI Crisis Negotiation Unit, http://www.fbi.gov/hq/isd/cirg/osb.htm#cnu. Accessed May 11, 2006.
5. Goolishian & Anderson, 1988.
6. Theroux, 2000, p. 4.
7. Ibid.
8. Stoller, 1997.
9. Ellis, 2004.
10. Rambo Ronai, 1995.
11. Ellis, 2004.
12. Goodall, 2000.
13. Ellis, 2004.
14. Ellis, 2004.

15. Ellis, 2004, p. 126.
16. I will discuss the decisions that informed my writing process, such as using composite characters, in Chapter 10.
17. Nugent, 2002, excuses the personal paragraphs he includes in his book on West Africa as necessary biography "not for reasons of academic self-indulgence dressed up as 'self-reflexivity,' but because the final product genuinely has resulted between dynamic interaction between the research and the subject of enquiry" (p. 5).
18. Ellis, 1995, p. 308.
19. Ellis, 1995, p. 3.
20. Ibid.
21. Goodall, 2000, p. 14.
22. Ibid.
23. Theroux, 2000.
24. Ellis, 2004.

Chapter 1

1. I am a Mestiza, born in Texas. Gloria Anzaldúa (1999) described mestizas/os as a new race, born in 1521, of people of mixed Indian and Spanish blood. My ancestors have been Texas Mestizos since 1894, when they first settled in the United States, immigrating from areas known at the time as Spanish Mexico and Mexican Texas. I think this unique migration, shaped by the geopolitical economics of the period, is why I consider myself Latina, Tejana, and Mestiza, rather than Hispanic, Mexican, Spanish, or Indian. Nor can I comfortably embrace the term Mexican American (see Charlés, 2003). I have not known Mexico well enough to claim her as my own—even partially; my ancestors who lived in what is now Mexico did so over 100 years ago.

   Despite these cultural complexities (of which I became highly conscious only after and precisely because of my experience in Togo), the Togolese saw me as a *blanche*, a white European, and treated me as such. In fact, even the black U.S. volunteers I worked with (one of whom actually was half-African, her mother a citizen of a West African nation), were considered *blanches* by the Togolese. This fascinated me (but frustrated her) to no end. It seemed that to the Togolese, our "economic ancestry," as privileged U.S. citizens, was much more relevant than our actual skin color or racial/ethnic heritage. Thus, they chose to identify all Peace Corps volunteers as *blanches*, ignoring the color distinctions routinely at issue for minorities in the United States.

2. Although our GEE group numbered only 12, we trained in Kpalimé simultaneously with six other volunteers in a Small Business Development program (SBD), sharing many training sessions (and numerous beers) together.

3. *Yovo* is a Togolese referent for *blanche*, white person, foreigner. *Yovo* is sung, hissed, yelled, shouted, or whined in a high voice, by children as well as adults. Packer (2001) noted the origin of the word is *yewu*, which comes from the words *aye* or *avu*, meaning "cunning dog" (p. 11).
4. Fufu is *l'igniames*, or yams, a root vegetable, pounded with a mortar and pestle into a gelatinous blob, served with various sauces such as chicken, eggplant, or peanut, and eaten by pinching bits of the pasty blob off with your fingers, then dipping it into the sauce.

Chapter 2

1. *Groupements* are women's groups founded to conduct activities and procure revenue. *Groupements* thrive in Togo because banks are much more likely to lend money to a group or cooperative of women than to an individual woman.
2. *Pâte* is ground corn flour, served up in pasty blob, often with an okra-based sauce.
3. As I came to know Antoine, I learned that many villagers did see him as an outsider, because he tended to impose unaccustomed rules on Sunday Mass. He caused quite an uproar once when he announced that he would lock the church doors at 7:30 the following Sunday morning to bar latecomers. He didn't do it, but even the suggestion caused much talk. Bernadette, Antoine, and I often joked about Antoine's behavior, because it was so strongly influenced by his time in Europe; however, perhaps not everyone felt comfortable joking about the village priest.
4. According to Marguerite, the role of the *sous-préfet* is that of law keeper in a community of several villages. He is there to prevent or settle any conflict between villages or among people in the village.
5. 13 Janvier is the date Gnassingbe Eyadema became president of Togo; he changed the original independence date to the day he began his 30-year term. The official name of the 13 Janvier holiday is *Fête de la Liberation*.
6. Although I think there are probably multiple explanations for origin of the term "dead *yovo*" to refer to Euro-American donated clothes at African markets, in Togo, the saying I heard most often is that only a dead person (that is, foreigner) would throw out such good clothes.
7. See Haley (1986).

Chapter 3

1. See Blake (1991).

Chapter 4

1. It was a requirement for Peace Corps service that applicants hold a baccalaureate degree. I was the sole volunteer with a PhD in my training group; a handful of volunteers held master's degrees.

Chapter 5

1. Along with alcohol pads, gauze bandages, ibuprofen, and antihistamines, my Peace Corps medical kit included contained exactly 100 condoms, provided to all Togo PCVs, courtesy of the U.S. government.
2. See John M. Chernoff's (2003) *Hustling Is Not Stealing: Stories of an African Bar Girl*, and (2005) *Exchange Is Not Robbery: More Stories of an African Bar Girl*, for an in-depth look at this complex phenomenon.
3. One art critic referred to Patricia's work as scary after interpreting an abstract painting of my mother laughing as a representation of a woman screaming in horror.
4. When my sister, now an adjunct professor of art, read this passage, she laughed and said, "It's true! I can't make a living at it!"
5. See Nwoye (2004) for a discussion of how the graphic differences between rural and urban cities in Africa give rise to a kind of "double society" in countries across the continent.

Chapter 6

1. Kasiram (2005) noted that TODTWD is now being implemented successfully in many developing nations. Exposing girls to the world of work may, according to Kasiram, expand their choices, encourage education, and improve their personal plight as well as contributing to their country's development.
2. To deal with life in Togo, I read a lot; a book a week, on average. I also write quotes from the books into my journals as a way to manage and think about my feelings. During this period with René, several books were especially thought provoking: a collection of Lorrie Moore's, with a story in it entitled "An Other Woman"; *Smilla's Sense of Snow*, by Peter Hoeg; *Les Liasons Dangereuses,* by Choderlos de Laclos; and *A Suitable Boy*, by Vikram Seth.
3. See Charlés (2004) for a thorough discussion of my transformation from Latina to white woman in Africa.

Chapter 7

1. See Barbara Tedlock (1994) for a discussion on how, in the early days of anthropology, figures such as Margaret Mead came to be seen as "surrogate" or "honorary" males in the field.

2. See Werner (1992).

3. I became more conscious of my alcohol use after I began to feel harassed by Antoine. I think the intense frustration and helplessness I felt exacerbated the drinking habit I had already cultivated as a coping skill while living in Togo. I noted the destructive nature of my newly acquired habits on this day at the pool in Kpalimé—as evidenced by my journal—but I developed the habits earlier in my tour. I just didn't see or feel them as destructive before the day at the pool.

   In Togo, many of my fellow PCVs and I often joked that you need alcohol to get through the Third World Peace Corps experience; we felt this was particularly true in Togo. PCVs like to debate which countries are most difficult; many of us cited Togo and certain other West African countries (Mauritania, for example), due to the intense poverty that is often the direct result of corrupt governments. For instance, when I arrived in Togo in 1999, the country had recently been denied EU assistance because of its human rights record and the fact that bodies (believed to be political dissidents) had recently been found floating in the sea near Lomé.

   It became painfully clear to me how much a country's political and economic stability influences the PCV experience when several of us traveled to nearby Ghana, meeting PCVs with markedly different (and quite cushy, we thought) sets of volunteer problems. Not coincidentally, Ghana is a more developed country than Togo, its democratic government is not accused of human rights abuses, and thus it continues to be a repository for foreign aid. The systemic effect of Togo's political situation seemed to make the desperation of the people more intense, which of course affects the way foreigners are treated.

   Never a big drinker, in Togo I eventually drank every day, particularly toward the end of my tour. Around the time I wrote this passage, I had also started to buy over-the-counter Valium when I couldn't sleep, which was often, and had used marijuana more than once (about which I wrote home to my Mom!). Alcohol was my biggest vice in Togo, however. When I lived in Djon, I kept a bottle of rum or gin in my home at all times, and I would sip a small glass every night before bed. Sometimes the Djon village authorities stopped by my house in the early evening for a short visit and a nightcap shot of whiskey. I was happy to oblige them after all they did for me each day, and my alcohol use was almost always social in the village.

   When I was socializing with other PCVs, however, I would drink much more, as many as three 16-ounce Togolese beers, something I could probably not now do without requiring medical attention. I rarely drank with Maxim or René, interestingly enough. But I did begin to smoke cigarettes.

   Finally, I am certain that other RPCVs reading this book have their own coping mechanisms for working in the developing world, involving any number of possible or imagined vices. As with everything else in this book, my story is just one version.

Chapter 8

1. This is an excerpt from Pascal's actual speech to the ambassador, which he typed up and provided to the village authorities. I am responsible for the translation.

Chapter 10

1. Theroux (2000).
2. Trujillo (2004).
3. Ellis (2007).
4. The most authentic writing I've found about the Peace Corps experience is that of Paul Theroux—who was kicked out of the Peace Corps. Recently, Sarah Erdman (2003) wrote a fine book about her experience in Côte d'Ivoire; in the text, she is much more vulnerable than previous RPCV writers have allowed themselves to be.
5. Bochner (2001).
6. Anzaldúa (2000).
7. See Charlés (2004, 2005).
8. Bochner, as cited in Ellis (2004).
9. Carolyn Ellis (1995) discusses this issue at length.
10. Ellis, (1995b).
11. Ellis (2004).
12. Ellis (1995).
13. Ibid.
14. Bochner (2001).
15. Medford (2006).
16. Ellis (2007).
17. Ibid.
18. Tillman-Healy (2003).
19. Ibid.
20. Newton (1996), p. 228.
21. Tillman-Healy (2003).
22. Tillman-Healy (2003) discusses doing this in her work.
23. Ellis, in press.
24. Ibid.
25. Ibid; Ellis (1995a).
26. Bateson (1972).

27. Duneier (1999) stated, "Ultimately I believe I should never publish something about an identifiable person which I cannot look him or her in the eye and read" (pp. 351–52).
28. Medford (2006).
29. Ellis (2007) discussed this issue.
30. Ellis (1995b).
31. Ibid.
32. Gunzenhauser (2006) stated that the researcher should consider relationships with participants as occurring in a context of two knowing subjects: "knower–knower," rather than "knower–known," or "researcher–participant."
33. However "cool" it was, Marguerite was cognizant of the book's possible reach in Togo. She was insistent that I change her family's name and that of her boyfriend, who I mention early in the book.
34. Duneier (1999).
35. Ibid., pp. 78–79).
36. Ellis (in press).
37. I remain responsible for any errors that remain in this text.
38. Stoller (1989).
39. My compliments to Carolyn Ellis for capturing these sensations for me so vividly.
40. Kulick (1995), p. 23.
41. Gunzenhauser (2006) stated that "the quality of qualitative research is based on the quality of relations developed" (p. 622).
42. Coffey (1999), p. 14.
43. Ibid., p. 32.
44. I think this is a universal principle; however, in the Western world we have many more things to distract us from head, heart, and body.
45. Coffey (1999), pp. 94–95.
46. Newton, (1996), p. 214.
47. Newton (1996), pp. 212–13.
48. Newton (1996).
49. Kulick (1995).
50. Zussman (2002).
51. Kulick (1995), p. 20.
52. Ibid., p. 22.
53. Zussman (2002), p. 475.
54. Kulick (1995).
55. Ibid.

56. Kulick (1995).
57. Kulick & Wilson (1995).
58. Ibid.

References

Anzaldúa, G. (2000). *Borderlands/La Frontera: The New Mestiza*, 2nd ed. San Francisco: Aunt Lute Books.

Blackwood, E. (1995). Falling in love with another lesbian: Reflections on identity in fieldwork. In Kulick, D., Wilson, M. (eds.). *Taboo: Sex, Identity, and Erotic Subjectivity in Anthropological Fieldwork* (51–75). New York: Routledge.

Blake, S. (1991). *Letters from Togo*. Iowa City: University of Iowa Press.

Boyd, W. (1994). *The Blue Afternoon*. London: Penguin.

Charlés, L. (2006). Young women struggling for an education: Systemic work with a village community in West Africa. *Journal of Feminist Family Therapy, 18*(3) 63–83.

Charlés, L. (2004). Stories from urban and rural landscapes: The development of a cultural identity. In Rastogi, M., Wieling, L. (eds.). *Voices of Color: First Person Accounts of Ethnic Minority Therapists* (169–87). Thousand Oaks, CA: Sage.

Charlés, L. (2005). A family therapist in the Peace Corps. *Family Therapy Magazine*. Washington DC: American Association for Marriage and Family Therapy.

Chernoff, JM. (2003). *Hustling Is Not Stealing: Stories of an African Bar Girl*. Chicago: University of Chicago Press.

Chernoff, JM. (2005). *Exchange Is Not Robbery: More Stories of an African Bar Girl*. Chicago: University of Chicago Press.

Coffey, A. (1999). *The Ethnographic Self: Fieldwork and the Representation of Identity*. London: Sage.

Duneier, M. (1999). *Sidewalk*. New York: Farrar, Straus, & Giroux.

Ellis, C. (1995a). Emotional and ethical quagmires in returning to the field. *Journal of Contemporary Ethnography, 24*(1), 68–98.

Ellis, C. (1995b). *Final Negotiations: A Story of Love, Loss, and Chronic Illness*. Philadelphia: Temple University Press.

Ellis, C. (2004) *The Ethnographic I: A Methodological Novel about Autoethnography*. Walnut Creek, CA: AltaMira Press.

Ellis, C. (2007). Telling secrets, revealing lives: Relational ethics in research with intimate others. *Qualitative Inquiry, 13*(1), 3–29.

Erdman, S. (2003). *Nine Hills to Nambonkaha: Two Years in the Heart of an African Village*. New York: Henry Holt.

Flemons, D., Green, S. (2002). Stories that conform/stories that transform: A conversation in four parts. In Bochner A., Ellis C. (eds.). *Ethnographically Speaking: Autoethnography, Literature, and Aesthetics*. (87–94). Walnut Creek, CA: AltaMira Press.

Goodall, H. (2000). *Writing the New Ethnography*. Walnut Creek, CA: AltaMira Press.

Haley, J. (1986). *Uncommon Therapy: The Psychiatric Techniques of Milton H. Erickson, M.D.* New York: Norton.

Gunzenhauser, MG. (2006). A moral epistemology of knowing subjects: Theorizing a relational turn for qualitative research. *Qualitative Inquiry 12*(3) 621–47.

Human Rights Watch. (2003). *Borderline Slavery: Child Trafficking in Togo* (Vol. 15, No. 8 A). Washington, DC: Author.

Hoeg, P. (1994). *Miss Smilla's Feeling for Snow*. London: Harvill.

Kasiram, M. (2005, June). *Human Rights Forum: The Changing Face of the AIDS Epidemic—Human Rights and Clinical Implications*. Meeting of the American Family Therapy Academy-International Family Therapy Association, Washington, DC.

Kulick, D. (1995) Introduction: The sexual life of anthropologists: Erotic subjectivity and fieldwork. In Kulick, D., Wilson, M. (eds.). *Taboo: Sex, Identity, and Erotic Subjectivity in Anthropological Fieldwork* (1–28). New York: Routledge.

Kundera, M. (1984). *The Unbearable Lightness of Being*. New York: HarperCollins.

Liftin, H., Montgomery, K. (1999). *Dear Exile: The True Story of Two Friends Separated (for a Year) by an Ocean*. New York: Random House.

Medford, K. (2006). Caught with a fake ID: Ethical questions about slippage in autoethnography. *Qualitative Inquiry 13*(1) 3–29.

Newton, E. (1996). My best informant's dress: The erotic equation in fieldwork. In Lewin E., Leap W. (eds.). *Out in the Field: Reflections of Lesbian and Gay Anthropologists* (212–35). University of Illinois Press: Urbana.

Nugent, P. (2002). *Smugglers, Secessionists and Loyal Citizens on the Ghana-Togo Frontier*. Oxford: James Currey.

Packer, G. (2001). *The Village of Waiting*. New York: Farrar, Strauss, & Giroux.

Rambo Ronai, C. (1995). Multiple reflections of child sex abuse: An argument for a layered account. *Journal of Contemporary Ethnography, 23*, 395–426.

Stoller, P. (1989). *The Taste of Ethnographic Things: The Senses in Anthropology*. Philadelphia: University of Pennsylvania Press.

Tedlock, B. (1994). Works and wives: On the sexual division of textual labor. In Behar, R., Gordon, DA. (eds.). *Women Writing Culture*. Berkeley and Los Angeles: University of California Press.

Theroux, P. (2000). *Fresh Air Fiend*. New York: First Mariner.

Tillman-Healy, L. (2003). Friendship as Method. *Qualitative Inquiry 9*(5):729–49.

Van Maanen, J. (1998). *Tales of the Field: On Writing Ethnography*. Chicago: University of Chicago Press.

Weston, K. (1996). Requiem for a streetfighter. In Lewin, E., Leap, W. (eds.). *Out in the Field: Reflections of Lesbian and Gay Anthropologists* (274–85). Urbana: University of Illinois Press.

Werner, D. (1992). *Where There Is No Doctor: A Village Health Care Handbook.* Palo Alto: Hesperian Foundation.

Williams, WL. (1996). Being gay and doing fieldwork. In Lewin, E., Leap, W. (eds.). *Out in the Field: Reflections of Lesbian and Gay Anthropologists* (70–85). Urbana: University of Illinois Press.

Zussman, R. (2002). Editor's introduction: Sex in research. *Qualitative Sociology* 25(4):473–77.

Index

About the Author

LAURIE L. CHARLÉS is an assistant professor of family therapy at the University of Massachusetts, Boston. She received her doctorate at Nova Southeastern University in Ft. Lauderdale, Florida, in 1999. Her master's degree was conferred at Our Lady of the Lake University in San Antonio, Texas, her hometown, in 1993. Charlés is the author of a forthcoming book on crisis (hostage) negotiation discourse, and author or co-author of numerous articles in the field of family therapy qualitative research, practice, and supervision.

Charlés' recent work focuses on how systemic family therapists can take a more global, citizen/activist, and human rights perspective to their work. She is currently tracing the migration of her ancestors, Aurelia and Alcario Charlés, to *Mexican Texas* from *Spanish Mexico* in 1894, with an emphasis on how *mestiza* women in Texas have balanced gender expectations throughout the past century.

Charlés enjoys talking about patterns of migration across cultures and continents, teaching therapists how to learn from the resilience of people often marginalized as "other," and studying conversations as a way to learn more about the ways we live, love, and work in contemporary society.

Her hobbies include traveling in various seas of diversity (*Globetrekker*-style) with her husband Eric, walking for miles in the city of Boston and then sitting down to a good Italian meal (accompanied by lots of red wine) in the North End, and, most of all, laughing over coffee with her mother whenever she can find time to migrate back to San Antonio.

For Product Safety Concerns and Information please contact our EU
representative GPSR@taylorandfrancis.com Taylor & Francis Verlag GmbH,
Kaufingerstraße 24, 80331 München, Germany

Batch number: 08153776

Printed by Printforce, the Netherlands